21世纪普通高等院校系列教材

国际贸易：理论与政策（双语）

International Trade: Theory and Policy (Bilingual)

主　编○李大鹏　刘晓远　黄　翔
副主编○陈京晶　李　玺　赵亚男　郑　南

西南财经大学出版社
Southwestern University of Finance & Economics Press
中国·成都

图书在版编目（CIP）数据

国际贸易：理论与政策：汉文、英文/李大鹏，刘晓远，黄翔主编．—成都：西南财经大学出版社，2021.8
ISBN 978-7-5504-4694-6

Ⅰ.①国…　Ⅱ.①李…②刘…③黄…　Ⅲ.①国际贸易理论—双语教学—高等学校—教材—汉、英②国际贸易政策—双语教学—高等学校—教材—汉、英　Ⅳ.①F74

中国版本图书馆 CIP 数据核字（2020）第 244643 号

国际贸易：理论与政策（双语）
GUOJI MAOYI：LILUN YU ZHENGCE（SHUANGYU）

主　编　李大鹏　刘晓远　黄　翔
副主编　陈京晶　李　玺　赵亚男　郑　南

责任编辑：植苗
封面设计：何东琳设计工作室
责任印制：朱曼丽

出版发行	西南财经大学出版社（四川省成都市光华村街 55 号）
网　　址	http://cbs.swufe.edu.cn
电子邮件	bookcj@swufe.edu.cn
邮政编码	610074
电　　话	028-87353785
照　　排	四川胜翔数码印务设计有限公司
印　　刷	四川五洲彩印有限责任公司
成品尺寸	185mm×260mm
印　　张	14
字　　数	400 千字
版　　次	2021 年 8 月第 1 版
印　　次	2021 年 8 月第 1 次印刷
书　　号	ISBN 978-7-5504-4694-6
定　　价	48.00 元

▶▶ Preface

With the development of world economic integration, all the countries are interlinked, interdependent and developing together. The Chinese economy is increasingly integrated into the world economy and has become an important link in today's world economic system. Due to the further development of reform and opening up in China in recent years as well as the frequent economic interactions with the world, international trade has had a huge development, but it is also facing enormous challenges at the same time. The market demand for inter-disciplinary talents possessing both solid professional knowledge and language skills has been increasing, but this kind of demand cannot be met by a pure professional education mode. Our goal is to cultivate international application-oriented "Profession + English" talents.

This textbook is bilingual in both English and Chinese. It analyzes the theories and policies of international trade in today's world. It not only strengthens students' professional knowledge of economic and trade practice, but also improves students' English level. At the same time, this textbook highlights the corresponding key and difficult points in teaching from different dimensions, with different contents and diversified perspectives, aiming at cultivating students' good learning habits of combining theory with practice and applying what they have learned in class to their real life.

The book is composed of 12 chapters. The specific division of work in this book is as follows: Chapters 1 & 5 are written by Xiaoyuan Liu from Chongqing Technology and Business University (CTBU), Chapters 2, 3, 4 & 6 by Jingjing Chen from CTBU, Chapters 7 & 8 by Xiang Huang from Zhejiang Institute of Mechanical & Electrical Engineering, Chapter 9 by Yanan Zhao from CTBU, Chapter 10 by Nan Zheng from CTBU, Chapter 11 by Dapeng Li from CTBU, and Chapter 12 by Xi Li from CTBU. The whole book is compiled by Xiaoyuan Liu and

Xiang Huang.

The strong support from the leaders of Chongqing Technology and Business University and International Business School is much appreciated in the process of writing this book. Due to the time limit and knowledge level of the compilers, some mistakes and errors in the book are unavoidable. Thus further criticism and correction are welcome from all the readers.

Author

July 2021

▶▶ 前言

随着世界经济一体化的发展，各个国家相互联系、相互依赖、共同发展，中国经济也不断融入世界经济，已构成当今世界经济体系重要一环。近年来我国改革开放的深入发展，与世界的经济互动日益频繁，国际贸易取得较大发展，同时也面临巨大挑战，市场上对既有扎实专业知识又掌握娴熟外语语言技能的复合型人才的需求不断扩大，而这种需求是单一专业教育模式所不能满足的。“专业+英语”的国际化应用型复合人才正是我们培养的目标。

本教材采用全英文版形式，对当今世界国际贸易进行了理论和政策分析，不仅夯实学生经贸实务的专业知识，而且提升学生英语的应用水平。同时，本教材从不同维度突出相应教学重难点，内容不雷同，角度多元化，旨在培养学生理论联系实际、学以致用的良好学习习惯。

全书共12章，具体编写分工如下：第1、5章由重庆工商大学刘晓远编写，第2、3、4、6章由重庆工商大学陈京晶编写，第7、8章由浙江机电职业技术学院黄翔编写，第9章由重庆工商大学赵亚男编写，第10章由重庆工商大学郑南编写，第11章由重庆工商大学李大鹏编写，第12章由重庆工商大学李玺编写。全书由刘晓远、黄翔统稿。

本书在编写过程中，得到了重庆工商大学及国际商学院各级领导的大力支持，在此致以诚挚的感谢。由于时间关系和编者水平所限，书中不当之处在所难免，恳请广大读者批评指正。

编者

2020年7月

▶▶ Contents

Part Two Policy of International Trade

▶▶ 目录

第二部分　国际贸易政策

1 Introduction to International Trade

International trade is the exchange of goods and services across national borders or territories. It is also known as world trade, import and export trade or overseas trade. In most countries, it represents a significant share of gross domestic product (GDP). While international trade has been present throughout much of history, its economic, social, and political importance has been on the rise only in recent centuries. Industrialization, advanced transportation, globalization, and multinational corporations are all having a major impact on the international trade system. Increasing international trade is crucial to the continuance of globalization. International trade is a major source of economic revenue for any nation that is considered as a world power. Without international trade, nations would be limited to the goods and services produced within their own borders or territories.

This chapter firstly illustrates the reasons for international trade, and then it discusses the major difference between international trade and domestic trade. Finally it defines some basic concepts relating to international trade.

1.1 The Reasons for International Trade

Why does international trade take place? There are numerous reasons.

1.1.1 Get the goods needed

No nation has all of the commodities it needs. Some countries are abundant in certain resources, while other nations may lack them. For example, Colombia and Brazil have the ideal climate for growing coffee beans. The United States is a major consumer of coffee, yet it does not have the climate to grow any on its (other than in Hawaii). Consequently, this has made Colombia and Brazil big coffee exporters, and the United States a big coffee importer. Raw materials are scattered around the world. Large deposits of copper are mined in Peru and Zaire and diamonds are mined in South Africa. Countries that do not have these resources within their own boundaries must import from countries that export them. In short, the uneven distribution of resources around the world is one of the basic reasons why nations trade with each other.

1.1.2 Gain economic benefits

With the development of manufacturing technology, there arose another incentive for nations to trade-economic benefits. In addition to getting the products they need, countries also wish to gain economically by trading with each other. China has been able to export large quantities of textiles and television sets because it can produce them more efficiently than other countries. It is cheaper for countries like the United States and Germany to buy these than to produce them domestically. According to economic theory, China should produce and export those items from which it derives a comparative advantage. It should also buy and import what it needs from those countries that have a comparative advantage in the desired items.

1.1.3 Other reasons

A country often does not have enough quantity of a particular item to meet its needs. Although China is a producer of oil, it consumes more than it can produce internally and thus must import oil. Even though a country can produce enough quantity of an item at reasonable costs to meet its own demand, it may import some from other countries for innovation or a variety of styles. For example, the United States produces more automobiles than any other country; it still imports large quantities of autos from Germany, Japan, and Sweden, primarily because there is a market for them in the United States. Sometimes, political objectives can outweigh economic considerations between countries. One country might trade with another to support the latter's government which upholds the same political doctrine.

To sum up, in today's complex economic world, neither individuals nor nations are self-sufficient. Nations have utilized different economic resources; people have developed different skills. This is the foundation of international trade and economic activities.

1.2 The Difference Between International Trade and Domestic Trade

International trade is in principle not different from domestic trade as both are exchange activities. Special problems that are not normally experienced when trading at home may arise in international trade.

1.2.1 More complex context

Under the context of international trade, deals might have to be transacted in foreign languages and under international or foreign laws, customs and regulations. Numerous cultural differences may have to be taken into account when trading with other nations. Before a corporation begins exporting products to other countries, it must first examine the norms, taboos and values of those countries. Control and communication systems are normally more complex for foreign than for domestic operations. Foreign currency transactions will be necessary. Exchange rate variations can be very wide and create many problems for international trade.

1.2.2 More difficult and risky

Due to the complex context of international trade, international trade is generally much more difficult and risky than domestic trade. In international trade, information on foreign countries needed by a particular firm may be difficult to obtain.

Risk levels might be higher in foreign markets. The risks include political risks such as war risks, risk of expropriation or confiscation of the importer's company, risk of the imposition of an import ban after the shipment of the goods, transfer risk and risk of different tax rates, etc.; economic risks like risk of insolvency of the buyer, risk of protracted default, risk of non-acceptance, risk of exchange rate as well as susceptibility to changing standards and regulations within other countries.

1.2.3 Higher skills required

Business professionals engaged in international trade need a broader range of professional skills than business professionals who are only concerned with domestic problems.

1.3 Basic Concepts Relating to International Trade

1.3.1 Visible trade and invisible trade

1.3.1.1 Visible trade: Trade in goods (merchandise)

When nations import or export goods, customs formalities will have to be carried out. Thus goods transactions are observable. The usual customs records or data are available for valuing these transactions. That is why these transactions are called visible trade. In 2011, the share of international visible trade was around 80% of the total value of international trade. For the purpose of collecting statistics of many varieties of goods in international trade, the UN Secretariat drafted the Standard International Trade Classification (SITC) in 1950, and made amendments in 1960, 1974, 1985 and 2006. The current version (Version 4) of SITC classifies international trade commodities into 10 sections, 67 divisions, 262 groups, 1023 sub-groups and 1924 basic headings. The 10 sections are: Food and live animals; Beverages and tobacco; Crude materials, inedible, except fuels; Mineral fuels, lubricantsand related raw material; Animal and vegetable oils, fats and wax; Chemicals and related products, n. e. s.; Manufactured goods chiefly classified by material; Machinery and transportation equipment; Miscellaneous manufactured articles; Commodities and transactions not classified elsewhere in the SITC.

1.3.1.2 Invisible trade: Trade in services

It is extremely difficult to obtain accurate estimates of the value of the transactions of trade in services. This results from the fact that there is no definition of what constitutes traded services, and the ways in which these transactions are measured are less precise than in the case for merchandise trade. Estimates are obtained by examining foreign exchange records and/or through surveys of establishments. Since many services are not observable (hence they are referred to as the "invisible" in international trade), the usual customs records or data are not available for valuing these transactions. Thus it is likely that the value of trade in commercial services is underestimated. However, there may also be instances when firms may choose to overvalue trade in services, so reported figures must be viewed with some caution.

International trade in services broadly consists of commercial services, investment income and government services, with the first two categories accounting for the bulk of services. Discussions of trade in services generally refer to trade in commercial services. During the 1970s, this category grew more slowly in value than merchandise exports did. However, during the 1980s, exports of commercial services outgrew merchandise exports, and the relative importance of commercial services is roughly the same today as it was in the early 1980s. The total value of commercial services in 2011 was US $4.2 trillion, accounting for 18.75% of the total value of international trade. Although trading of services is still a relatively small part of the international trade, its growth rate is getting more and more rapid. Today, especially in developed societies, services account for large portions of national outputs. In 2011, the United States was the world's largest exporter and importer of commercial services.

The two main categories of world trade in commercial services are travel and transportation and services. In 2011, the value of exports of travel was US $1.63 billion, accounting for 25.3% of all commercial services and the value of exports of transport was US $855 billion, accounting for 20.4% of all commercial services.

Trade in services has been virtually ignored in trade negotiations and trade agreements. However, because of its increasing importance, there has been a growing concern for the need to establish some general guidelines for international transactions in services. Consequently, discussions regarding the nature of the service trade and various country restrictions that may influence it were included in the last completed round of trade negotiations (the Uruguay Round) conducted under the auspices of the General Agreement on Tariffs and Trade (GATT), which became the World Organization in 1995. Achieving a General Agreement on Trade in Services (GATS) was a major focus of the Uruguay Round of GATT negotiations. Developing nations (led by India and Brazil) opposed such an agreement because they viewed it as a one-way street benefiting the developed world, particularly its banking, insurance, telecommunications and professional business. GATS does not define services, but does define trade in services. Paragraph 2 of Article defines trade in services as the supply of a service through any of four modes of supply: cross border supply of services, consumption abroad, commercial presence in the consuming country, and presence of natural persons.

According to the department of international trade in services, it includes: ①Transportation, for example, sea transportation, air transportation, other transportation. ② Travel. ③Other commercial services, for example, communication services, construction services, insurance services, financial services, computer and information services, royalties and licence fees services, other business services, personal cultural and recreation services.

1. 3. 2 Favorable balance of trade and unfavorable balance of trade

The balance of trade (or net exports, sometimes symbolized as NX) is the difference between the monetary value of exports and imports of output in an economy over certain period. A favorable balance of trade is known as a trade surplus or positive balance of trade and consists of exporting more than is imported; an unfavorable balance of trade is known as a trade deficit or negative balance of trade and consists of importing more than is exported. The balance of trade is sometimes divided into merchandise and service balance.

The balance of trade is an important part of current account of a nation's balance of payment. The current account includes other transaction such as income from the international investment positions as well as international aid. If the current account is in surplus, the country's net international asset position increases correspondingly. Conversely, a deficit decreases the net international asset position.

Factors that can affect the balance of trade include: The cost of production (land, labor, capital, taxes, incentives, etc.) in the exporting economy to those in the importing economy; Exchange rate movements; Multilateral, bilateral and unilateral taxes or restrictions on trade; Non-tariff barriers such as environmental, health or safety standards; The availability of adequate foreign exchange with which to pay for imports, etc. In addition, the trade balance is likely to differ across the business cycle. In export led growth (such as oil and early industrial goods), the balance of trade will improve during an economic expansion. However, with domestic demand led growth (as in the United States and Australia), the balance of trade will worsen at the same stage in the business cycle.

In China, the trade in goods was in deficit for most of the years prior to 1994. Since 1994, with large-scale industrial outsourcing and relocation, China enhanced its competitiveness in manufactured goods. Growth in exports overtook that of imports, turning the overall deficit to a surplus in trade in goods. In 2005, China's surplus in trade in goods reached US $ 100 billion for the first time.

A higher saving rate generally corresponds to a trade surplus. Correspondingly, the United States with its lower saving rate has tended to run high trade deficits, especially with Asian nations. Since the mid-1980s, the United States has had a growing deficit in tradable goods, especially with Asian nations (China and Japan) which now hold large sums of US debt that has funded the consumption of the United States.

1.3.3 General trade system and special trade system

Two systems of recording merchandise exports and imports are in common use. They are referred to as general trade system and special trade system.

1.3.3.1 General trade system

This is a system under which statistic figures are collected on the basis of economic territory of country. In other words, the general trade system is in use when the statistic territory of a country consists of the geographical territory administered by a government. This system covers all types of inward and outward movement of goods through an economic territory including movements through customs warehouses and free trade zones.

1.3.3.2 Special trade system

This is a system under which statistic figures are collected on the basis of customs territory. It covers all types of inward and outward movement of goods through a country or territory excluding movements through customs warehouses and free trade zones. In the majority of countries, data collection is based on customs procedures, and many of these countries adopt their customs territory (boundary) as their statistical boundary. Customs territory is the geographical territory upon which a sovereign nation imposes its exports and imports regulations and duties. Certain territorial possession and special economic zones (such as free trade zones) are often considered outside the customs territory of a nation.

The general trade system provides a more comprehensive recording of the external trade flows than the special system does. It is recommended, therefore, by the UN that countries use the general trade system for compilation of their international merchandise trade statistics and international reporting. Thestatistical territory of China is, generally, defined by the economic territory, comprising of areas of bonded warehouses and free trade zones.

1.3.4 Volume of international trade and quantum of international trade

1.3.4.1 Volume of international trade

Volume of international trade refers to the total value of international trade in merchandise and services. Since one nation's export is another nation's import, the total volume of international trade in merchandise and services is thus the aggregated value of either the imports or exports of all nations all over the world. As exports of goods are usually valued at transaction value which excludes the cost of transportation and insurance to bring the merchandise to the frontier of the importing country or territory ("free on board" valuation), and imports are valued at transaction value plus the cost of transportation and insurance to the port of destination of the importing country or territory ("cost, insurance and freight" valuation), the total volume of international exports of merchandise is therefore the aggregated volume of exports rather than imports of all nations throughout the world.

As the prices of merchandise fluctuate frequently, the value of international trade cannot reflect the real development of international trade, thus the volume of international trade in different period is incomparable.

1.3.4.2 Quantum of international trade

International trade has grown rapidly in the recent decades. A large part of the increase, however, was due to inflation. For the purpose of reflecting the real development of international trade, the quantum of international trade is used.

The quantum of international trade is the value of international trade calculated according to constant prices, which is the value of international trade multiplied by the price index in the base year and divided by the price index in the calculation year. For example, in the base year 1950, the volume of international trade in merchandise and the price index was US $ 60.7 billion and 100 respectively. In the calculation year 1997, the volume of international trade in merchandise and the price index was US $ 5 450 billion and 600 respectively. The quantum of international trade in 1997 was thus US $ 9 083 billion (5 450 multiplied by 100 and divided by 600).

1.3.5 Commodity composition of international trade

Commodity composition of international trade refers to the share of all categories or kinds of merchandise in international trade within a certain period of time. It consists of the commodity composition of both exports and imports. The commodity composition of international trade usually reflects the level of economic development as well as the industrial structure of the whole world. In 2010, the share of manufactures was the largest in world merchandise trade. For a particular nation, the commodity composition of foreign trade is the share of each category or kind of goods in the nation's foreign trade within a certain period of time. It also consists of the commodity composition of both export and import.

1.3.6 Geographical composition of international trade

Geographical composition of international trade or direction of international trade, refer to the share of nations, regions or economies in international trade. For a particular country, the share of each region or country in its exports or imports constitute the geographical composition of its exports or imports.

1.3.7 Ratio of dependence on foreign trade

It is important not only to recognize the absolute level of international trade but also to recognize that the relative importance of trade has been growing for nearly every country. The relative size of trade is often measured by comparing the size of a country's exports and imports of merchandise with its GDP. The ratio of dependence on foreign trade is the total volume of foreign trade (exports and imports) to GDP, which can be represented by the following formula: $Z = (X+M)/\mathrm{GDP} \times 100\%$, where Z is the ratio of the volume of exports and imports to GDP, X is the volume of exports and M is the volume of imports.

Although the ratio of dependence on foreign trade varies considerably among countries, the relative importance of exports has increased in almost all individual cases and for every country grouping where data are available. This means not only that individual countries are experiencing the economic benefits but also that their own economic prosperity is dependent upon economic prosperity of the world as a while.

The ratio of exports and imports to GDP is often used to indicate the openness of an economy. However, results should not be interpreted as a trade policy indicator. For example, the United States shows a relatively low ratio despite its openness to trade—as reflected, for example, by its low tariffs. This reflects the fact that service-oriented and larger economies tend to show a relatively small ratio. An increase in the value of trade may not be a consequence of trade liberalization. For example, oil price increases lead to an increase in the value of exports of oil exporters that do not fully reflect an increase in an economy's GDP. The situation is even more marked for importing countries because the rise in the value of fuel imports may depress domestic economic activity, leading to a higher trade to GDP ratio. Exchange rate fluctuations also have an impact on making comparisons among countries.

1 国际贸易概论

国际贸易是指国家之间或者地区之间进行的商品和服务的交换活动，它也称为“世界贸易”“进出口贸易”，或者像英国、日本等这样的国家也称其为“海外贸易”。大多数国家中，国际贸易在该国的GDP（国内生产总值）中占有重要的地位。虽然国际贸易贯穿大部分历史的发展中，然而，只有近几个世纪来，国际贸易的经济、社会和政治的重要性才得以上升。工业化、先进的运输、全球化和跨国公司都对国际贸易体系有着重要的影响。日益增长的国际贸易对全球化的持续至关重要。对认为具有世界影响力的一国而言，国际贸易是其经济收入的一个重要来源。如果没有国际贸易，国家就会被限制在只能在其国内或区内进行商品和劳务的活动。

这一章首先分析了国际贸易的原因，其次讨论了国际贸易与国内贸易的主要区别，最后分析了相关国际贸易的基本概念。

1.1 国际贸易的原因

为什么会产生国际贸易？有以下几个原因：

1.1.1 获得需要的商品

没有一个国家会拥有它需要的所有商品。一些国家在某些资源上丰裕，而其他一些国家则可能稀缺。例如，哥伦比亚和巴西拥有生产咖啡豆的理想气候。美国是咖啡的主要消费国，然而却没有生产一些它自己的咖啡豆的适宜气候（夏威夷除外）。因此，这就使得哥伦比亚和巴西成为大量出口咖啡的出口国，而美国成为大量进口咖啡的进口国。在世界范围内，自然资源是分散的，如人们在秘鲁和赞比亚开采铜矿，在南非开采钻石。在其国内不拥有这些资源的国家必须从出口这些资源的国家进口。总之，世界范围内参差不齐的资源分布是国际贸易产生的基本原因之一。

1.1.2 获得经济收益

随着生产技术的不断提高，则产生了另外一个导致国际贸易的诱因——经济收益。国家除了获得他们所需要的产品之外，他们还希望通过彼此的贸易获得经济收益。中国出口了大量的纺织品和电视机，是因为中国比其他的国家更能高效地生产这些产品。像美国和德国这些国家，它们购买这些产品相比自己生产而言更便宜些。根据经济学理论，中国应该生产并出口具有比较优势的产品。一国也应该从具有比较优势的国家购买和进口其所需要的产品。

1.1.3 其他原因

通常，一国并没有足够数量的特定产品以满足该国的需求。虽然中国是石油生产国，但是其对石油的消费比国内的生产要多，所以还必须进口石油。甚至，一国能够在合理的成本上生产出满足其需求的足够数量的产品，该国还仍然从别的国家进口该产品，是因为该产品的创新或者样式的多样性。例如，美国比别的国家生产更多的汽车，而仍然从德国、日本和瑞典进口大量的汽车，其主要是因为美国国内市场有需求。有时候，国家之间的政治因素的力量能超过经济因素的影响。一国和另一国进行贸易往来，可能是为了支持另一国足够数量的特定产品来维护彼此间相同的政治信条。

总之，在当今复杂的经济世界中，没有哪一个人或者哪一个国家是自给自足的。国家使用着不同的经济资源，人们发展了不同的技能，这是国际贸易和经济活动的基础。

1.2 国际贸易与国内贸易的区别

虽然国际贸易和国内贸易都是交换活动，但两者基本上还存在着很大的区别。国际贸易区别于国内贸易的根本特征是：国际贸易包括了跨国界的贸易活动。在国内贸易中不常发生的一些特殊问题，却常常在国际贸易中发生。

1.2.1 更复杂的环境

在国际贸易环境下，交易可能不得不在面临外国的语言、国际或外国的法律、习惯和规则的情况下进行。和别的国家做贸易时可能要考虑到大量的文化差异。一个公司准备向别的国家出口产品之前，该公司必须要考察这些国家的行为规范、禁忌和价值观等。国外的指挥和通信系统通常比国内的运营要复杂得多。外汇交易会必然发生，汇率变动也时常发生，并且产生许多相关国际贸易的问题。

1.2.2 更具有难度和风险

因为国际贸易的复杂环境，所以国际贸易常常比国内贸易更具有难度和风险。在国际贸易中，我们往往可能难以获得国外特定公司的信息。

在国外市场风险更大。这些风险包括：政治风险，如战争风险、进口公司被征收和没收的风险、装货后实施进口禁令的风险、转移风险（进口国实施外汇管制或者外汇短缺）和不同税率的风险；经济风险，如进口人破产的风险、违约的风险（付款日期到后买方拖欠债务）、拒绝承兑的风险、汇率风险以及其他国家不断变化的标准和规则。

1.2.3 要求更高的技能

从事国际贸易的商务专业人才，相比仅从事国内贸易的商务专业人才而言，则需要更为宽广的专业技能。

1.3 相关国际贸易的基本概念

1.3.1 有形贸易与无形贸易

1.3.1.1 有形贸易：货物贸易（商品）

进出口货物时，我们必须要履行海关手续。因此，货物的交易能够观察得到，统计这些交易的海关记录和资料也通常能够得到。所以，这是为什么这些交易被称为“有形贸易”的原因。2011 年，有形贸易的份额在全部国际贸易总值中所占的比重达 80%。国际贸易中的货物种类繁多，为了便于统计，联合国秘书处起草了 1950 年《国际贸易标准分类》，并于 1960 年、1974 年、1985 年和 2006 年进行了修订。《国际贸易标准分类》的新版本（第四版）将国际货物贸易分为 10 大类、67 章、262 组、1 023 个分组和 1 924 个基本项目。这 10 类商品为：食品和活动物；饮料及烟类；燃料以外的非食用原料；矿物燃料、润滑油及有关原料；动植物油脂及蜡；未列名化学品及有关产品；主要按原料分类的制成品；机械及运输设备；杂项制品；《国际贸易标准分类》中没有分类的其他商品和交易。

1.3.1.2 无形贸易：服务贸易

要获得准确的服务贸易额是非常困难的，这主要是因为我们没有对服务贸易界定出一致的定义，并且测算服务贸易的方法没有像测算货物贸易那样精确。服务贸易是通过外汇记录或/和对企业的调查而估算出的。既然许多服务不能够观察得到（因此在国际贸易中被称为“无形”），统计这些交易的海关记录和资料也通常不能够得到。因此，服务贸易额可能被低估了。然而，也有些企业选择高估服务贸易额的情况，所以我们对报道出来的数据必须谨慎对待。

国际服务贸易广义上包括商业性服务、投资收益服务和政府服务，其中前两者在服务中占绝大部分。对服务贸易的讨论常常是指商业性服务贸易。20 世纪 70 年代，相比货物的出口，服务的出口增长缓慢。然而，20 世纪 80 年代，商业性服务出口的发展速度超过了货物的出口，其早期的商业性服务的重要性如同今天一样。2011 年，商业性服务贸易总额为 4.2 万亿美元，占到了国际贸易总额的 18.75%。虽然服务贸易仍然是国际贸易中的小部分，但是它的增速越来越迅猛。今天，尤其是发达国家，服务在一国的产出中占有大的比重。2011 年，美国是世界上商业性服务最大的出口方和进口方。

旅游和运输是全球商业性服务贸易的两个主要类别。2011 年，旅游的出口额为 10 630亿美元，在全部的商业性服务贸易额中的占比为 25.3%；运输的出口额为 8 550 亿美元，在全部的商业性服务贸易额中的占比为 20.4%。

实际上，服务贸易曾经在贸易协定和贸易协议中被忽略了。然而，因为它的重要性日益增加，需要为国际服务贸易建立一些统一的准则就成了我们日益关注的一个话题。最终，在关贸总协定的支持下，在最后一轮完成的贸易协商（乌拉圭回合）中，就包含有服务贸易的特征和影响服务贸易的各种国家限制措施。1995 年，关贸总协定演变成了世界贸易组织。在关贸总协定协商的乌拉圭回合中达成的《服务贸易总协定》（GATS），成了这轮协商的一个主要聚焦点。发展中国家（由印度和巴西主导）反对这项协定，因为他们认为这项协定只对发达国家有利，尤其是这些国家的银行、保险、电信和专门业务。GATS 并没有对服务下定义，但是却对服务贸易给予了定义。第 1 款第 2 章将服务贸易定义为：通过任何四种提供方式所提供的服务，即跨境交付服务、境外消费、设在消费国的商业存在和自然人存在。

按照部门分类，国际服务贸易可分为：①运输服务，如海运服务、空运服务、其他运输形式服务；②旅游服务；③其他商业性服务，如通信服务，建筑服务，保险服务，金融服务，计算机与信息服务，特许与许可服务，其他商业服务，个人、文化与娱乐服务。

1.3.2 贸易顺差与贸易逆差

贸易差额（或净出口，有时也表示为 NX）是指一定时期内一个经济体产品出口额与产品进口额之差。顺差称为“贸易盈余”或者“出超”，指出口超过进口；逆差称为“贸易赤字”或者“入超”，指进口超过出口。有时候，贸易差额分为货物贸易和服务贸易差额。

贸易差额是国际收支平衡表中经常项目的一个重要部分。经常项目包括其他一些交易，如来自国际投资头寸和国际援助产生的收入。如果经常项目处于盈余的状态，则该国的国际净资产头寸相应地增加；反之，赤字会减少该国的国际净资产头寸。

影响贸易差额的因素有：出口国经济相对于进口国经济的生产成本（土地、劳动力、资本、税收、激励等）；汇率变动；多边、双边和单边的税收或者贸易限制；非关税壁垒如环境、健康和安全标准；为支付进口的充裕外汇的可获性等。此外，随着商业周期的不同，贸易差额也会有所不同。出口带动的增长（如石油和早期的工业品）中，经济高涨时，其贸易差额会改善。然而，国内需求带动的增长（如美国和澳大利亚）中，同样阶段的商业周期时，其贸易差额却会恶化。

在1994年之前的大多数年份中，中国的货物贸易处于赤字状态。1994年以来，随着大规模的工业产业外包和转移，中国增强了工业品的竞争力。出口的增长超过了进口，将整个贸易赤字扭转为了贸易盈余。2005年，中国货物贸易的盈余额首次达到1 000亿美元。

高储蓄率通常会与贸易顺差相一致。相应地，美国的低储蓄率导致了大的贸易逆差，尤其对东亚国家的贸易逆差。20世纪80年代中叶以来，美国的货物贸易逆差尤其是与东亚国家（中国和日本）的贸易逆差逐渐增加，这些东亚国家目前持有美国大量的债务，从而支撑起了美国的消费。

1.3.3 总贸易体系与专门贸易体系

目前，两种统计进出口商品的制度被广泛使用，即总贸易体系和专门贸易体系。

1.3.3.1 总贸易体系

总贸易体系是指以货物通过一国的国境作为统计的标准。换句话说，当一国的国境与它的经济领土一致时，则使用总贸易体系。一国的经济领土由该国政府管理的地理区域构成，总贸易体系涵盖了所有商品经过该国经济领土的进出，包括通过保税仓库和自由贸易区的流动。

1.3.3.2 专门贸易体系

专门贸易体系是指以货物通过一国的关境作为统计的标准。该体系涵盖了所有商品经过该国或者领土的进出口，但不包括通过保税仓库和自由贸易区的流动。在大多数国家中，收集资料是建立在海关流程基础之上的，并且许多国家都采用关境（边界）作为他们的统计标准。关境是一个地理区域，在此区域一国实施他的进出口规则并征收关税。某些领地或者特殊的经济区域（如自由贸易区）常常被认为是在一国的关境之外。

相比专门贸易体系，总贸易体系提供了更加详尽的外部贸易流动的统计。因此，联合国推荐使用总贸易体系，用该体系对国际贸易统计和国际贸易公布进行编辑。

1.3.4 国际贸易额与国际贸易量

1.3.4.1 国际贸易额

国际贸易额是指国际商品和服务贸易的总额。由于一个国家的出口就是另一个国家的进口，把世界上所有国家的商品进口总额或商品出口总额加在一起，即得到国际货物和服务贸易总额。货物的出口常常按交易额计算，并去掉运费和保险费（FOB价）；而货物的进口按交易额计算，并加上运费和保险费（CIF价）。因此，国际商品贸易总额是指世界出口总额，而不是指世界进口总额。

由于商品的价格经常波动，国际贸易额不能真正地反映出国际贸易的增长水平，因此，不同时期的国际贸易额不具有可比性。

1.3.4.2　国际贸易量

近10年来，国际贸易增长迅速。然而，增长中的许多部分却归结于通货膨胀。为了真正地反映出国际贸易的增长水平，我们使用“国际贸易量”这一概念。

国际贸易量是指根据不变价格计算出来的国际贸易价值，用国际贸易额乘以基期年份的价格指数，然后再除以计算年份的价格指数。例如，1950年为基期年份，该年的商品国际贸易额和价格指数分别为607亿美元和100；计算年份为1997年，该年的商品国际贸易额和价格指数分别为54 500亿美元和600，则1997年的国际贸易量为9 083亿美元（54 500亿美元乘以100，再除以600）。

1.3.5　国际贸易商品结构

国际贸易商品结构是指一定时期内所有货物或者各类货物在国际贸易中所占的比重，它由出口商品结构和进口商品结构组成。国际贸易商品结构通常反映整个世界的经济发展水平、产业结构状况。2010年，在全球商品贸易中，制成品所占的比重最大。对一个特定的国家而言，对外贸易商品结构是指一定时期内一国进出口贸易中每一类或者各类货物所占的比重，它也由出口商品结构和进口商品结构组成。

1.3.6　国际贸易地区分布

国际贸易地区分布或者国际贸易地理方向是指各个国家、地区或经济体在国际贸易中所占的比重。对一个特定的国家而言，每一个地区或国家在其出口或进口中所占的比重构成出口地理方向或进口地理方向。

1.3.7　对外贸易依存度

几乎每一个国家不但要认识到国际贸易发展的绝对水平的重要性，而且还要认识到国际贸易发展的相对水平日益增长的重要性。贸易发展的相对规模常常通过比较一国商品的进出口额和该国的GDP来衡量。对外贸易依存度是指一国的对外贸易额（出口额加进口额）除以GDP，我们可以用下面的公式来表达：$Z=(X+M)/GDP\times100\%$。这里的Z代表进出口额除以GDP的比率，X代表出口额，M代表进口额。

虽然在各国之间对外贸易依存度的差别很大，但是，根据可查的资料来看，在几乎所有的个体或每一个国家集团中，出口的相对重要性增加了许多。这就意味着，不但单个国家正在获得经济收益，而且单个国家的经济繁荣都需要依赖于世界整体的经济繁荣。

进出口额除以GDP的比率常常用来反映一个经济体的开放程度，然而该比率不应作为解释一国贸易政策的标志。例如，美国这一比率相对较低，但美国贸易开放程度高是通过它的低关税反映出来的。这说明了一个事实：服务导向型的国家或经济体大国倾向于相对低的比率。贸易额的增长可能并不是贸易自由化带来的效果。例如，石油价格上涨后，会导致石油出口商出口额的增加，但不会充分地反映在该国的GDP上。对进口国而言，这种形势更加明显，因为燃料进口的增加可能使国内的经济活动变得萧条，从而导致一个更高的贸易对GDP的比率。在不同国家之间进行该比率的比较时，汇率的变动也具有影响力。

Part One
The Theory of International Trade

2 Mercantilism & Theory of Absolute Advantage

2.1 Mercantilism

The systematic study of international trade originated in the Mercantilism era (from the end of the 14th century to the 18th century). The 15th century was a period of primitive accumulation of capital. With the development of productivity in western European countries, the commodity economy for the purpose of exchange gradually became the way for western European countries to accumulate monetary (gold) wealth. In the late 15th and early 16th centuries, great geographical discoveries brought new opportunities to western European countries that had limited gold reserves. These European countries accumulated reserves of gold by expanding international trade and pillaging overseas colonies. This is the historical background of mercantilism.

Mercantilism went through two stages, early and late. The early mercantilism was from the 15th century to the middle of the 16th century, and the late mercantilism was from the second half of the 16th century to the late 18th century. Both early and late mercantilism held the basic view that the wealth was gold and silver, and that the gold and silver currency was the only form of national wealth. The economic activity of domestic market was a kind of zero sum game, and the gain of one party brought the loss of the other party. Domestic transactions did not increase total wealth, but rather redistributed it among groups. The only contribution to the national wealth came from foreign trade. Mercantilism held the view that a country could increase its wealth by exporting its goods and obtaining foreign currency (trade surplus), while importing foreign goods and paying foreign currencies (trade deficit) would decrease its wealth. Therefore, the main point of mercantilism was that the state must actively intervene in the economy, in other words, to encourage the export of goods and suppress the import of goods, so as to increase the social wealth.

Early mercantilists emphasized absolute trade surpluses, advocated the principle of "sell more, buy less" or "do not buy", and advocated the adoption of administrative legistation measures to prohibit the outflow of gold and silver, to control the import of goods, and to encourage the export of goods in order to accumulate monetary wealth. The early mercantilists focus their policies on the strict control of currency inflow and owtflow, hence namely monetary equilibrium theory. Its representative figures included John Hales, William Stafford, A. Monthretien and so on.

Different from the early mercantilism, the late mercantilism advocated that the currency should be viewed from the perspective of development, and the trade surplus of all countries should not be required. As long as the trade surplus of all countries was maintained, the currency would eventually flow back to the domestic. Also the late mercantilism did not insist on obtaining trade surplus in a certain period of time, as long as there was a trade surplus finally. Therefore, this idea of late mercantilism was also known as trade balance theory. Its representative figure was the British economist, Thomas Mun. His book *England's Treasure by Foreign Trade* comprehensively and systematically elaborated the thought of Mercantilism.

Although the trade theory of mercantilism has many defects and limitations, it has begun to regard foreign trade as an important part of the economic system, which has laid a foundation for the later international trade theory.

2.2 Theory of Absolute Advantage

2.2.1 Adam Smith and the theory of absolute advantage

In 1776, Adam Smith, a British classical economist, published a study, *An Inquiry into the Nature and Causes of the Wealth of Nations*. The book became the cornerstone of the classical political economy theory. In *An Inquiry into the Nature and Causes of the Wealth of Nations* (*the National Wealth* for short), Adam Smith stated his ideas on competition and trade. The benefits of division of labor and cooperation among different individuals or families within a country could also be used to explain the causes of international trade. Since every household thought it was cost-effective to produce only a fraction of what it needs and to use what it can produce to buy other goods, the same principle should apply to every country: households should not produce a commodity if it costs less to buy it than to produce it. And if every family within a country acted rationally, so did the country as a whole. For example, Country A could produce more Commodity C with the same resources than Country B, so that the production cost of Commodity C of Country A was lower than that of Country B. Then Country B could exchange for Commodity C with the goods which Country B had more cost advantage or technological advantage on.

Adam Smith argued that national differences in natural conditions such as the geography, soil, and climate – that is, better natural endowments – made a country the best at producing something and the most advantageous in an industry. This led to differences in labor productivity among countries. If a country had higher labor productivity (lower production cost) than other countries on a certain product, then it had an absolute advantage in this product. On the contrary, the product with lower labor productivity (higher production cost) did not have absolute advantage, that is, it had absolute disadvantage. The absolute advantage (lower production cost) that a country had in producing specific products provided the foundation international division of labor. Each country produced and exported the products with the highest "absolute advantage" in labor productivity and the least production cost, and imported the products without "absolute advantage". The exchange between the two parties was beneficial to both parties involved in the trade. In trade theory, this doctrine is called "the absolute advantage theory".

2.2.2 Absolute advantage model

2.2.2.1 Theoretical assumption

Similar to the research method of economics, the theoretical analysis of international trade simplifies the unimportant conditions as much as possible without affecting the analysis conclusion. The basic assumption of Adam Smith's theory of absolute advantage is as follows:

(1) From the perspective of supply: ①two countries and two tradable products, the production of both products has only one input-labor, namely 2×2×1 model; ②supply of labor factors is given; ③the return to scale remains unchanged; ④there is an absolute difference in labor productivity in the two countries.

(2) From a demand perspective: income budget constraints.

(3) From the perspective of trade: ①No transportation and transaction costs; ②Trade between the two countries is balanced, namely exports equal imports; ③The elements of labor may move freely in different sectors within a country, but not between countries.

(4) From the perspective of market structure: production and transaction are carried out in the perfectly competitive market and there is no economic profit.

2.2.2.2 Model analysis

To illustrate the absolute advantage theory more clearly, we provide a model that assumes that Country A and Country B produce wine and cloth, and that the only input factor is the labor factor. According to the division of labor from the principle of Adam Smith, the division before, the division after and after trade between two countries are shown in the following table:

Table 2.1 **Case analysis**

	Country	Wine		Cloth	
		Q_W	L_W	Q_C	L_C
the division before	Country A	1	120	1	70
	Country B	1	80	1	110
the division after	Country A			2.7	190
	Country B	2.375	190		
after trade	Country A	1	1.7		
	Country B	1.375	1		

According to the trade theory of absolute advantage, countries should specialize in producing and export the products with "absolute advantage", and not produce but import the products with "absolute disadvantage". There are two ways to define absolute advantage: the labor productivity and the production cost.

When the labor productivity is used to measure absolute advantage, it refers to the output rate (Q/L) per unit factor input where Q is output and L is labor input. If a country has higher labor productivity than other countries on a certain product, then it has an absolute advantage in that product.

In the model shown above, suppose there are two countries (Country A and Country B). Both countries produce "wine" and "cotton", but with different techniques. Labor is the only factor of production. "Country A" and "Country B" have the same total labor resources of 190 people. According to the distribution of labor resources on different products in the table and the definition of labor productivity, "Country A" can produce 1/120 units of wine and 1/70 units of cloth per person per year, and "Country B" can produce 1/80 units of wine and 1/110 units of cloth per person per year. Therefore, Country A has the absolute advantage of producing cotton cloth. Country B has the absolute advantage of producing wine. According to absolute advantage which takes into account only extreme division of labor and barter, Country A should use all the 190 units of labor to produce the cloth (2.7 units) and then exchange some of the cloth for wine with Country B. Country B should devote 190 units of labor to wine production (2.375 units) and then exchange some of the wine for cotton from Country A.

The benefits of this production specialization and exchange are obvious. Without barter trade, Countries A and B are self-sufficient closed economies. So, in order to satisfy different consumption (the basic assumption of microeconomics is that consumers are always inclined to diversity of goods), each country produces two products–cloth and wine. In a closed economy, what each country produces is what each country consumes.

After two countries open up to free trade and specialization, Country A produces 2.7 units of cloth and Country B produces 2.375 units of wine. Meanwhile, Country A still wants to maintain self-sufficient wine consumption (1 unit), it needs to take out the rest of cloth to exchange wine with Country B. Country B wants to guarantee the original consumption of cloth (1 unit), and exchange the rest of the wine with Country A.

Suppose that the exchange ratio between Country A's cloth and Country B's wine is one unit of cloth for one unit of wine (in practice, this exchange ratio "price" depends on the supply and demand of two products in the international market). After the exchange, Country A now has 1.7 units (of its own production) and 1 unit of wine (imported), 0.7 more cotton than when it was self-sufficient. While Country B also has 1.375 units of wine and 1 unit of cotton, 0.375 more wine than when it was self-sufficient. Both countries have increased consumption than before trade, and both have achieved a level of consumption that is impossible to achieve when they are self-sufficient.

From the example above, it can be found that both sides exchange the products with high production efficiency and low production cost for the products with low production efficiency and high production cost in their own countries, so that the quantities of products owned by each country has been improved compared with the quantities before division of labor. Through the specialized production and international trade, the factors of production are used more effectively, and the consumption and welfare level of both countries are correspondingly improved. That's the gain from trade.

In addition, the production cost can be used to measure the absolute advantage, that is, the number of inputs required to produce a unit of product (unit labor requirement, $a_L = L/Q$). If, in the production of a product, unit labor requirement of one country is less than that of another country, then that country has an absolute advantage in that product. If you are interested in this, you can check by yourself whether you can get the same conclusion as above by comparing the costs of production.

2.2.2.3 Summary using the simple formula

In order to present the main content of the absolute advantage theory more intuitively, the theory is summarized by the simple formulas as follows:

Table 2.2 Formula Summary

Conclusion	Criterion	Formula	Symbol
Compared with Country B, Country A has an absolute advantage in producing specific product j	Labor productivity (output rate per unit labor factor input) $\frac{Q_j}{L}$	$\frac{Q_j^A}{L} > \frac{Q_j^B}{L}$	Q is output, L is labor input; Labor is the only factor of production, and both countries have the same labor resources
	Production cost (the number of factor inputs needed to produce one unit of product j) $a_{Lj} = \frac{L}{Q_j}$	$a_{Lj}^A < a_{Lj}^B$	a_{Lj}: Unit labor requirement, production cost

2.2.2.4 Theoretical meaning of absolute advantage

The emergence of the theory of absolute advantage explains some of the reasons for trade. It played a key role in the replacement of mercantilism by classical economic theory. Its main significance is that international trade can be a "positive-sum game", and both sides of participating countries can benefit from specialized division of labor and exchange, rather than the foreign trade advocated by mercantilism as a "zero-sum game". The cumulative benefit of international trade is an increase in goods with the same amount of labor, not an increase in precious metals such as gold and silver, as mercantilism would have it. At the same time, countries in international trade benefit from the higher labor productivity of a particular product produced than other trading partners, rather than the trade surplus emphasized by mercantilism. In addition, Adam Smith brought the theory of international trade into the theoretical system of market economy. He believed that the economic behavior of trade should also be regulated by the market, rather than the policies of state control, emphasis on exports and inhibition of imports advocated by mercantilism.

However, it must be noted that the absolute advantage theory still has great limitations in explaining the actual phenomenon of international trade. For example, it cannot account for the causes of trade between strong countries with absolute advantage in the production of all kinds of products and weak countries with no absolute advantage in the production of all kinds of products. This is the main limitation of Adam Smith's theory of absolute advantage.

第一部分
国际贸易理论

2 重商主义和绝对优势理论

2.1 重商主义

国际贸易的系统研究萌芽于重商主义时代（14 世纪末到 18 世纪）。15 世纪正好是资本主义原始资本积累阶段。伴随西欧国家生产力发展，以交换为目的的商品经济逐渐变成西欧国家累积货币（黄金）财富的途径。15 世纪末至 16 世纪初的地理大发现，为本身黄金储备有限的西欧国家带来了新的机遇。这些欧洲国家通过扩大国际贸易和掠夺海外殖民地来积累储备黄金。这就是重商主义发展的时代背景。

重商主义的发展历经早期和晚期两个阶段，从15 世纪到 16 世纪中叶，属于重商主义的早期阶段，16 世纪下半叶到 18 世纪属于重商主义的晚期阶段。无论早期还是晚期的重商主义，它们均持有的基本观点是：财富即金银，金银货币是国家财富的唯一形态。国内市场的经济活动是一种零和博弈，一方的获利带来另一方的损失。国内的交易并没有增加社会总财富，而只是社会财富在不同集团之间再分配。而国家财富的改变，唯一来源于对外的贸易活动。重商主义认为一国可以通过出口本国商品并从外国获取货币（贸易顺差），增加国家的财富，而进口外国商品并向外国支付货币（贸易逆差）则会减少国家的财富。因此，重商主义的主要观点就是国家必须要积极干涉经济，换句话说，唯有鼓励商品出口、抑制商品进口，才会增加社会财富。

早期的重商主义者强调绝对的贸易顺差，主张“多卖少买”或者“不买”原则，主张通过立法采取行政手段，严禁金银流出，控制商品进口，同时鼓励商品出口，以累积货币财富。早期的重商主义者将政策重心集中在货币输入、输出的严格管制上，因此又被称为“货币平衡论”。其代表人物有英国的约翰·海尔斯、威廉·斯坦福德和法国的安徒安·孟克列钦等。

与早期重商主义不同，晚期重商主义主张用发展的眼光看待货币，不强求所有国家的贸易都要获得贸易顺差，只要保持总和的贸易顺差，货币最终流回国内即可；也不强求在一定时期内均要获得贸易顺差，只要最终贸易顺差即可。因此，晚期重商主义的这种思想又被称为“贸易平衡论”。其代表人物有英国的托马斯·孟，他的著作《英国得自对外贸易的财富》全面系统地阐述了重商主义的思想。

尽管重商主义的贸易理论存在不少瑕疵和局限性，但重商主义已经开始将对外贸易看成经济系统中的一个重要组成部分，为后世的国际贸易理论奠定了基础。

2.2 绝对优势理论

2.2.1 亚当·斯密与绝对优势理论

1776 年，英国古典经济学家亚当·斯密出版了《国民财富的性质和原因的研究》（简称《国富论》）一书，该书成为古典政治经济学理论的奠基之作。《国富论》中，亚当·斯密陈述了其自由竞争和自由贸易的贸易思想。一国内部不同个体或家庭从分工合作带来的好处同样可以用来解释国际贸易的成因。既然每个家庭都认为只生产一部分它自己需要的产品而用那些它能出售的产品来购买其他产品是合算的，同样的道理应该适用于每个国家。对于家庭而言，如果一件商品的购买支出低于自己的生产成本，那么就不应该自己生产。而如果一个国家内部每一个家庭的行为是理性的，那么整个国家的行为也是理性的。举例而言，国家A可以用同样的资源比国家B生产出更多的商品C，从而使单位商品C的生产成本低于国家B。那么国家B可以用自己更有成本优势或者技术优势的商品同国家A交换商品C。

亚当·斯密认为，诸如地理环境、土壤、气候等自然条件的国别差异——有利的自然禀赋，使某个国家最擅长生产某样东西、最具有某个产业的优势，这就形成了国家间的劳动生产率的差异。一国如果在某种产品上具有比别国高的劳动生产率（低生产成本），该国在这一产品上就具有绝对优势；相反，劳动生产率低的产品（高生产成本）就不具有绝对优势，而是具有绝对劣势。国家在生产特定产品上具有的绝对优势（低生产成本），为国际分工提供了生长的土壤。各国分别生产并出口自身最具劳动生产率和生产成本“绝对优势”的产品，进口其不具有“绝对优势”的产品。双方交换后，对参与贸易的所有交易方均是有利的。在贸易理论上，这一学说被称为“绝对优势理论”。

2.2.2 绝对优势模型

2.2.2.1 理论假设

与经济学的研究方法类似，国际贸易理论分析在不影响分析结论的基础上，将不重要的条件尽可能简化。亚当·斯密的绝对优势理论的基本假设如下：

（1）从供给角度而言。①两个国家和两种可贸易产品，两种产品的生产都只有一种要素投入——劳动，即2×2×1模型；②劳动要素供给给定；③规模报酬不变；④两国在不同产品上的生产技术不同，存在着劳动生产率上的绝对差异。

（2）从需求角度而言，主要是收入预算约束。

（3）从贸易角度而言。①无运输成本和交易费用；②两国贸易均衡，即出口额等于进口额；③劳动要素可以在一国之内的不同部门自由流动，但不能在国家之间流动。

（4）从市场结构而言。生产和交易均在完全竞争市场下进行，无经济利润。

2.2.2.2 模型分析

为了更清楚地说明绝对优势理论，我们提供了一个模型：假定国家A和国家B两个国家生产葡萄酒和棉布，投入要素为劳动要素。按照亚当·斯密的分工原则进行分工，两国分工前、分工后和交换后的情况如表2.1所示。

表2.1 两国分工前、分工后和交换后的情况

分工阶段	国家	葡萄酒		棉布	
		产量/单位（Q）	劳动投入/人·年（L）	产量/单位（Q）	劳动投入/人·年（L）
分工前	国家A	1	120	1	70
	国家B	1	80	1	110

表2.1(续)

分工阶段	国家	葡萄酒		棉布	
		产量/单位(*Q*)	劳动投入/人·年(*L*)	产量/单位(*Q*)	劳动投入/人·年(*L*)
分工后	国家A			2.7	190
	国家B	2.375	190		
交换后	国家A	1		1.7	
	国家B	1.375		1	

根据绝对优势贸易理论，各国应该专门生产并出口其具有“绝对优势”的产品，不生产但进口其具有“绝对劣势”的产品。有两种方式可以定义绝对优势：劳动生产率和生产成本。

用劳动生产率来衡量绝对优势时，即指用单位要素投入的产出率（Q/L）来衡量，其中 Q 表示产量，L 表示劳动投入。一国如果在某种产品上具有比别国高的劳动生产率，该国在这一产品上就具有绝对优势。

表2.1的模型里，假设有两个国家（国家A和国家B），它们都生产“葡萄酒”和“棉布”，但生产技术不同。劳动要素是唯一的生产要素，国家A和国家B的劳动力资源总量相同，都是190人。根据表2.1的劳动资源在不同产品上的分配，结合劳动生产率的定义可知，国家A每人每年可以生产1/120单位的葡萄酒和1/70单位的棉布，国家B每人每年可以生产1/80单位的葡萄酒和1/110单位的棉布。因此，国家A具有生产棉布的绝对优势，国家B具有生产葡萄酒的绝对优势。根据亚当·斯密的绝对优势理论（此处仅考虑极端分工和以物易物的贸易交换模式），国家A应该将190个单位的劳动要素专门生产棉布（2.7单位），然后用其中的一部分去跟国家B交换葡萄酒。国家B则应将190个单位的劳动要素专门生产葡萄酒（2.375单位），然后用一部分葡萄酒去交换国家A的棉布。

这种专业化分工生产和交换的益处是显而易见的：如果没有以物易物的贸易交换，国家A和国家B都是自给自足的封闭经济。那么，为了满足不同的消费（微观经济学的基本假设——消费者总是倾向于商品的多样性），每个国家都要生产两种产品——棉布和葡萄酒。在封闭经济中，各国的生产量也是各国的消费量。

在两国开放自由贸易和专业化分工之后，国家A生产2.7个单位的棉布，而国家B生产2.375个单位的葡萄酒。同时，国家A仍然希望保持自给自足时的葡萄酒消费量（1个单位），则需要拿出富余的棉布去跟国家B交换葡萄酒；而国家B则希望保证原来的棉布消费量（1个单位），将富余的葡萄酒去跟国家A交换。假设，国家A的棉布与国家B的葡萄酒的交换比例是1∶1，即用1个单位的棉布交换1个单位的葡萄酒（实际过程中，这个交换比例“价格”取决于国际市场上两种产品的供给与需求）。贸易交换后，国家A现有1.7个单位（自己生产的）和1个单位葡萄酒（进口的），比自给自足时多了0.7个单位的棉布。而国家B也有1.375个单位的葡萄酒和1个单位的棉布，比自给自足时多了0.375个单位的葡萄酒，两国都比贸易前增加了消费，都得到了在自给自足时不可能达到的消费水平。

从上例可以看出，贸易双方都用本国效率高且成本低的产品去交换本国效率低且成本高的产品，使各国所拥有的产品产量都比分工以前提高了。两国通过专业化生产和国际贸易，使生产要素得到最有效的利用，其消费和福利水平均获得了相应的提高。这就是贸易所得。

另外，如果用生产成本，即生产一个单位产品所需的要素投入数量来衡量（unit labor requirement，单位产品劳动要素投入，$a_L = L/Q$）。如在某种产品的生产中，一国单位产量所需的要素投入低于另一国，该国在这一产品上就具有绝对优势。因此，感兴趣的同学，可以自行通过比较生产成本的方式，检验是否与以上比较劳动生产率时得到同样的结论。

2.2.2.3　简易公式总结

为了使绝对优势理论的主要内容有更直观的呈现，我们将内容用简易公式进行总结，见表 2.2。

表 2.2　公式总结

结论	判断依据	公式	符号含义
相较于国家 B，国家 A 在生产特定产品 j 上具有绝对优势	劳动生产率（单位劳动要素投入的产出率）$\frac{Q_j}{L}$	$\frac{Q_j^A}{L} > \frac{Q_j^B}{L}$	Q 表示产量，L 表示劳动投入；劳动是唯一的生产要素，两国有相同的劳动力资源
	生产成本（生产一单位产品 j 所需的要素投入数量）$a_{Lj} = \frac{L}{Q_j}$	$a_{Lj}^A < a_{Lj}^B$	a_{Lj}，即单位产品劳动要素投入，生产成本

2.2.2.4　绝对优势理论意义

绝对优势理论的诞生解释了产生贸易的部分原因。它在古典经济学说取代重商主义思想的过程中起到了关键作用。其主要意义在于，国际贸易可以是一个“正和博弈”，参与贸易的国家双方均可以从专业化分工与交换中获益，而不是重商主义宣扬的对外贸易是一个“零和游戏”。国际贸易中国家累积的利益是劳动量不变情况下的商品增加，而不是重商主义思想认为的黄金白银等贵金属的增加。同时，国际贸易中国家的获益来自所生产的某个特定产品高于其他贸易伙伴的劳动生产率，而不是重商主义强调的贸易顺差。此外，亚当·斯密把国际贸易理论纳入了市场经济的理论体系，他认为贸易这种经济行为也应受市场调节而不是重商主义提倡的国家控制、重视出口、抑制进口等政策。

但是，必须要注意的是，亚当·斯密的绝对优势理论在解释国际贸易实际现象时仍然存在很大的局限性。例如，它无法解释在各种产品的生产上都具有绝对优势的强国和在各种产品的生产上均不具有绝对优势的弱国之间的贸易成因。这是亚当·斯密的绝对优势理论的主要遗憾。

3 Theory of Comparative Advantage

3.1 Ricardo and the Theory of Comparative Advantage

As an important figure in classical political economy, David Ricardo, like Adam Smith, was a strong supporter of free trade. In April 1817, David Ricardo's masterwork *On the Principles of Political Economy and Taxation* was published. The book contains a wealth of his economic thoughts and has made pioneering contributions to the theory of international trade. In the chapter *on Foreign Trade*, David Ricardo used the classic examples of "wine" and "cloth" to illustrate comparative advantage, and concluded that free trade benefits all trading countries, namely the most well-known doctrine in classical economics – the law of comparative advantage. This basic idea was later adopted and developed by numerous economists.

David Ricardo believed that countries should adopt the division of labor according to the law of comparative advantage. If one country has an absolute advantage in the production of both goods, but the degree of advantage position is not the same, while, another country has an absolute disadvantage in the production of both goods, but the degree of disadvantage position is not the same, Then the former should be specialized production, which is relatively more advantageous.

Ricardo believed that free trade and specialized division of labor increased the total amount of goods in a country and brought benefits to society. International trade increases the quantity and variety of goods purchased with income and provides incentives for economy and capital accumulation due to the abundance and low prices of goods. Like Adam Smith, Ricardo recognized the benefits of imports.

3.2 Analysis of Theory of Comparative Advantage

3.2.1 Theoretical Assumptions

(1) There are only two countries producing two kinds of goods, 2×2 model.

(2) The factors of production may flow freely within a country, but not between countries.

(3) Trade is in the form of barter.

(4) The production costs of both parties of the transaction remain unchanged, and there are no returns to scale, transportation costs and transaction costs.

(5) There is no technological progress or economic development.

(6) The market for factors of production and the market for products are perfectly competitive markets.

(7) There is no change in income distribution.

(8) Adhere to the labor theory of value, that is, labor determines the value of goods. All labor is homogeneous.

3.2.2 Model Analysis

David Ricardo used the example of wine and cloth produced in Britain and Portugal to explain the theory of comparative advantage. Suppose that labor is the only input. Portugal has absolute advantage in wine and cloth production. According to Ricardo's principle of division of labor, the division before, the division after trade between two countries is shown in Table 3.1.

Table 3.1 Case analysis

	Country	Wine		Cloth	
		Q_W	L_W		Q_W
the division before	Britain	1	120	1	100
	Portugal	1	80	1	90
the division after	Britain			2.2	220
	Portugal	2.375	170		
after trade	Britain	1	1.2		
	Portugal	1.125	1		

Whether a product has a comparative advantage in production can be measured by the opportunity cost of the product. Opportunity cost refers to the amount of other products (cloth) that must be given up in order to produce an extra unit of one product (wine, for example). The opportunity cost of producing one unit of wine in terms of cloth is: the opportunity cost of wine = Reduced cloth production (ΔQc) / Increased wine production (ΔQw).

In a given period of time (or land), each British labor can produce 2.2 units of cloth or 1.833 3 units of wine. That is, to produce one more unit of cloth in Britain, a farmer would have to produce 0.833 3 more units of wine. The opportunity cost of producing an extra unit of cloth is 0.833 3 units of wine. In Portugal, to produce one more unit of cloth, a farmer must produce 1.125 fewer units of wine. The opportunity cost of producing an extra unit of cloth is 1.125 per unit of wine. Similarly, we can calculate the opportunity cost of wine (the inverse of the opportunity cost of cloth): 1.2 units of cloth in the UK and 0.888 9 units in Portugal. The opportunity cost of producing cloth in Britain is lower and has a comparative advantage. Portugal has a comparative advantage in producing wine because of its lower opportunity cost.

3.2.3 Summary Using the Simple Formula

In addition to using the opportunity cost of products to measure whether a product has a comparative advantage in production, we can also use the relative labor productivity and relative cost of products to judge the comparative advantage. The main determination methods of comparative advantage are summarized by simple formula as follows:

Whether it is the product's relative labor productivity, relative cost or opportunity cost, the conclusion of comparative advantage measured by the three methods is the same.

According to David Ricardo, trade is caused by differences in production technology and relative cost among countries. A country may have an absolute advantage in the production of all products, but it will not have a comparative advantage in the production of all products. Conversely, a country must have a comparative advantage in the production of certain products. Then, according to David ricardo's theory of comparative advantage, a country with a comparative advantage in the production of a certain product must be able to participate in the international division of labor, export its products with comparative advantage and import its products with comparative disadvantage, so as to obtain trade gains.

Many of the conclusions of economics are consistent with "common sense". Are there any economic conclusions that contradict "common sense"? Yes, the theory of comparative advantage is a typical economic conclusion that contradicts popular perception. For example, developed countries like the United States have high labor productivity in the production of many goods, while less developed countries like India have low labor productivity in the production of the same goods. According to "common sense", there would be no trade between the US and India. That is not the case at all. In the previous example, Portugal had an absolute advantage in producing cotton as well as wine. According g to the law of absolute advantage, Portugal should produce both products and export them to Britain, while Britain should produce nothing but import both products. It is practically impossible, because trade itself is bidirectional. A country cannot import without exporting. If Britain could only export profitably under conditions of absolute advantage, it could not export anything, and it would not trade with Portugal.

Table 3.2 Formula Summary

Conclusion	Criterion	Formula
Compared with Country B, Country A has a comparative advantage in producing specific product j	Relative labor productivity of products (labor productivity ratio of different products or the ratio of output per capita of two different products)	Labor productivity of product i: $\frac{Q_i}{L}$ Labor productivity of product j: $\frac{Q_j}{L}$ Relative labor productivity of product i in Country A (relative to product j) $= \frac{\frac{Q_i^A}{L}}{\frac{Q_j^A}{L}}$ Relative labor productivity of product i in Country B (relative to product j) $= \frac{\frac{Q_i^B}{L}}{\frac{Q_j^B}{L}}$ If the relative labor productivity of product i in Country A is higher than that of the same product in Country B, then Country A has a comparative advantage in product i: $\frac{\frac{Q_i^A}{L}}{\frac{Q_j^A}{L}} > \frac{\frac{Q_i^B}{L}}{\frac{Q_j^B}{L}}$
	Relative cost (the ratio of unit factor input of one product to unit factor input of another product)	Unit labor requirements for product i: $a_{Li} = \frac{L}{Q_i}$ Unit labor requirements for product j: $a_{Lj} = \frac{L}{Q_j}$ If the relative cost of product i in Country A is lower than that of the same product in Country B, then Country A has a comparative advantage in product i: $\frac{a_{Li}^A}{a_{Lj}^A} < \frac{a_{Li}^B}{a_{Lj}^B}$
	Opportunity cost (the number of other products that must be given up in order to produce one more unit of a product)	Opportunity cost of product i: $\frac{\Delta Q_i}{\Delta Q_j}$ If the opportunity cost of product i in Country A is lower than that of the same product in Country B, then Country A has A comparative advantage in product i: $(\frac{\Delta Q_i}{\Delta Q_j})^A < (\frac{\Delta Q_i}{\Delta Q_j})^B$

However, according to the theory of comparative advantage, trade can still occur between two countries. Britain has a comparative advantage in cloth production, although Britain does not have an absolute advantage in any products. The opportunity cost of producing one unit of cloth is 1. 125 units of wine in Portugal and just 0. 833 3 units of wine in the Britain. That is to say, you can get one unit of cloth with 0. 833 3 units of wine in the Britain but with 1. 125 units of wine in Portugal.

Therefore, Britain could concentrate on cloth production and export cloth to Portugal, importing wine from Portugal. There was trade between the two countries. Through this example, we can see that the theory of comparative advantage is more general than the theory of absolute advantage. Not only does it more broadly demonstrate the basis of trade in theory, but also partly explains the reasons for trade between developed countries and less developed countries in practice.

3.2.4 Graphical Analysis

The theory of comparative advantage can be illustrated by graphs and curves. Suppose there are only two countries, domestic country and foreign country; there is only one factor of production, labor; only two products, wine and cloth; labor productivity represents the level of production technology of each country; labor productivity is expressed as unit labor requirement.

The notation a_{LC} and a_{LW} represent unit labor requirement of cloth and wine produced in the domestic country respectively. L is the total supply of labor in the domestic country. The notation a_{LC}^* and a_{LW}^* respectively represent unit labor requirement of cloth and wine produced in foreign countries. L^* is the total supply of foreign labor.

According to the above assumptions, the production possibility frontier of domestic and foreign countries can be formed. The production possibilities frontier (PPF) shows that a country's resources are limited and the products it can produce are limited. Therefore, there is product substitution: producing one more product means sacrificing the output of another. The production possibilities frontier (PPF) of an economy shows the maximum combination of quantities of goods that can be produced from a fixed quantity of resources.

Q_W and Q_C are the output of domestic wine and cloth respectively. The labor input that can be used for wine production in the domestic country is $a_{LW}Q_W$, and the labor input for cotton production is $a_{LC}Q_C$. The total labor supply in the country is L. Therefore, the restriction of domestic resources on output: $a_{LC}Q_C+a_{LW}Q_W \leqslant L$. Under the condition of single factor of production (labor), the production possibility frontier is a straight line, where the opportunity cost of cloth in terms of wine is fixed. To produce one more unit of cloth requires a_{LC} labor, and each labor can produce $1/a_{LW}$ unit of wine. Therefore, the opportunity cost of cloth measured by wine is a_{LC}/a_{LW}, which is equal to the negative slope of the production possibilities frontier (Figure 3.1).

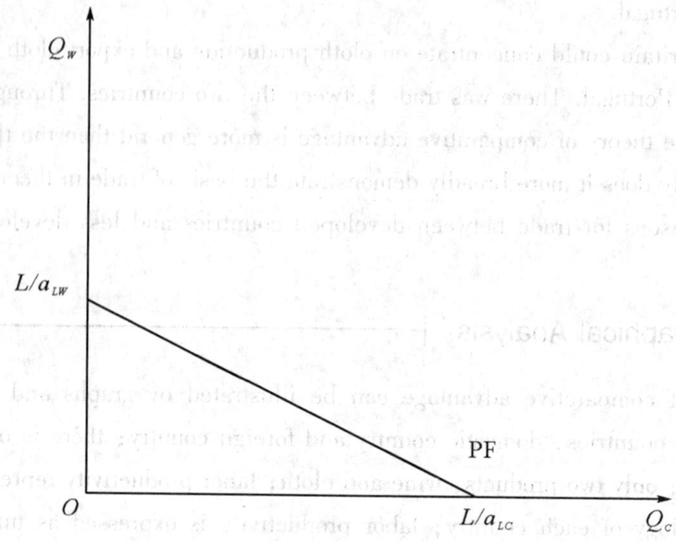

Figure 3. 1 The Production Possibilities Frontier (PPF) of Domestic Country

Similarly, let Q_W^* and Q_C^* be the output of foreign wine and cloth respectively. The labor input of foreign countries for wine production is $a_{LW}^* Q_W^*$, and the labor input for cloth production is $a_{LC}^* Q_C^*$. The total labor supply of foreign countries is L^*. Therefore, the restriction of foreign resources on output: $a_{LC}^* Q_C^* + a_{LW}^* Q_W^* \leqslant L^*$. Under the condition of single factor of production (labor), the production possibility boundary is a straight line, where the opportunity cost of cloth represented by wine is fixed. To produce one more unit of cloth requires an input of a_{LC}^* labor, and each unit of labor can produce $1/a_{LW}^*$ unit of wine. Therefore, the opportunity cost of cloth measured by wine is a_{LC}^*/a_{LW}^*, equal to the negative slope of the production possibilities frontier (Figure 3. 2).

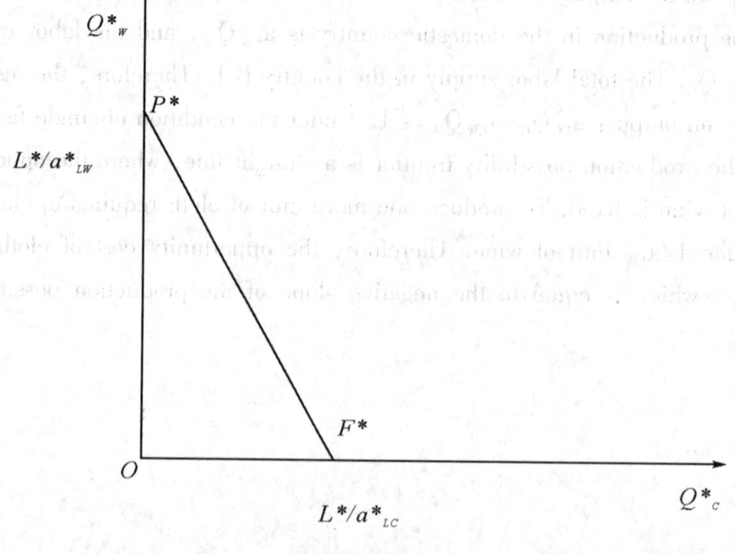

Figure 3. 2 The Production Possibilities Frontier (PPF) of Foreign Country

The current model is simplified: labor is the only factor of production, and the labor supply of cloth and wine is determined by the flow of labor, which always goes to higher-wage sectors.

Let P_W represent the price of wine and P_C represent the price of cloth. There is no economic profit in the single-factor model. The hourly wage rate in the cloth industry is equal to the value created by a worker in 1 hour P_C/a_{LC}. Therefore, the hourly wage rate in the wine industry is equal to P_W/a_{LW}. When $P_C/a_{LC}>P_W/a_{LW}$, namely $P_C/P_W> a_{LC}/a_{LW}$, it implies that the wage rate of cloth industry is higher and everyone wants to work in the industry with higher wages. Then the country will only specialize in the production of cloth; When $P_C/P_W< a_{LC}/a_{LW}$, the wage rate in the wine industry is relatively high and everyone wants to work in the wine industry. Therefore, the country will only specialize in wine production. When $P_C/P_W=a_{LC}/a_{LW}$, the cloth and wine industries have the same wage rates. The labor would flow arbitrarily to either industry, so the country would produce cloth and wine both.

a_{LC}/a_{LW} is the opportunity cost of cloth in terms of wine, while P_C/P_W is the relative price of cloth. Thus, a country specializes in producing cloth when its relative price is higher than its opportunity cost. When the relative price of cloth is below its opportunity cost, the country specializes in wine (cloth is unprofitable). In the absence of international trade, countries have to produce both products by themselves (the basic assumption of economics is that there is always a preference for diversified commodity combination), and the relative price of products is equal to their relative unit labor requirement (opportunity cost).

Suppose that $a_{LC}/a_{LW}< a^*_{LC}/a^*_{LW}$, that is, the opportunity cost of domestic cloth production is less than that of foreign cloth production, which indicates that the country has a comparative advantage in producing cloth. In addition, since a_{LC}/a_{LW} and a^*_{LC}/a^*_{LW} represent the negative slopes of the domestic and foreign production possibilities frontier respectively, another implication of the hypothesis is that the foreign production possibilities frontier is steeper than the domestic production possibilities frontier.

It must be clear when a country can produce the same units of goods with less labor input than other countries, we say that the country has an absolute advantage in producing such goods, such as $a_{LC}< a^*_{LC}$ and $a_{LW}< a^*_{LW}$. If we say that our country has a comparative advantage in producing cloth, we mean $a_{LC}/a_{LW}< a^*_{LC}/a^*_{LW}$ or $a_{LC}/ a^*_{LC}< a_{LW}/a^*_{LW}$.

If there is no international trade, the relative price of cloth against wine in each country is determined by their relative unit labor requirement. The relative price of domestic cloth is a_{LC}/a_{LW}, and the relative price of foreign cotton is a^*_{LC}/a^*_{LW}. Once international trade is conducted, domestic factors are no longer the sole determinant of prices. If the relative price of foreign cloth is higher than that at home country, it is profitable to ship cloth from home or wine from abroad. However, as domestic cloth exports increase, the relative price of cloth will rise and the relative price of foreign cloth will fall. Eventually, the relative prices of domestic and foreign countries will converge, and imports and exports will reach equilibrium at this point. So how should this relative price of trade be determined?

The relative price of domestic and foreign cloth ultimately equal to each other. The demand and supply model determines this relative price. Suppose there are only two countries in the world market: domestic and foreign. The relative price of cloth to wine is determined by the intersection of the relative demand curve of cloth to wine and the relative supply curve of cloth to wine. The relative demand curve of cloth to wine is a normal relative demand curve, and the demand curve slopes downward. In this case, the relative supply curve of cloth to wine is different from that of normal upward-slopping supply curve. The relative supply curve here is a ladder (Figure 3.3). How does this work?

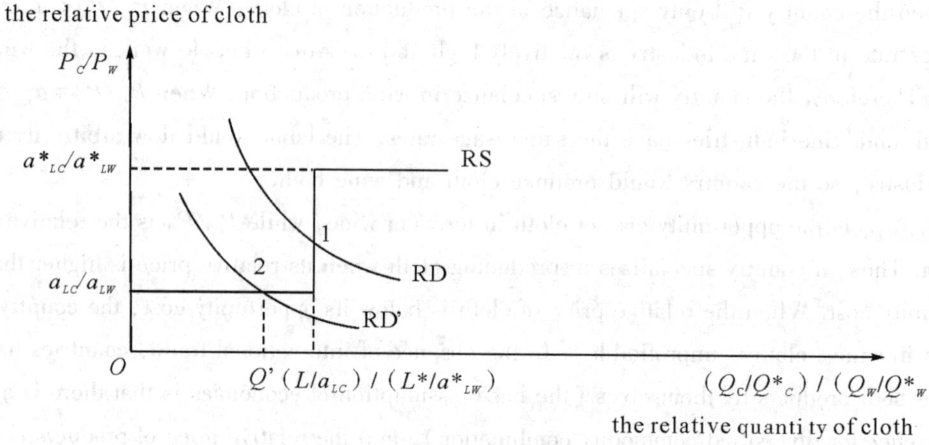

Figure 3.3 **Relative supply and relative demand of cloth in the world**

First, in the world, when the relative price of cloth is $0< P_C/P_W< a_{LC}/a_{LW}$, it means that the relative price of cloth is less than the opportunity cost of cloth production. Then the relative supply of cloth worldwide is zero.

Second, when the relative price of cloth $P_C/P_W = a_{LC}/a_{LW}$, the relative price of domestic cloth is equal to the opportunity cost of cloth production. Domestic workers can get the same salary no matter whether they produce cloth or wine. Therefore, the relative supply of domestic cloth can be arbitrary value, so the relative supply curve is horizontal. In addition, the world relative price of cloth is lower than the opportunity cost of producing foreign cloth, so the production of foreign cloth is 0.

Third, when the relative price of cloth is between the opportunity cost of domestic and foreign cloth production, or when $a_{LC}/a_{LW} < P_C/P_W < a^*_{LC}/a^*_{LW}$, the domestic country will specialize in the production of cloth. The quantity of cloth produced is a fixed number, L/a_{LC}. Foreign country will specialize in the production of wine, L^* / a^*_{LW}. At this point, the relative supply quantity of cloth is (L/a_{LC}) / (L^* / a^*_{LW}). This is a constant value, so the relative supply curve is vertical.

Fourth, when the relative price of cloth is equal to the opportunity cost of producing foreign cloth, $P_C/P_W = a^*_{LC}/a^*_{LW}$. The country will specialize in producing wine and not cloth. However, foreign workers can get the same salary whether they produce cloth or wine. The relative supply of foreign cloth can be arbitrary value, so the relative supply curve is again horizontal.

Finally, when the relative price of cloth is greater than the opportunity cost of foreign cloth production, $P_C/P_W > a^*_{LC}/a^*_{LW}$. Both domestic and foreign workers choose to work in the cloth sector because of the higher payment in the cloth sector. At this time, the world output of wine is 0, and the relative supply of cloth becomes infinite.

Based on the analysis above, we can find out why the relative supply curve of cloth presents a ladder shape.

Then look at the two relative demand curves in the previous figure. RD and RS intersects at point 1. At this point, the relative price of cloth P_C/P_W is between the opportunity cost of domestic cloth a_{LC}/a_{LW} and the opportunity cost of foreign cloth a^*_{LC}/a^*_{LW}. If RD ′and RS intersects at point 2, the relative price of cloth P_C/P_W is equal to the opportunity cost of domestic cloth a_{LC}/a_{LW}, and less than the opportunity cost of foreign cotton a^*_{LC}/a^*_{LW}. It means that the domestic country may produce both wine and cloth products, while the foreign country only produces wine. This is an incomplete specialization.

3.2.5 Gains from Trade

In the theory of absolute advantage, it is easier for people to see clearly the gains from trade. Because the absolute value of production cost of a country's exports must be lower than that of other countries and the products imported must be the products whose production cost is absolutely higher than that of other countries. You can make or save money from trade. However, in the theory of comparative advantage, the gains from trade are not so intuitive. It is possible for a country to export products with higher production costs than foreign countries, or to import products with lower production costs from foreign countries. In this case, what does a country gain from participating in international trade?

In fact, the trade gains of each country are obtained through specialization and exchange.

If the country wanted to consume the wine, it could produce $1/a_{LW}$ of wine with 1 unit of labor factor. It is also possible to produce $1/a_{LC}$ units of cloth with 1 unit of labor factor, and export the cloth in exchange for wine. The terms of trade is 1 unit of cloth for P_C/P_W units of wine, so one unit of labor can produce $(1/a_{LC}) \times (P_C/P_W)$ units of wine. In the world market equilibrium, if no country produces two products at the same time, there must be $P_C/P_W > a_{LC}/a_{LW}$, or $(1/a_{LC}) \times (P_C/P_W) > 1/a_{LW}$. It implies that the amount of wine indirectly produced by cloth production and export is more than the amount of wine directly produced by one unit of labor. This shows that the domestic country benefits from specialization and international trade. Similarly, the foreign country can "produce" cloth more efficiently by producing and exporting wine in exchange for cloth. Therefore, domestic and foreign countries can get win-win results from international trade cooperation.

Trade also enlarges domestic and foreign consumption possibilities. Before trade, the consumption possibility frontier is consistent with the production possibility frontier. Once international trade occurs, countries can consume a different mix of products than they produce. In both countries, trade has expanded the range of consumption options. Therefore, it is bound to improve the welfare of their citizens (Figure 3.4).

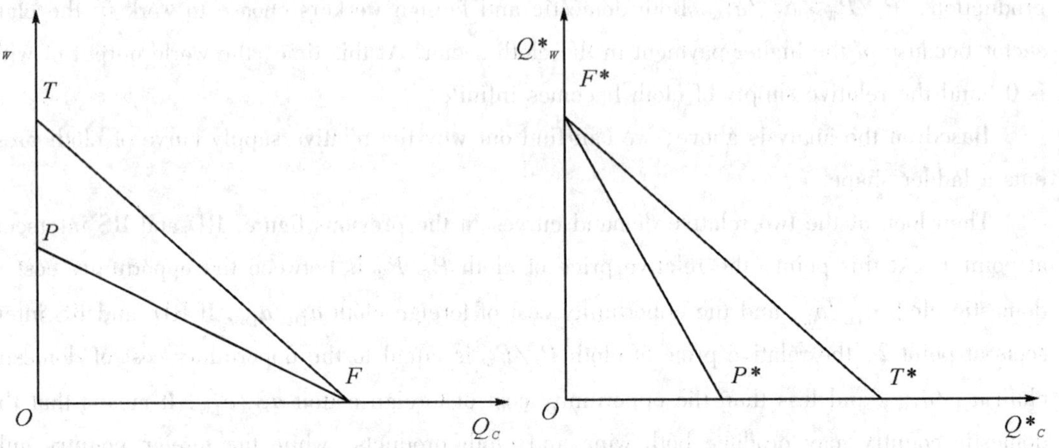

Figure 3.4 **Domestic and Foreign Consumption Possibilities**

Through the analysis above, the effects and gains of trade on a country's economy in Ricardo's comparative advantage model can be summarized as follows:

(1) After the occurrence of trade, countries export products with comparative advantages and import products without comparative advantages, resulting in an increase in the relative price of products with comparative advantages (export products) (or a decrease in the relative price of imported products without comparative advantages).

(2) Changes in relative prices encourage each country to specialize in the production of products with a comparative advantage and not produce products with no comparative advantage.

(3) Under the trade, the social welfare level of all countries has been improved. Gain from trade comes from the efficient allocation of both consumption and production of products. Through trade, a country can consume more than it can produce.

3 比较优势理论

3.1 大卫·李嘉图与比较优势理论

作为古典政治经济学的重要人物，大卫·李嘉图和亚当·斯密一样，是贸易自由的坚决支持者。1817年4月，大卫·李嘉图的名著《政治经济学及赋税原理》出版。该书包含了他丰富的经济思想，对国际贸易理论有开创性的贡献。在《政治经济学及赋税原理》的《论对外贸易》一章中，大卫·李嘉图用经典例子“葡萄酒”和“棉布”说明了比较优势，并得到了自由贸易使贸易国均有所得的结论，即古典经济学中最广为人知的学说——比较优势原则。这个基本思想在后来被无数经济学者引用并发展。

大卫·李嘉图认为，国家之间应该按照比较优势原则进行分工。如果一个国家在两种商品的生产上均处于绝对有利地位，但有利的程度不一样；而另一个国家在两种产品的生产上都处于绝对不利地位，但不利的程度不同；那么前者应专门生产比较更有利。

大卫·李嘉图认为，自由贸易与专业分工使一国商品总量的增长，给社会带来利益。国际贸易增加了用收入购买的物品的数量和种类，并且由于商品丰富和价格低廉而为节约和资本积累提供刺激。同亚当·斯密一样，大卫·李嘉图同样肯定了进口带来的好处。

3.2 比较优势理论的分析

3.2.1 理论假设

（1）只有两个国家，生产两种商品，2×2模型；

（2）生产要素在一国之内可以自由流动，但不能在国家之间流动；

（3）贸易是以物易物的形式；

（4）交易双方生产成本不变，没有规模收益，无运输费用和交易费用；

（5）不存在技术进步和经济发展；

（6）生产要素市场和产品市场是完全竞争市场；

（7）收入分配未发生变化；

（8）坚持劳动价值论，即劳动决定商品价值，所有劳动都是同质的。

3.2.2 模型分析

大卫·李嘉图用英国和葡萄牙两个国家生产葡萄酒和棉布的例子来解释比较优势理论。其假定投入要素为劳动要素，则葡萄牙在葡萄酒和棉布的生产上均具有绝对优势。我们按照大卫·李嘉图的分工原则进行分工，两国分工前、分工后和交换后的情况如表3.1所示。

表 3.1　两国分工前、分工后和交换后的情况

分工阶段	国家	葡萄酒		棉布	
		产量/单位（Q）	劳动投入/人·年（L）	产量/单位（Q）	劳动投入/人·年（L）
分工前	英国	1	120	1	100
	葡萄牙	1	80	1	90
分工后	英国			2.2	220
	葡萄牙	2.375	170		
交换后	英国	1		1.2	
	葡萄牙	1.125		1	

一种产品是否具有生产上的比较优势可以用该产品的机会成本来衡量。所谓“机会成本”，指的是为了额外多生产一个单位的某产品（如葡萄酒）而必须放弃的其他产品（棉布）的数量。用棉布来衡量的每单位葡萄酒产量的机会成本为：葡萄酒的机会成本=减少的棉布产量（$\triangle Qc$）/增加的葡萄酒产量（$\triangle Qw$）。

在给定的时间（或土地）里，每个英国劳动要素可以生产 2.2 个单位棉布，也可以生产 1.833 3 个单位的葡萄酒，但不能同时生产 2.2 个单位棉布和 1.833 3 个单位的葡萄酒。也就是说，在英国，一个农民要想多生产 1 个单位棉布，他就不得不少生产 0.833 3 个单位的葡萄酒。每单位棉布的“机会成本”是 0.833 3 个单位的葡萄酒。在葡萄牙，一个农民要想多生产一个单位的棉布，就必须少生产 1.125 个单位的葡萄酒。每单位棉布的“机会成本”是 1.125 个单位的葡萄酒。同样，我们可以算出葡萄酒的机会成本（棉布机会成本的倒数）：英国为 1.2 个单位的棉布，葡萄牙为 0.888 9 个单位的棉布。英国生产棉布的机会成本低，具有比较优势。葡萄牙生产葡萄酒的机会成本低，具有生产葡萄酒的比较优势。

3.2.3　简易公式总结

我们除了用产品的机会成本来衡量一种产品是否具有生产上的比较优势外，还可以用产品的相对劳动生产率和相对成本来判断比较优势。我们将比较优势的主要判定方法用简易公式进行总结，见表 3.2。

表 3.2　公式总结

结论	判断依据	公式
相较于国家 B，国家 A 在生产特定产品 j 上具有比较优势	产品的相对劳动生产率（不同产品劳动生产率比率或两种不同产品的人均产量之比）	产品 i 的劳动生产率：$\frac{Q_i}{L}$ 产品 j 的劳动生产率：$\frac{Q_j}{L}$ A 国，产品 i 的相对劳动生产率（相对于产品 j）$=\frac{\frac{Q_i^A}{L}}{\frac{Q_j^A}{L}}$ B 国，产品 i 的相对劳动生产率（相对于产品 j）$=\frac{\frac{Q_i^B}{L}}{\frac{Q_j^B}{L}}$ 如果 A 国产品 i 的相对劳动生产率高于 B 国同样产品的相对劳动生产率，则 A 国在产品 i 上拥有比较优势，即 $\frac{\frac{Q_i^A}{L}}{\frac{Q_j^A}{L}} > \frac{\frac{Q_i^B}{L}}{\frac{Q_j^B}{L}}$
	相对成本（一个产品的单位要素投入与另一产品单位要素投入的比率）	单位产品 i 的要素投入量：$a_{Li}=\frac{L}{Q_i}$ 单位产品 j 的要素投入量：$a_{Lj}=\frac{L}{Q_j}$ 如果 A 国产品 i 的相对成本低于 B 国同样产品的相对成本，则 A 国在产品 i 上拥有比较优势，即 $\frac{a_{Li}^A}{a_{Lj}^A} < \frac{a_{Li}^B}{a_{Lj}^B}$
	机会成本（为了额外多生产一个单位的某产品而必须放弃的其他产品的数量）	产品 i 的机会成本：$\frac{\triangle Q_i}{\triangle Q_j}$ 如果 A 国生产产品 i 的机会成本低于 B 国同样产品的机会成本，则 A 国在产品 i 上拥有比较优势，即 $(\frac{\triangle Q_i}{\triangle Q_j})^A < (\frac{\triangle Q_i}{\triangle Q_j})^B$

无论是用产品的相对劳动生产率还是相对成本（或机会成本），它们衡量的比较优势结论都是一样的。

大卫·李嘉图认为，贸易之所以产生是各国的生产技术差异和相对成本差异。一个国家可能会在所有产品的生产上具有绝对优势，但是不会在所有产品的生产上具有比较优势；反过来，一个国家一定在某些产品的生产上具有比较优势。那么，根据大卫·李嘉图的比较优势理论，在某产品生产上具有比较优势的国家，一定能参与国际分工，出口其具有比较优势的产品，进口其具有比较劣势的产品，从而获得贸易所得。

经济学的很多结论都是与"常识"相符的。那么，有没有与"常识"相悖的经济学结论呢？有的，比较优势理论就是一个典型的，会与大众认知相悖的经济学结论。例如，像美国这样的发达国家，在很多的商品生产上具有极高的劳动生产率，而印度这样的欠发达国家，在同商品的生产上，劳动生产率偏低。按照大众的"常识"，美国和印度之间就不会存在贸易。但事实并非如此。又比如，在前面的例子中，葡萄牙不但拥有生产葡萄酒的绝对优势，也拥有生产棉布的绝对优势。根据"绝对优势"学说，葡萄牙应该生产所有两种产品并向英国出口，英国应该什么也不生产只是进口。但是，这种情况实际是不可能发生的，因为贸易本身是双向的。一个国家不可能只有进口没有出口。如果只有在绝对优势的条件下才能出口获利的话，英国什么东西都不能出口，英国和葡萄牙就不会产生贸易。

但是，根据比较优势学说，贸易仍能在两国间产生。英国虽然在所有两种产品上都不拥有绝对优势，却在棉布生产上拥有比较优势。生产一个单位棉布的机会成本，在葡萄牙是 1.125 个单位的葡萄酒，在英国只是 0.833 3 个单位的葡萄酒。也就是说，用 0.833 3 个单位的葡萄酒在英国就可以换到一个单位棉布，在葡萄牙则要用 1.125 个单位的葡萄酒。从而，英国可以集中生产棉布并出口葡萄牙，同时从葡萄牙进口葡萄酒，两国之间产生了贸易。通过此例，我们可以看到，"比较优势"学说比"绝对优势"理论更有普遍意义，不仅在理论上更广泛地论证了贸易的基础，在实践上也部分解释了发达国家与欠发达国家之间产生贸易的原因。

3.2.4 图形分析

比较优势理论可以用图形和曲线来说明。假设只有本国和外国两个国家；只有一种生产要素，即劳动；只生产两种产品——葡萄酒和棉布；劳动生产率代表各个国家的生产技术水平；劳动生产率用单位产品劳动要素投入来表示。

a_{LC}和a_{LW}分别表示本国生产棉布和葡萄酒的单位产品劳动投入；L表示本国的劳动总供给。a_{LC}^*和a_{LW}^*分别表示外国生产棉布和葡萄酒的单位产品劳动投入；L^*表示外国的劳动总供给。

根据以上假设，可得本国和外国的生产可能性曲线。生产可能性边界（PPF）指的是：一个国家的资源是有限的，它所能生产的产品也是有限的。因此就存在着产品替代的问题：多生产一种产品就意味着要牺牲另一种产品的产量。一个经济体的生产可能性边界（PPF）显示了其固定数量资源所能生产的商品的最大数量。

Q_W和Q_C分别为本国葡萄酒和棉布的产量。本国可以用于葡萄酒生产的劳动投入为$a_{LW}Q_W$，用于棉布生产的劳动投入为$a_{LC}Q_C$，而本国的劳动总供给为L。因此，本国资源对产出的限制为$a_{LC}Q_C+a_{LW}Q_W \leqslant L$。单一生产要素（劳动）条件下生产可能性边界是一条直线，此时用葡萄酒表示的棉布的机会成本是固定的。多生产 1 个单位棉布需要投入a_{LC}人/小时的劳动，而每单位/人 · 小时的劳动能产生$1/a_{LW}$单位的葡萄酒，因此用葡萄酒来衡量的棉布的机会成本为a_{LC}/a_{LW}，等于生产可能性边界的负斜率。本国的生产可能性边界见图 3.1。

类似，令Q_W^*和Q_C^*分别表示外国葡萄酒和棉布的产量。外国可用于葡萄酒生产的劳动投入为$a_{LW}^* Q_W^*$，用于棉布生产的劳动投入为$a_{LC}^* Q_C^*$，而外国的劳动总供给为L^*。因此，外国资源对产出的限制为$a_{LC}^* Q_C^*+a_{LW}^* Q_W^* \leqslant L^*$。单一生产要素（劳动）条件下生产可能性边界是一条直线，此时用葡萄酒表示的棉布的机会成本是固定的。多生产 1 个单位棉布需要投入 a_{LC}^{*}人·小时的劳动，而每单位/人·小时的劳动能产生 $1/a_{LW}^{*}$单位的葡萄酒，因此用葡萄酒来衡量的棉布的机会成本为 a_{LC}^{*}/a_{LW}^{*}，等于生产可能性边界的负斜率。外国的生产可能性边界见图 3.2。

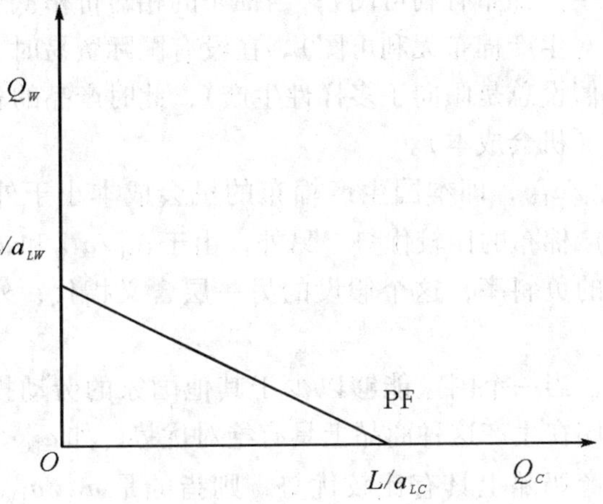

图 3.1 本国的生产可能性边界

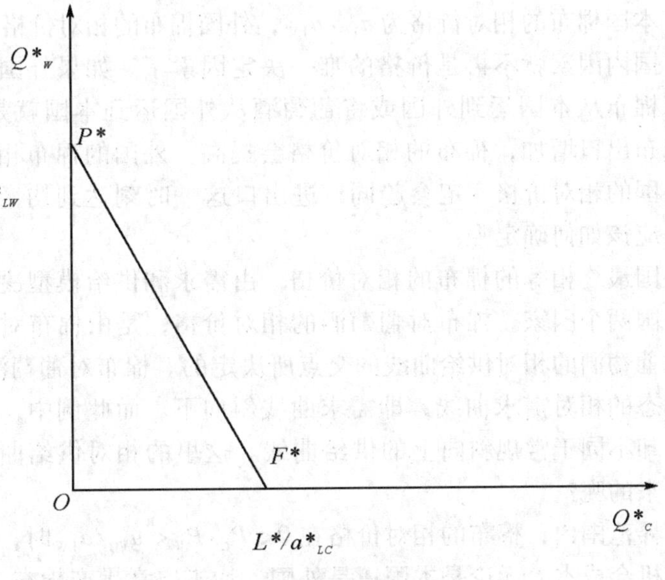

图 3.2 外国的生产可能性边界

由于现阶段的模型是一个简化模型：仅有劳动这种生产要素，棉布和葡萄酒的供给由劳动力的流向决定，而劳动力总会流向工资比较高的部门。

令 P_W表示葡萄酒的价格，P_C表示棉布的价格。单一要素模型中不存在利润，棉布行业中每小时工资率等于一个工人在 1 小时内创造的价值 P_C/a_{LC}，葡萄酒行业每小时的工资率等于 P_W/a_{LW}。当 $P_C/a_{LC} > P_W/a_{LW}$，即 $P_C/P_W > a_{LC}/a_{LW}$时，棉布行业的工资率更高，每个人都想去工资更高的行业工作，因此该国只会专业化生产棉布；当 $P_C/P_W < a_{LC}/a_{LW}$时，葡萄酒行业的工资率就比较高，每个人都想去葡萄酒行业工作，这时该国

只会专业化生产葡萄酒；当 $P_C/P_W=a_{LC}/a_{LW}$ 时，棉布行业和葡萄酒行业的工资率相等。劳动要素会任意流向两个行业，因此这时该国会生产棉布和葡萄酒两种产品。

a_{LC}/a_{LW} 是以葡萄酒来衡量的棉布的机会成本，而 P_C/P_W 是棉布的相对价格。因此，价格与生产之间的核心在于：当一个国家的棉布的相对价格高于它的机会成本时，该国就专门生产棉布（生产棉布有利可图）；当棉布的相对价格低于它的机会成本时，该国就专门生产葡萄酒（生产棉布无利可图）。在没有国际贸易时，本国只能自己生产两种产品（经济学基本假设总是倾向于多样性生产），此时产品的相对价格等于它们的相对单位产品劳动投入（机会成本）。

假设 $a_{LC}/a_{LW}< a^*_{LC}/a^*_{LW}$，即本国生产棉布的机会成本小于外国生产棉布的机会成本，说明本国具有生产棉布的比较优势。另外，由于 a_{LC}/a_{LW} 和 a^*_{LC}/a^*_{LW} 分别表示本国和外国生产可能性边界的负斜率，这个假设的另一层含义指代，外国的生产可能性边界比本国的陡。

必须要明确的是，当一个国家能够以少于其他国家的劳动投入生产出同样单位的商品时，我们就说本国在生产这种商品上具有绝对优势，如 $a_{LC}< a^*_{LC}$ 和 $a_{LW}< a^*_{LW}$。而如果我们说，本国在生产奶酪上具有比较优势，则指的是 $a_{LC}/a_{LW}< a^*_{LC}/a^*_{LW}$ 或 $a_{LC}/ a^*_{LC}< a_{LW}/a^*_{LW}$。

如果没有国际贸易，各国的棉布对葡萄酒的相对价格由它们的相对单位产品劳动投入来确定。本国棉布的相对价格为 a_{LC}/a_{LW}，外国棉布的相对价格为 a^*_{LC}/a^*_{LW}。一旦进行国际贸易，国内因素就不再是价格的唯一决定因素了。如果外国棉布的相对价格比本国高，则将棉布从本国运到外国或将葡萄酒从外国运到本国就是有利可图。但是，随着本国的棉布出口增加，棉布的相对价格会提高，外国的棉布相对价格会降低。最终，本国和外国的相对价格一定会趋同，进出口这一时刻达到均衡。那么，贸易中的这一相对价格应该如何确定呢？

本国和外国最终相等的棉布的相对价格，由需求和供给模型决定。假设世界市场只有本国和外国两个国家。棉布对葡萄酒的相对价格，是由棉布对葡萄酒的相对需求曲线和棉布对葡萄酒的相对供给曲线的交点所决定的。棉布对葡萄酒的相对需求曲线，是一条常规形态的相对需求曲线，即需求曲线斜向下。而此例中，棉布对葡萄酒的相对供给曲线，却不同于常规斜向上的供给曲线。这里的相对供给曲线，呈阶梯状。这是如何推导出来的呢？

第一，世界范围内，棉布的相对价格在 $0< P_C/P_W< a_{LC}/a_{LW}$ 时，棉布的相对价格小于棉布生产的机会成本，无论是本国还是外国，均不愿意生产棉布。此时世界范围内，棉布的相对供给为 0。

第二，当棉布的相对价格 $P_C/P_W=a_{LC}/a_{LW}$ 时，本国棉布的相对价格等于棉布生产的机会成本，本国工人无论生产棉布还是葡萄酒均可获得同样的薪酬，因此本国的棉布相对供给量可以是任意值，从而相对供给曲线呈水平状。另外，此时棉布的世界相对价格低于外国的棉布生产的机会成本，因此外国的棉布生产量为 0。

第三，当棉布的相对价格位于本国和外国棉布生产的机会成本之间时，即 $a_{LC}/a_{LW}< P_C/P_W< a^*_{LC}/a^*_{LW}$ 时，本国将专门化生产棉布，并且数量为定值，共生产 L/a_{LC} 单位的棉布；外国将专门生产葡萄酒，共生产 L^*/ a^*_{LW} 单位的葡萄酒。此时，棉布的相

对供给量为 $L/a_{LC}/L^*/a_{LW}^*$，此为定值，因而相对供给曲线为垂线。

第四，当棉布的相对价格等于外国棉布生产的机会成本之间时，即$P_C/P_W=a_{LC}^*/a_{LW}^*$时，本国将专门化生产葡萄酒，不生产棉布；而外国工人无论生产棉布还是葡萄酒均可获得同样的薪酬，因此外国的棉布相对供给量可以是任意值，从而相对供给曲线再次呈水平状。

第五，当棉布的相对价格大于外国棉布生产的机会成本之间时，即$P_C/P_W>a_{LC}^*/a_{LW}^*$时，本国和外国的工人因为棉布行业更高的报酬，均选择到棉布行业工作，此时葡萄酒的世界产量为0，而棉布的相对供给就变成了无穷大。

综合上述分析，可以分析出为什么棉布的相对供给曲线呈现为阶梯状。世界的相对供给和相对需求见图 3.3。

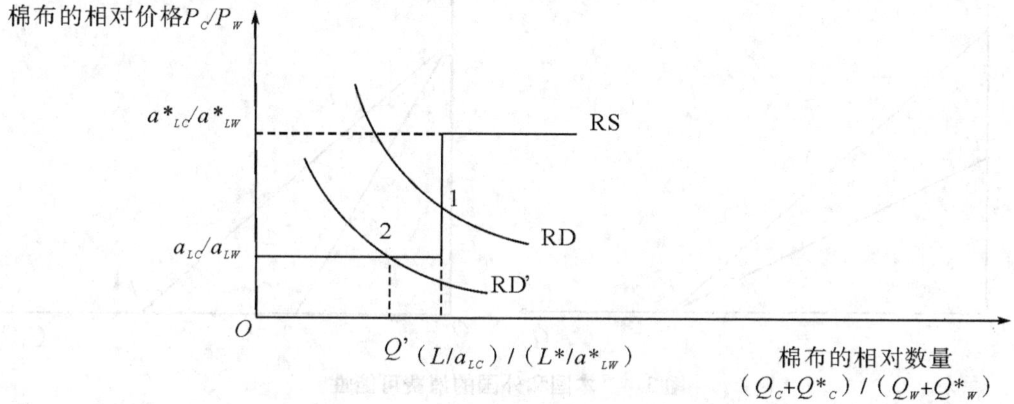

图 3.3 世界的相对供给和相对需求

再看图 3.3 中的两根相对需求曲线，*RD* 与 *RS* 相交于点 1，此时棉布的相对价格P_C/P_W在本国棉布的机会成本 a_{LC}/a_{LW}和外国棉布的机会成本 a_{LC}^*/a_{LW}^*之间，从而本国和外国都只生产自己最具有比较优势的产品，实现了完全分工。而 *RD'* 与 *RS* 相交于点 2，棉布的相对价格 P_C/P_W等于本国棉布的机会成本 a_{LC}/a_{LW}，并且小于外国棉布的机会成本 a_{LC}^*/a_{LW}^*，这意味着本国可能会同时生产葡萄酒和棉布两种产品，外国只生产葡萄酒。这种情况属于不完全专业化分工。

3.2.5 贸易所得

在绝对优势贸易理论中，人们对贸易所得比较容易看得清楚，因为一国出口产品的绝对生产成本一定比别国低，而且进口的也一定是自己生产成本绝对比别国高的产品，所以贸易一定能够赚钱或省钱。但在比较优势理论中，贸易所得就不是那么直观了。本国有可能出口比外国生产成本高的产品，也有可能从外国进口生产成本不如本国低的产品。在这种情况下，一国参与国际贸易的收益何在呢?

事实上，每个国家的贸易所得是通过专业化分工和交换获得的。

如果本国希望持有葡萄酒，那么本国可以用 1 个单位的劳动要素自己生产 $1/a_{LW}$个单位的葡萄酒；也可以通过 1 个单位的劳动要素生产 $1/a_{LC}$个单位的棉布，并出口这些棉布来换取葡萄酒，交换条件是 1 个单位的棉布交换 P_C/P_W个单位的葡萄酒，这样，1 小时劳动就可以生产（$1/a_{LC}$）×（P_C/P_W）加仑葡萄酒。而在世界市场均衡时，如果没有一个国家同时生产两种产品，就一定有 $P_C/P_W>a_{LC}/a_{LW}$，则（$1/a_{LC}$）×（P_C/P_W）$>1/a_{LW}$，则生产并出口棉布间接生产的葡萄酒就比 1 小时劳动直接生产的葡萄酒要多。这说明了本国从专业化分工和国际贸易中获利了。同样，外国也可以通过生产并出口葡萄酒来换取棉布的方式更高效地“生产”棉布。故本国和外国可以从国际贸易合作中得到双赢的结果。

同时，贸易还使本国和外国的消费可能性变大了。贸易前，消费可能性边界与生产可能性边界是一致的。而一旦国际贸易产生，各国便可以消费与其产出不同的产品组合。在两国，贸易都扩大了消费选择的范围，因此也必将提高各国居民的福利水平。本国和外国的消费可能性见图 3.4。

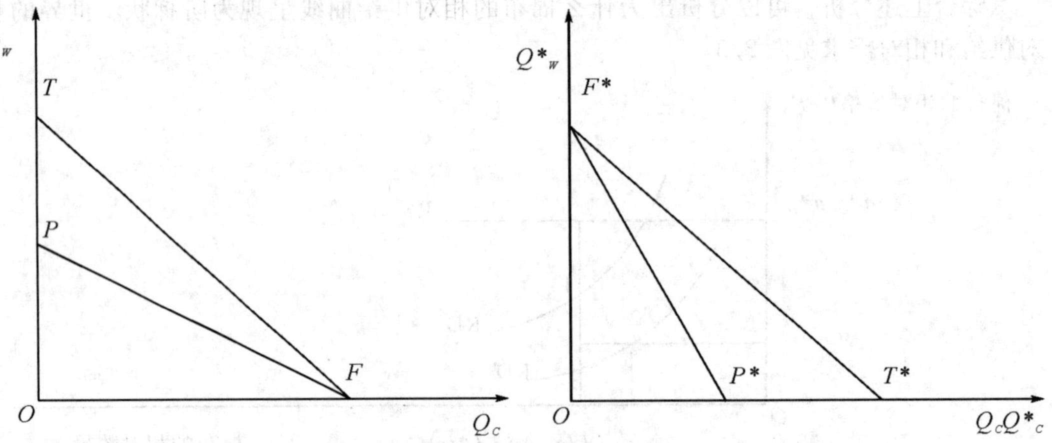

图 3.4　本国和外国的消费可能性

通过以上分析，大卫·李嘉图的比较优势模型中贸易对一国经济的影响和所得可以总结如下：

（1）发生贸易后各国出口具有比较优势的产品，进口没有比较优势的产品，造成具有比较优势产品（出口产品）的相对价格上升（或没有比较优势的进口产品的相对价格下降）。

（2）相对价格的变化促进各国实行专业分工，专门从事本国具有比较优势的产品的生产，不生产不具有比较优势的产品。

（3）在新的贸易下，各国的社会福利水平提高。贸易所得来自产品的消费和生产两个方面的有效配置。通过贸易，一国可以消费超出其生产能力的产品。

4 Heckscher-Ohlin Theorem

4.1 Heckscher, Ohlin and H-O Theory

Both Smith's theory of absolute advantage and Ricardo's theory of comparative advantage belong to the classical school. In explaining the causes, patterns and influences of international trade, the classical school has an important enlightening effect on the later theoretical policies. However, classical trade theory is based on classical economics. Its limitation is that the analysis process only admits one kind of factor input - labor factor. With two or more inputs, many analytical processes and conclusions are no longer valid. Therefore, the neoclassical economics, which is no longer determined by a single factor of product production, gradually took shape, and the neoclassical trade theory, which analyzes international trade under the framework of neoclassical economics, came into being.

Swedish economists Eli F. Heckscher and Bertil Ohlin are the most important contributors to the neoclassical theory of international trade. In the model of Adam Smith and David Ricardo, differences in labor productivity caused by technological level led to huge differences in the production costs of each country, so that trade could benefit all the participating countries. In the early 20th century, countries interact more closely, exacerbating technological spillovers. Because of technology spillover, technological differences between countries are becoming smaller and smaller. However, the cost differences between countries are still confusingly large. Therefore, he explained the causes of international trade by the differences in resources among countries.

In 1919, Heckscher published *Effect of Foreign Trade on the Distribution of Income*. In this paper, Heckscher put forward the theory of comparative advantage based on the situation of relative resource endowment and the proportion of factors in production. He thinks that the difference in the endowments of factors of production and the different proportion of factors of production are the prerequisites for international trade. Heckscher further argues that trade must equalize the prices of relatively scarce factors of production under the assumption that all countries have the same level of technology.

As a student of Heckscher, Ohlin further perfected Heckscher's theory of resource endowments in the book *Interregional and International Trade* published in 1933.

4.2 H-O Model

4.2.1 Theoretical Assumptions

(1) There are two countries (Country A and Country B), two products (C and F) and two factors of production (capital and labor), sometimes called the 2×2×2 model.

(2) Assume that both countries use the same technology in production.

(3) In any country, assume that Product C is labor-intensive and Product F is capital-intensive.

(4) In any country, it is assumed that the two countries have an incomplete division of labor in production.

(5) Assume that the return to scale for the production of both commodities is constant regardless of the country.

(6) Assume that the commodity market and the factor market are perfectly competitive in all countries.

(7) In any country, it is assumed that factors can flow freely within one country, but not between two countries.

(8) Assume that there are no transportation costs, tariffs or other barriers in the transaction.

(9) Assume that the needs of the two countries are the same.

(10) Assume that both countries are in full employment.

(11) Suppose the two countries maintain trade balance.

4.2.2 Model Analysis

A country's capital stock K and labor supply L is fixed and distributed among production in both sectors. The amount of capital and labor invested in the production of a unit of product *C* and a unit of product F is fixed, that is, the unit factor requirement is fixed. The parameters, a_{KC}, a_{LC}, a_{KF}, a_{LF}, are constant parameters. The output of each product is determined by its production function: $Q_C = Q_C(K_C, L_C)$ and $Q_F = Q_F(K_F, L_F)$. These parameters are defined as follows:

a_{KC} = The capital invested to produce a unit of product C

a_{LC} = The labor invested to produce a unit of product C

a_{KF} = The capital invested to produce a unit of product F

a_{LF} = The labor invested to produce a unit of product F

Q_C = product C

Q_F = product F

K= the aggregate supply of capital in a country

L= the aggregate supply of labor in a country

The production possibility curve and the social indifference curve are used to analyze the overall equilibrium of trade influence.

The Heckscher-Ohlin model's assumptions about the production possibilities of a country differ from the classical trade models of Adam Smith and David Ricardo in two ways. The classical trade model thinks that the two countries′ ability to produce various commodities is different in production technology, while the Heckscher-Ohlin model thinks that the factor endowments are different. Second, as for the assumption about the opportunity cost of production, the classical model assumes that labor is the only factor of production and the unit labor requirement is constant. So the opportunity cost of producing an extra product is fixed, and the production possibilities curve is a straight line. However, the Heckscher-Ohlin model assumes thatthere are two kinds of production factors, capital and labor, so there is a certain room for the choice of input factors, and the production possibility curve is no longer a straight line.

Resource constraints on capital: the total amount of capital used in the production of products C and F cannot exceed the total supply of capital.

$$a_{KC}Q_C+a_{KF}Q_F\leqslant K$$

Labor resource constraints: the total amount of labor used in the production of product C and product F shall not exceed the total supply of labor.

$$a_{LC}Q_C+a_{LF}Q_F\leqslant L$$

Suppose that the ratio of labor to capital required to produce product C is greater than that required to produce product F, then

$$a_{LC}/a_{KC}>a_{LF}/a_{KF}$$

After a little adjustment of the above equation, it can be changed into

$$a_{LC}/a_{LF}>a_{KC}/a_{KF}$$

The latter equation can be regarded as the slope value of the resource constraint line. That is, the resource constraint line of labor is steeper than that of capital. See the picture below.

The bold polyline in the figure is the production possibility frontier when the factors are irreplaceable. An important feature of this production possibilities frontier is that the opportunity cost of each additional unit of product C, in terms of product F, is variable and increases as the country's production portfolio tilts towards product F. Therefore, the more F the country produces, the greater the opportunity cost of producing C.

If capital and labor are interchangeable, then the production possibilities frontier is no longer a broken line, as shown in the figure above. However, as the output of product C increases and the output of product F decreases, the opportunity cost of product C, as measured by product F, continues to rise, which is still true. So the question at what point on the production possibilities frontier is the whole society producing? The answer is to produce at the point where the total output value is the largest, determined by the prices of the two products (Figure 4. 1 and Figure 4. 2).

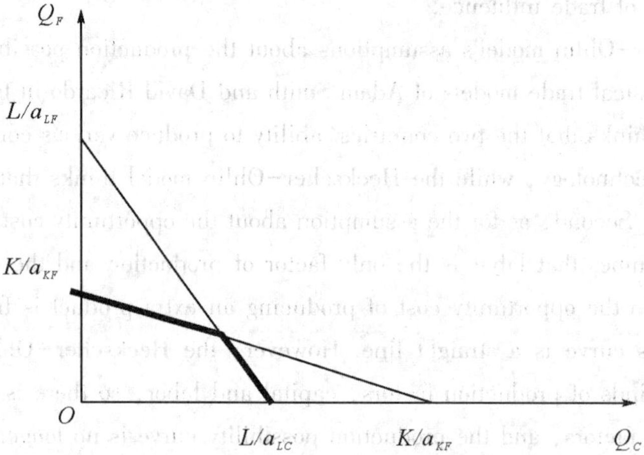

Figure 4. 1 **the Production Possibility Frontier When the Factors are Irreplaceable**

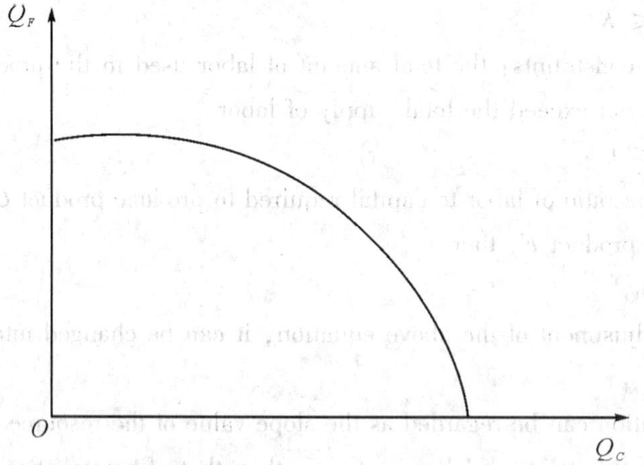

Figure 4. 2 **the Production Possibility Frontier When the Factors are Interchangeable**

Suppose the value of the country's output is: $V=P_CQ_C+P_FQ_F$

V、P_C、P_F are parameters, and Q_C、Q_F are variables. The maximization point of output value is located where the highest iso-value line tangent to the production possibility frontier. At the tangent point, the slope of the iso-value line is equal to the slope of the production possibilities frontier. At this point, the slope of the iso-value line is $-P_C/P_F$, and the slope of the production possibilities frontier is equal to the forgoing product F of producing one additional unit of product C. Therefore, at the point of maximizing output value, the opportunity cost of producing one more unit of product C, as measured by product F, is equal to the relative price of product C to product F.

In the two-factor model, the manufacturer can freely choose the combination of input factors. For any fixed amount of the output, the firm can choose the input combination with more capital factors and less labor factors, or the combination with less capital factors and more labor factors. In reality, the manufacturer's choice of input combination depends on the relative price of factors.

The difference in relative prices of factors of production results from the different endowments of various factors of production. The difference of endowment of factor of production is an important cause of international trade. A country exports goods for which it intensively use its abundant factors of production and imports goods for which it intensively use its scarce factors of production. The comparative advantage of each country is determined by the relative abundance of factors of production owned by each country. For a country, a relatively large supply of resources is the country's abundance factor; The relatively small supply of resources is the country's scarcity factor.

If w is used to represent the wage rate of labor and r is used to represent the interest rate of capital, then the combination of factors will depend on the prices of these two factors, the ratio w/r (Figure 4. 3).

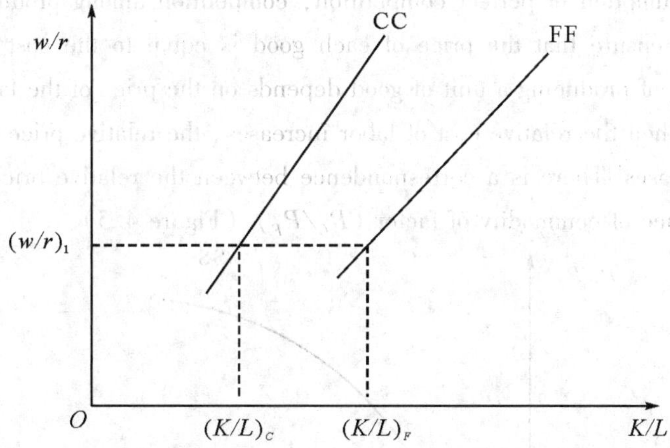

Figure 4. 3 **the Relative Inputs and Price of Capital and Labor**

The FF curve represents the capital-labor ratio of product F production corresponding to different factor price ratios. The CC curve represents the capital-labor ratio in production ofproduct C corresponding to different factor price ratios. When the price ratio (w/r) increases, it means that the cost of capital is relatively low, while the cost of labor is relatively higher. Manufacturers will use more capital to replace labor to produce products, resulting in the relative increase of capital. Therefore, FF curve and CC curve are inclined upward.

For any given wage-rent rate ratio, production of product F uses a higher capital-labor ratio. In this case, we call the production of product F capital-intensive and the production of product C labor-intensive.

Note: whether a product is labor-intensive or capital-intensive depends on the ratio of capital input to labor input in production, not the ratio of labor input or capital input to output. A product cannot be both capital-intensive and labor-intensive.

Suppose Country B is a capital-abundant country with relatively cheap capital. Then w/r of Country B is greater than that of Country A. For the same Product C and Product F, K/L of Country B is greater than that of Country A. The figure is as follows (Figure 4.4).

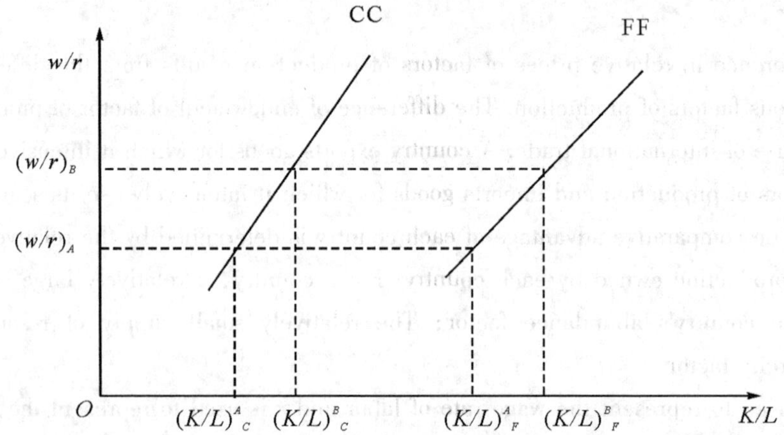

Figure 4.4 the Relative Inputs and Price of Capital and Labor in two countries

Under the assumption of perfect competition, competition among producers in each production sector will ensure that the price of each good is equal to the cost of producing that good, and the cost of producing a unit of good depends on the price of the factor. Product C is labor-intensive. When the relative cost of labor increases, the relative price of labor-intensive products also increases. There is a correspondence between the relative price of factor (w/r) and the relative price of commodity of factor (P_C/P_F) (Figure 4.5).

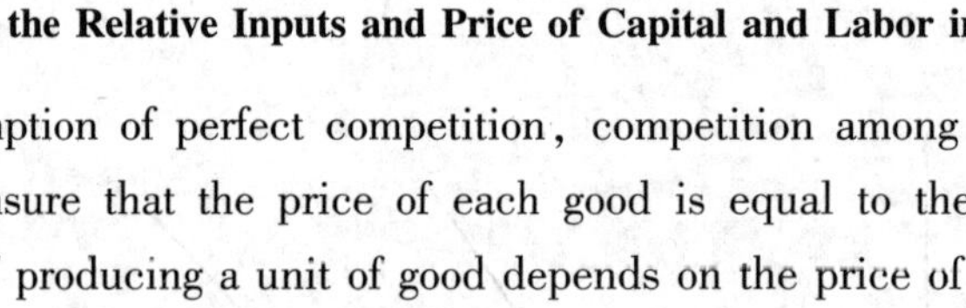

Figure 4.5 the Relative Price of Factors and Commodities

Combining two graphs, we can see the relationship between the relative price of goods, the relative price of factors and the capital to labor ratio invested in the production of each commodity:

Since Country B is a capital-abundant country, the relative wages in Country B are higher than those in Country A. The relative costs of Product C in Country B are higher than that in Country A. Factor prices and commodity prices have a one-to-one correspondence relationship. Therefore, the relative price of Product C in Country B is higher than that in Country A. According to the law of comparative advantage, the difference in relative price indicates their respective comparative advantages. That is, Country B has a comparative disadvantage in Product C and a comparative advantage in Product F. Country A has a comparative advantage in Product C and a comparative disadvantage in Product F. So Country B should export Product F and import Product C. Country A should export Product C and import Product F. Note that Product F and Product C are capital-intensive and labor-intensive, respectively. so the H-O model can be summarized: a country should export products that intensively use its relatively abundant resources, while imports products that intensively use its relatively scarce resources (Figure 4. 6).

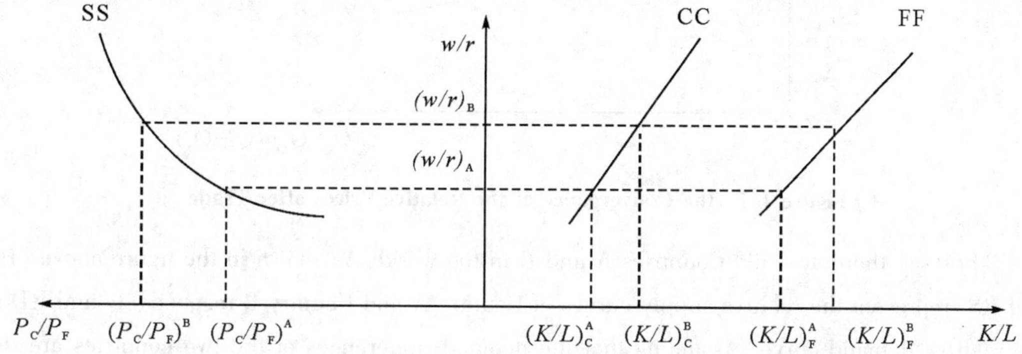

Figure 4. 6　the Choices of Factors and the Relative Price of Commodities

Given that the relative price of Product C goes up, the ratio of wage-rent rate will also go up. At this time, labor is relatively expensive and capital is relatively cheap, so the capital-labor ratio invested in the production of Product C and product F will go up accordingly. It can be concluded that a rise in the relative price of product C to Product F leads to an increase in the income of workers relative to the owners of capital. This change in relative prices would unequivocally increase the purchasing power of workers and reduce the purchasing power of owners of capital by raising real wages as measured by both goods and lowering real rents as measured by both goods. In the H-O model, not only does the change in the relative price of goods impacts the income distribution, but also always benefits the owner of one factor of production and damages the owner of another factor of production.

4. 3　H-O Theory Expansion

Heckscher-Ohlin's factor endowment theory (H-O model) shows that resource endowment is the determinant of comparative costs, and international trade causes the changes of factor prices. Heckscher proposed that international trade might lead to equalization of factor prices. Ohlin explained in detail that equal prices of factors of production in the world are sometimes unattainable because of the lack of liquidity of factors of production in each country. However, commodity trade can partially replace the flow of factors of production to make up for the lack of liquidity of factors of production. Therefore, international trade will still lead to the convergence of factor prices (Figure 4.7).

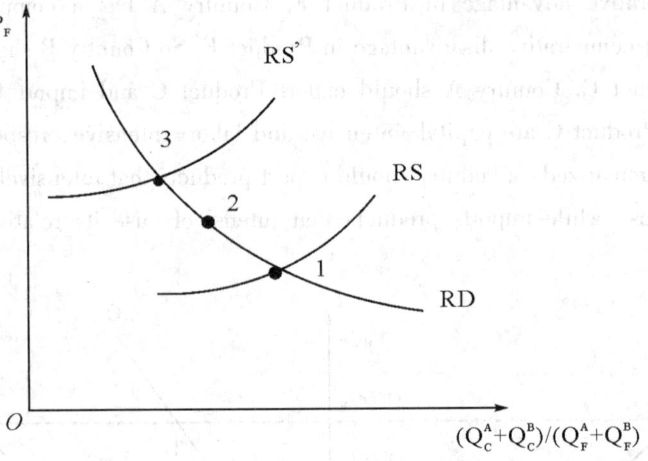

Figure 4.7 **the Convergence of the Relative Prices after Trade**

Let's say there are only Countries A and B in the world. As shown in the figure above, RS and RS′ represent the relative supply curves of Country A and Country B respectively and RD is the relative demand curve. Assuming that the demand preferences of the two countries are the same, the relative demand of Country A and Country B can therefore be represented by the same curve. Before trade, the equilibrium point between demand and supply in Country A's domestic market is point 1, while the equilibrium point between demand and supply in Country B's domestic market is point 3. If there is no trade, the relative price of Product C in Country A is lower than that in Country B. When trade occurs, the prices of the two countries converge. The new world relative price will lie between the relative prices of the two countries before trade, shown as point 2 in the graph.

There is a one-to-one correspondence between the relative price of goods and the relative price of inputs. After trade, the convergence of relative prices of product leads to the convergence of relative prices of labor and capital. Since the relative prices of X against Y and the relative factor prices in Country A and Country B are the same after trade, the wage rates and rental rates of the two countries will become exactly the same. Therefore, the equalization theorem of the price of factors of production can be expressed as: under all the assumptions of the theory of factor endowment, international trade will equalize the absolute and relative prices of the same factors by equalizing the relative prices of goods.

In the practice, because the hypothesis cannot be completely established in the real world, the relative prices of factors in each country are not equal.

Many scholars have extended the theory of factor endowment.

For example, Stolper-Samuelson theorem thinks that when all the assumptions of the factor endowment theory are satisfied, international trade causes the relative prices of abundant factors to rise and the relative prices of scarce factors to fall, by affecting the relative prices of import and export commodities. Each commodity must be a final product, not an intermediate product producing another commodity.

Samuelson and Jones states that if a factor is used more regularly in the production of the export commodities, the return of that factor increases with the advance of exporting. On the contrary, if a factor is used more regularly in the production of the import commodities, the return of that factorwill decrease as the import trade progresses.

Rybczynski Theorem illustrates that Changes in factor abundance also change the shape of the production possibilities curve. The theorem can be expressed as follows: if the price of a commodity remains unchanged, an increase in one factor of production will increase the output of goods that use this factor intensively, and at the same time, decreasethe output of another product.

4.4 The Leontief Paradox

The theory of factor endowment was generally accepted by the western academic circles, because the explanation of this theory was consistent with people's common sense. According to the H-O model, the United States has relatively abundant capital and relatively scarce labor, so it should export capital-intensive products and import labor-intensive products. This conclusion is the same as the public understanding. Leontief, a famous American economist, tried to verify the H-O model with empirical data. He analyzed the output of 200 American industries in 1947 and 1951. The results show that export goods of US are less capital intensive than import goods. In other words, US exports labor-intensive goods and imports capital-intensive goods, which is the exact opposite of what the H-O model predicted. This is known as the "Leontief Paradox".

The "Leontief Paradox" has aroused a great deal of discussion in the academic circle. These discussions promoted the development of international trade theory to some extent.

4.4.1 Factor Density Reversal

Suppose that in Country A, labor is relatively scarce due to abundant capital, making capital cheap and labor expensive. Therefore, Country A might use more capital than labor in the production of something, which is conventionally considered labor-intensive. In this way, the product becomes capital-intensive in Country A, while in other countries, the product remains labor-intensive because local capital is more expensive and labor is cheaper. This is a case of factor density reversal and this contradicts the assumptions of the H-O trade model about factor density.

In addition, Leontief estimates the capital-labor ratio of imported goods using the capital-labor ratio for similar goods produced in the United States, rather than the capital-labor ratio for imported goods actually used in the exporting country. Leontief counts imports as capital-intensive by U.S. standards, leading to a factor-intensive reversal.

In reality, some scholars have proved that the probability of factor - intensive reversal is small.

4. 4. 2 Human Capital

In H-O model, factors of production are simply divided into labor and capital without further subdivision of factors. Some economists argue that labor in production is of a different nature. This heterogeneity is embodied in the difference of labor efficiency determined by labor proficiency. More human capital investment in the United States leads to higher labor efficiency. America exports goods using more skilled labor factor. If we capitalize the difference part of the income earned by skilled labor over unskilled labor and add it to physical capital, the capital intensity of US exports is indeed higher than that of imports. The skills of technologists and skilled workers are the factors among the most abundant factors in the United States. This conclusion is called human capital theory.

4. 4. 3 Tariffs and other Trade Barriers

US tariff policy is also an important cause of the Leontief Paradox. A tariff is essentially a tax on imports. It reduces imports and stimulates the production of domestic import substitutes. Research shows that the most heavily protected industries in the United States are labor-intensive, which affects the trade pattern of the United States and reduces the labor intensity of import substitutes in the United States. This helps to explain the Leontief Paradox.

4. 4. 4 natural resources

The Leontief Paradox only calculated the ratio of capital to labor in trade and did not include natural resources. The types and quantities of natural resources vary greatly from country to country.

Leontief found, one reason for U.S. imports capital-intensive, is that the U.S. is a major importer of minerals. These products use large amounts of both natural resources and non-human capital. On the export side, the U.S. exports agricultural products that use relatively a lot of land and labor. Coincidentally, the natural resource products imported by the United States happen to have a high capital-labor ratio, while the natural resource products exported happen to have a low capital-labor ratio, thus forming the phenomenon that the United States imports capital-intensive products and exports labor-intensive products.

4 赫克歇尔—俄林理论

4.1 赫克歇尔、俄林与 H-O 理论

无论是亚当·斯密的绝对优势理论还是大卫·李嘉图的比较优势理论，均属于古典学派。古典学派在解释国际贸易成因、模式、影响等方面，均对后来的理论政策有着重要的启示作用。但是，古典贸易理论立足于古典经济学，它的局限在于分析过程只承认一种要素投入——劳动要素。在有两种或两种以上要素投入的情况下，许多分析过程和结论不再有效。因此，不再由单一要素决定产品生产的新古典经济学逐渐形成，在新古典经济学框架下，对国际贸易进行分析的新古典贸易理论也随之产生。

瑞典经济学家埃利·赫克歇尔和伯尔蒂尔·俄林对新古典国际贸易理论的贡献最大。亚当·斯密和大卫·李嘉图的模型里，技术水平导致的劳动生产率的不同，使各国生产成本出现了巨大差异，进而贸易才可以使参与国均有所获。但是，20 世纪初，各国往来密切，加剧了技术外溢。技术外溢带来的结果是各国的技术差异日趋减小。但令人疑惑的是，各国的成本差异仍然巨大。因此，赫克歇尔用各国之间的资源差异来解释国际贸易的成因。

1919 年，赫克歇尔发表了《国际贸易对收入分配的影响》。该文中，赫克歇尔提出了建立在相对资源禀赋情况和生产中要素比例基础上的比较优势理论。他认为，各国生产要素的禀赋差异和产品生产中投入的生产要素比例不同是国际贸易产生的前提条件。赫克歇尔进一步指出，在所有国家技术水平相同的假设下，贸易必然会令相对稀缺的生产要素价格出现均等化。

作为赫克歇尔的学生，俄林在 1933 年出版的《区间贸易和国际贸易论》中进一步完善了赫克歇尔的资源禀赋论。

4.2 H-O 理论模型

4.2.1 理论假设

（1）贸易中存在两个国家（A 国和 B 国）、两种产品（C 和 F）及两种生产要素（资本和劳动），有时称之为“2×2×2”模型；

（2）无论在哪国，假设两国在生产中使用相同的技术；

（3）无论在哪国，假设产品 C 是劳动密集型产品，产品 F 是资本密集型产品；

（4）无论在哪国，假设两国在生产中均为不完全分工；

（5）无论在哪国，假设两种商品的生产均是规模报酬不变的；

（6）无论在哪国，假设商品市场和要素市场是完全竞争的；

（7）无论在哪国，假设要素可以在一国之内自由流动，但是不能在两国之间流动；

（8）假设交易中没有运输成本、关税或其他壁垒；

（9）假设两国需求相同；

（10）假设两国资源均是充分就业状态；

（11）假设两国贸易平衡。

4.2.2 模型分析

一国资本存量 K 和劳动供给 L 都是固定的，被分配于两个部门的生产当中。生产一单位的产品 C 和一单位的产品 F 所投入的资本和劳动的数量是固定的，即单位产品要素投入是定值，即参数 a_{KC}，a_{LC}，a_{KF}，a_L 是不变参数，每种产品的产量由其生产函数来确定：$Q_C=Q_C(K_C, L_C)$ 和 $Q_F=Q_F(K_F, L_F)$。这些参数的定义如下：

a_{KC}=生产一个单位产品 C 所需要投入的资本

a_{LC}=生产一个单位产品 C 所需要投入的劳动

a_{KF}=生产一个单位产品 F 所需要投入的资本

a_{LF}=生产一个单位产品 F 所需要投入的劳动

Q_C=产品 C

Q_F=产品 F

K=一国资本总供给

L=一国劳动总供给

这里用生产可能性曲线和社会无差异曲线来对贸易影响进行总体均衡分析。

赫克歇尔—俄林模型对一国生产可能性的假设与亚当·斯密和大卫·李嘉图的古典贸易模型相比有两点不一样：第一，关于两国生产各种商品能力不同的原因。古典贸易模型认为，两国生产各种商品能力的不同在于生产技术上的不同，而赫克歇尔—俄林模型则认为是生产要素禀赋的不同。第二，关于产品生产机会成本的假定。古典模型假设劳动是唯一的生产要素，每单位劳动投入的产出是不变的，因此每单位产品的机会成本是固定的，生产可能性曲线是一条直线；而赫克歇尔—俄林模型假设有两种生产要素（资本和劳动），对投入要素的使用可以有一定的选择空间，生产可能性曲线不再是一条直线了。

资本方面的资源约束：产品 C 和产品 F 生产所使用的资本总量不能超过资本总供给。即

$$a_{KC}Q_C+a_{KF}Q_F\leqslant K$$

劳动方面的资源约束：产品 C 和产品 F 生产所使用的劳动总量不能超过劳动总供给。即

$$a_{LC}Q_C+a_{LF}Q_F\leqslant L$$

假设生产产品 C 所需要的劳动与资本的比例大于生产产品 F 的比例，则

$$a_{LC}/a_{KC}>a_{LF}/a_{KF}$$

将上式做一点调整后，可变为 $a_{LC}/a_{LF}>a_{KC}/a_{KF}$

后式可视为资源约束线的斜率值，即劳动的资源约束线较资本的资源约束线更陡一些。当要素不可替时的生存可能性曲线见图 4.1。

图 4.1 中加粗的折线即要素不可替代时的生产可能性边界。该生产可能性边界的一个重要特点是：用产品 F 衡量的每多生产一单位的产品 C 的机会成本是可变的，它随着该国的生产组合向产品 F 倾斜，逐渐增大。因此，该国生产的产品 F 越多，生产产品 C 的机会成本越大。

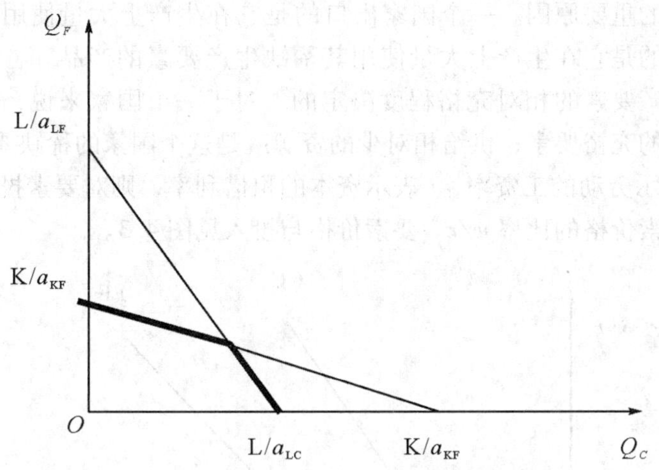

图 4.1　当要素不可替时的生存可能性曲线

如果资本与劳动可以相互替代，那么生产可能性边界就不再是折线（见图 4.2）。但是，随着产品 C 产量的增加和产品 F 产量的减少，以产品 F 衡量的产品 C 的机会成本不断上升，这一点仍然成立。那么问题是，整个社会究竟会是在生产可能性边界的哪一点生产呢？答案是：由两种产品价格确定的总产值最大的一点生产。

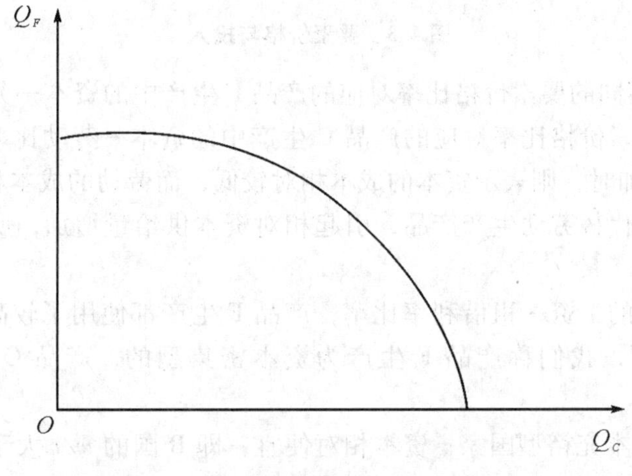

图 4.2　当要素可替时的生存可能性曲线

假设该国产出的价值为：$V=P_CQ_C+P_FQ_F$

其中 V、P_C、P_F 为参数，Q_C、Q_F 为变量，产出价值最大化的点位于与生产可能性边界相切的最高的一条等价值线上。在切点处，等价值线的斜率等于生产可能性边界在该点处的斜率。此时，等价值线的斜率是 $-P_C/P_F$，而生产可能性边界的斜率等于额外多生产 1 个单位产品 C 的放弃的产品 F。因此，在产出价值最大化的点，用产品 F 衡量的额外多生产 1 个单位产品 C 的机会成本就等于产品 C 对产品 F 的相对价格。

在两要素模型中，厂商可以自由选择投入要素的使用组合，即对于每单位的产出，厂商既可以选择较多的资本要素与较少的劳动要素，也可以选择较少的资本要素与较多的劳动要素。现实生活中，厂商对投入要素的选择取决于要素的相对价格。

生产要素相对价格的不同，源于各种生产要素的禀赋不同。生产要素的禀赋差异是国际贸易产生的重要原因。一个国家出口的是它在生产上大量使用其充裕生产要素的产品，而进口的是它在生产上大量使用其稀缺生产要素的产品。各国的比较优势是由各国拥有的生产要素的相对充裕程度决定的。对于一个国家来说，供给相对多的资源就是这个国家的充裕要素；供给相对少的资源就是这个国家的稀缺要素。

若用 w 来表示劳动的工资率，r 表示资本的租借利率，则对要素投入组合的选择将取决于这两种要素价格的比率 w/r。要素价格与投入见图 4.3。

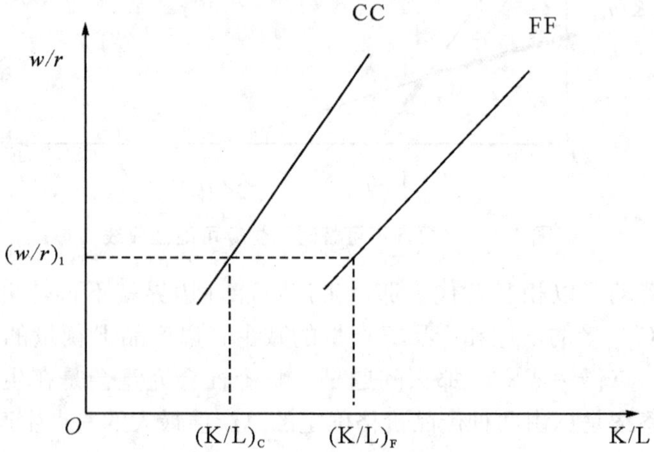

图 4.3 要素价格与投入

FF 曲线表示不同的要素价格比率对应的产品 F 生产中的资本—劳动比率选择；CC 曲线表示不同的要素价格比率对应的产品 C 生产中的资本—劳动比率选择。当要素价格比率（w/r）增加时，则表示资本的成本相对较低，而劳动的成本相对提高，厂商会使用更多的资本来代替劳动生产产品，引起相对资本供给量增加，所以 FF 曲线与 CC 曲线均是斜向上。

对于任意给定的工资—租借利率比率，产品 F 生产都使用了较高的资本—劳动比率。在这种情况下，我们称产品 F 生产为资本密集型的，产品 C 生产为劳动密集型的[①]。

假设 B 国是资本充裕型国家，资本相对便宜，即 B 国的 w/r 大于 A 国，对于同种产品 C 和产品 F，B 国的 K/L 均大于 A 国。不同国家要素价格与投入见图 4.4。

在完全竞争的假设条件下，每个生产部门中的生产者之间的竞争将保证每一商品的价格等于该商品的生产成本，而生产一个单位的商品成本取决于要素的价格。产品 C 是劳动密集型，当劳动相对成本提高的时候，劳动密集型产品的相对价格也在提高，要素相对价格（w/r）和要素的商品相对价格（P_C/P_F）存在一一对应关系。要素和商品的相对价格见图 4.5。

---

① 一种产品是劳动密集型的还是资本密集型的，取决于生产中资本投入量对劳动投入量的比例，而不是劳动投入量或资本投入量相对于产出的比例。一种产品不可能同时是资本密集型产品和劳动密集型产品。

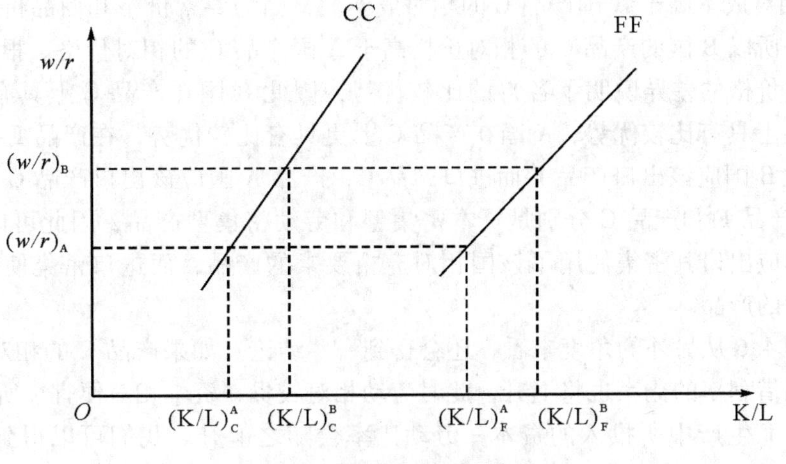

图 4.4　不同国家要素价格与投入

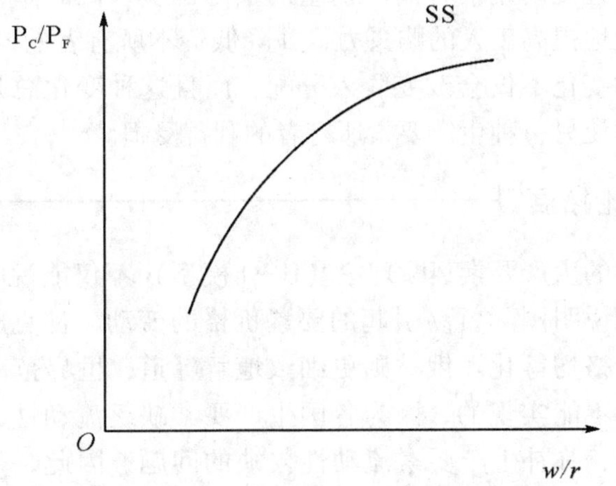

图 4.5　要素和商品的相对价格

将图 4.4 和图 4.5 合并在一起，就可以看出商品的相对价格、要素的相对价格和每种商品在生产中所投入的资本—劳动比率之间存在的关系。要素投入选择与商品价格见图 4.6。

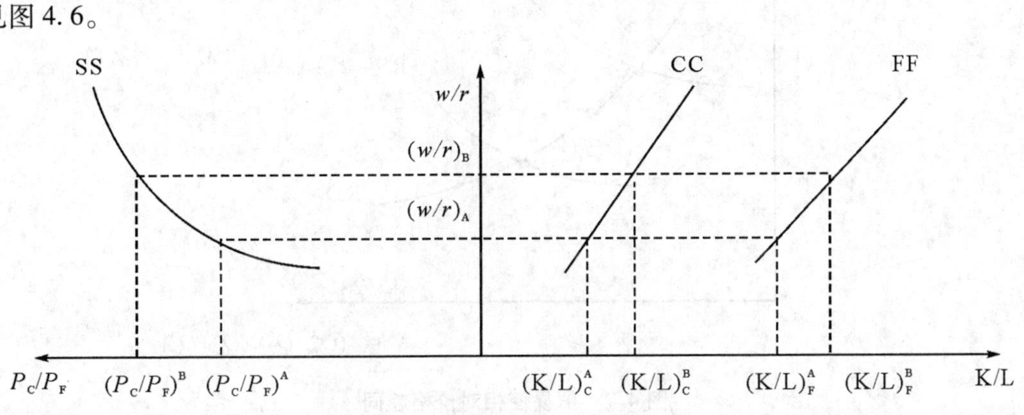

图 4.6　要素投入选择与商品价格

由于 B 国是资本充裕型国家，所以 B 国的相对工资高于 A 国的相对工资，B 国的产品 C 的相对成本高于 A 国产品 C 的相对成本。又因为要素价格和商品价格有一一对应的关系，所以 B 国的产品 C 的相对价格高于 A 国产品 C 的相对价格。根据比较优势原理，相对价格的差异说明了各自的比较优势，因此 B 国在产品 C 上具有比较劣势，而在产品 F 上具有比较优势；A 国在产品 C 上更具有比较优势，在产品 F 上具有比较劣势。因此 B 国应该出口产品 F 而进口产品 C，产品 A 国应该出口产品 C 而进口产品 F。注意，产品 F 和产品 C 分别是资本密集型和劳动密集型产品，因此可以概括 H-O 模型：一国应出口其密集使用了该国相对充裕要素的产品，而进口密集使用了该国相对稀缺要素的产品。

如果图 4.6 从另外的角度来看，还会得到一些结论。如果产品 C 的相对价格上升，则工资—租借利率的比率也将上升，此时劳动相对较贵，资本相对便宜，所以在产品 C 生产和产品 F 生产中所投入的资本—劳动比率会随之上升。我们可以得到的结论是：产品 C 对产品 F 的相对价格上升会导致劳动工人相对于资本所有者的收入增加。这种相对价格的变化将通过提高用两种商品衡量的实际工资，同时降低用两种商品衡量的实际租金，明确无疑地提高工人的购买力，并降低资本所有者的购买力。在 H-O 模型中，商品相对价格的变化不仅会改变收入分配，而且这种变化总是使得一种生产要素的所有者获利，同时使另一种生产要素所有者的利益受损。

4.3 H-O 理论拓展

赫克歇尔—俄林的生产要素禀赋理论（H-O 模型）不仅能说明资源禀赋是比较成本的决定因素，还能说明国际贸易引起的要素价格的变动。赫克歇尔首先提出，国际贸易可能导致要素价格均等化。俄林则更细致地解释道，世界范围内生产要素价格相等的理想状态有时是不能实现的，因为各国生产要素缺乏流动性，但商品贸易可以部分替代生产要素流动，弥补生产要素流动性欠缺的问题。因此，整体而言，国际贸易还是会使要素价格存在趋同性。贸易使相对价格趋同见图 4.7。

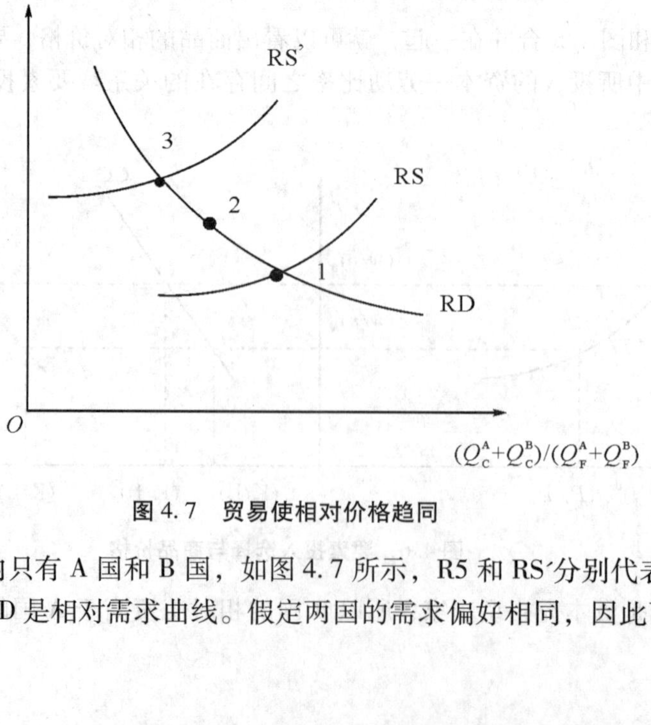

图 4.7 贸易使相对价格趋同

假设世界范围内只有 A 国和 B 国，如图 4.7 所示，R5 和 RS′分别代表 A 国和 B 国的相对供给曲线，RD 是相对需求曲线。假定两国的需求偏好相同，因此可以用同一条曲线来表示A国和B国的相对需求。贸易前，A国国内市场的需求和供给的均衡点在1处，而B国国内市场的需求和供给的均衡点在3处。如果没有贸易，A国产品C的相对价格比B国产品C的相对价格低。当贸易发生后，两国的价格会趋同。新的世界相对价格会位于两国贸易前的相对价格之间，在图中表示为点2。

由于商品的相对价格和投入要素的相对价格存在一一对应的关系。在贸易后，产品相对价格的趋同导致了生产要素劳动和资本相对价格的趋同，贸易后存在着要素价格均等化的趋势。即既然A、B两国的贸易后存在相同的X对Y的相对价格，那么他们的相对要素价格也相同，两国的工资率和租借利率就会变得完全相同。所以，生产要素价格均等化定理可以表述为：在满足生产要素禀赋理论的全部假定条件下，国际贸易将通过商品相对价格均等化，使同种要素的绝对和相对价格趋于均等。

但在实际过程中，由于模型假设不能完全在现实世界中成立，所以各国要素相对价格并不相等。

关于生产要素禀赋理论，还有很多学者做出了拓展。如斯托尔伯—萨缪尔森定理认为，在满足生产要素禀赋理论的全部假设条件时，国际贸易通过影响进出口商品（每一种商品都必须是最终产品，即不是生产另一种商品的中间品）的相对价格使充裕的生产要素相对价格上涨而稀缺的生产要素相对价格下降。或者说，从没有贸易转移到自由贸易，会使在商品相对价格上升的行业（出口行业）中密集使用的生产要素的报酬提高，而使在商品相对价格下跌的行业（进口竞争行业）中密集使用的生产要素的报酬降低；反之，对进口竞争品的保护会提高该部门密集使用的生产要素的收入。

这些命题都是基于不同生产要素具有同等的完全的流动性的条件下，讨论国际贸易对生产要素报酬的长期影响。当生产要素不具有同等的完全流动性时，即有些生产要素是可流动的，有些生产要素则不可流动，那么国际贸易对生产要素报酬的影响是什么呢？萨缪尔森和琼斯认为，如果某一要素被较为固定地使用在出口部门的商品生产中，那么该要素的报酬会随着出口贸易的推进而提升；相反，如果某一要素被较为固定地使用在进口部门的商品生产中，那么该要素的报酬会随着进口贸易的推进而降低。

雷布津斯基定理则说明，要素充裕程度的改变也会改变生产可能性曲线的形状。雷布津斯基定理可以表述为：假定商品价格不变，如果一种生产要素增加，会使密集使用这种生产要素的商品的产量增加，同时，使另一种产品的产量减少。例如，如果A国的劳动增加，在产品C（劳动密集型产品）与产品F（资本密集型产品）的价格均不改变的情况下，产品C的产量将以更大的幅度增加，而产品F的产量将下降。因为商品价格在单一要素增加时保持不变，所以要素价格（工资和利率）也必须不变。但是，仅在资本/劳动比率及两种商品的劳动和资本的生产率都不变时，要素价格才不变。要使增加的劳动充分就业，并保持两种商品资本/劳动不变的唯一方法，就是降低产品F（资本密集型商品）的产量以转移出足够的资本（和小部分的劳动）在产品C（劳动密集型商品）的生产中吸收所有增加的劳动。这样在商品价格不变的情况下，产品C的产量增加而产品F的产量下降。事实上，产品C的产量增加的比例大于劳动增加的比例，因为有一部分生产产品F的劳动和资本也转移到产品C的生产上来了。

4.4 里昂惕夫之谜

赫克歇尔—俄林的生产要素禀赋理论提出后，逐渐被西方学界普遍接受，因为这个理论模型解释的道理与人们的常识是一致的。根据 H-O 模型，美国的资本相对丰裕而劳动相对稀缺，所以美国应该出口资本密集型产品，而进口劳动密集型产品。这个结论与普通民众的理解是相同的，美国著名经济学家里昂惕夫就利用经验数据来进行验证，试图进一步证实 H-O 模型。他对美国 200 个产业 1947 年和 1951 年的生产情况进行了分析，比较了每生产百万美元的出口商品和与进口相竞争的替代品的所有资本有机构成的高低。其检验结果显示，出口商品的资本密集程度低于进口商品。显然，据此可以认为美国出口的是劳动密集型商品，而进口的是资本密集型商品。这与 H-O 模型的预测完全相反，这就是著名的"里昂惕夫之谜"（The Leontief Paradox）

"里昂惕夫之谜"引发了学界的讨论热潮，众多学者试图解开这个谜。这些讨论在一定程度上促进了战后西方国际分工和国际贸易理论的发展。

4.4.1 要素密集型逆转

赫克歇尔—俄林贸易模型假定，在给定某一生产要素价格比率时，某一商品的某种要素的密集度比另一商品高，则在任意生产要素价格比率下，这种商品的这种要素密集度都要比另一商品高。这是对要素密集型的基本假定。但是，事实的情况可能不是这样。假定在 A 国由于资本充裕而劳动相对稀缺导致资本便宜和劳动力昂贵。那么，A 国可能在某种常规认定为劳动密集型的产品生产中使用更多的资本而非劳动。这样的话，该产品在 A 国就变成了资本密集型商品，而在其他国家，由于资本较贵和劳动力比较便宜，该产品仍然是劳动密集型商品。这就是生产要素密集性逆转的一种情况。

另外，里昂惕夫在估算进口商品的资本—劳动比率时使用的是美国生产同类商品的资本—劳动比率，而不是进口商品在出口国国内实际使用的资本—劳动比率。如果在产品 C 的劳动对资本的替代弹性很大，其他出口国因为本国工资水平低，更倾向于用劳动密集型技术来生产产品 C。但美国因为本国的工资水平高，更倾向于用相对便宜的资本来生产产品 C。结果就是美国进口产品 C 实际上是进口劳动密集型商品，但里昂惕夫以美国的标准把进口的产品 C 估算成进口资本密集型商品，这就导致了生产要素密集型逆转。

现实中，有部分学者已经证实生产要素密集型逆转出现的概率较小。

4.4.2 人力资本

在赫克歇尔—俄林的模型中，生产要素被简单地分为劳动和资本，并没有进行下一步细分生产要素。一些经济学家认为，生产过程中的劳动是不同质的。这种异质具体体现在由劳动熟练程度决定的劳动效率差异上。对劳动者的培训、教育和其他有关的智力开发投资水平，决定了劳动者的劳动熟练程度。因此，较高的劳动效率最终是对人力投资的结果。由于美国投入了较多的人力资本，因而拥有更多的熟练劳动力，因此，美国出口产品中含有较多的熟练劳动。如果把熟练劳动高出非熟练劳动的收入部分资本化，并同有形资本相加，美国出口产品的资本（人力资本）密集度确实高于进口产品的资本密集度。科技人员和熟练工人的技能相对来说是美国最充裕的要素之一。该结论被称之为"人力资本说"（Human Capital Theory）。

4.4.3 关税和其他贸易壁垒

美国的关税政策也是产生里昂惕夫之谜的一个重要原因。关税实际上就是对进口商品征税，它减少了进口，刺激了国内进口替代品的生产。研究表明，美国受贸易保护最严格的产业就是劳动密集型产业，这就影响了美国的贸易模式，降低了美国进口替代品的劳动密集度。这对解释里昂惕夫之谜有一定的帮助。

4.4.4 自然资源

里昂惕夫之谜中只计算了贸易中的资本和劳动的比率而没有包括自然资源。不充分注意到各国自然资源的不同以及它们与资本和劳动力的关系，就不能完全解开资本劳动比率计算结果中出现的大部分奥秘。各国的天赋资源的种类和数量有很大不同。

为了判断自然资源在一国比较优势中的作用和对贸易模式的影响，我们首先应该对每一产业部门中所用耕地的地租、消耗的矿藏量的价值以及森林立木的价值等进行估计；其次应把这些资源地租的部分通过投入—产出系统过滤一下，以找出出口商品生产和与进口竞争的商品生产中的自然资源量。但在实践中，自然资源地租是很难计量的。因此，有些经济学家试图仅通过鉴定某些部门是资源密集的并把它们同其他部门分开，来判断自然资源在贸易中的作用。

关于自然资源在贸易中作用的研究，的确有助于解释为什么会出现“里昂惕夫之谜”。里昂惕夫发现，美国进口产品之所以是资本密集型的一个原因，就是美国是大量矿产的进口国。这些产品既使用大量的自然资源，也使用大量的非人力资本。在出口方面，美国出口的农产品相对来说主要使用的是土地和大量的劳动力。从这个意义上说，里昂惕夫之谜看来是一种幻景：美国进口的自然资源产品碰巧是资本劳动比率较高的，而出口的自然资源产品碰巧是资本劳动比率较低的，从而形成了美国进口资本密集型产品出口劳动密集型产品的现象。

5 New International Trade Theory

5.1 Scale Economies Theory

5.1.1 Increasing returns to scale

Even if two nations face identical production and demand conditions (i.e., they have identical production frontiers and community indifference curves) so that relative commodity prices are identical in the two nations before trade (i.e., there is no comparative advantage or disadvantage), there is still a basis for mutually beneficial trade between the two nations based on increasing returns to scale.

Increasing returns to scale refer to the production situation where output grows proportionately more than the increase in inputs or factors of production. For example, output may more than double with a doubling of inputs. Increasing returns to scale may occur because at a larger scale of operation a greater division of labor and specialization becomes possible. That is, as each worker specializes in performing a simple repetitive task, labor productivity increase. Furthermore, a larger scale of operation permits the introduction of more specialized and productive machinery than would be feasible at a smaller scale of operation. About a third of all goods-producing industries are characterized by increasing returns to scale in the world today.

5.1.2 Internal scale economies

Where do scale economies come from? There are actually two types of scale economies. First, scale economies can be internal to the individual firm. The actions and decisions of the individual firm itself result in internal scale economies. A larger firm may have a lower average cost for a number of different reasons. Here are a few examples. ①There are often up-front costs before any production occurs. For instance, the cost of designing and developing a new large civilian aircraft is often close to \$ 10 billion. As more planes of this model can be produced, the average cost of each airplane will be lower because the up-front fixed development cost is spread over the larger number of planes. ②There are sometimes advantages to using large, specialized capital equipment that operates at high volume. Bottling or canning beer achieves lowest cost per unit using high-speed automated filling and sealing machines, but use of such a machine is economical only if it can be run to produce more than a thousand bottles or cans per minute. ③Tanks, vats, and pipes are a source of scale economies in producing chemicals. The cost of this type input is based largely on its surface area, but its contribution to output is based on the volume that it contains. As size increases, volume increases proportionately more than surface area.

Scale economies that are internal to the firm can drive an industry away from textbook-perfect competition because they drive individual firms to be larger than the (very) small firms that populate perfectly competitive industries. But howis far away? This depends on the size or extent of the scale economies. How large does a firm have to be to achieve all or most of the scale economies? The answers to these questions are important for the type of structure that arises on the seller side of the market.

If scale economies are modest or moderate, the there is room in the industry for a large number of firms. If, in addition, products are differentiated, then we have a mild form of imperfect competition called monopolistic competition, a type of market structure in which a large number of firms compete vigorously with each other in producing and selling varieties of the basic product. Because each firm' product is somewhat different, each firm has some control over the price that it charges for its product. This contrasts with the perfectly competitive market structure used in standard trade theory. With perfect competition, each of the industry' many small firms produce an identical commodity-like product, takes the market price as given, and believes that it has no direct control or influence on this market price.

If scale economies are substantial over a large range of output, then it is likely that a few firms will grow to be large in order to reap the scale economies. If a few large firms dominate the global industry, perhaps because of substantial scale economies, then we have an oligopoly. The large firms in an oligopoly know that they can control or influence prices. A key issue in an oligopoly is how actively these large firms compete with each other. If they do not compete too aggressively, then it is possible for the firms to earn economic (or pure) profit, profit greater than the normal return to invested capital.

5.1.3 External scale economies

The second type of scale economies is external to any individual firm. External scale economiesare based on the size of an entire industry within a specific geographic area. The average cost of the typical firm producing the product in this area declines as the output of the industry (all the local firms producing this product) within the area is larger. External economies explain the clustering of the production of some products in specific geographic areas. What are the sources of external scale economies? There are several possibilities.

External economies can arise if concentration of an industry' firms in a geographic area attracts greater local supplies of specialized services for the industry or larger pools of specialized kinds of labor required by the industry. One reason that filmmaking firms cluster in Hollywood is that a deep pool of workers skilled in the various aspects of filmmaking and a range of companies providing special services to facilitate filmmaking are available in these locations. (You can also see the self-reinforcing aspect of external scale economies-if you want to break into films and filmmaking, or to offer services to film companies, you know where you need to go) External economies can also results as new knowledge about product and production technology (or other useful business information) diffuses quickly among firms in the area, through direct contacts among the firms or as skilled workers transfer from firm to firm. Knowledge diffusion is rapid and personnel are continually shifting among the high-technology computer, software, semiconductor, and related firms in Silicon Valley. Other examples of clustering driven by external scale economies include banking and finance in London and in New York City; stylish clothing, shoes, and accessories in Italy; and watches in Switzerland.

5.2 Intra-industry Trade Theory

5.2.1 How to understand Intra-Industry Trade?

According to our basic theories of comparative advantage, if a country trades in a product, it should either mostly export the product (based on its relatively low production costs) or mostly import the product (as a result of its relatively high production costs). We should see only inter-industry trade, in which a country exports some productions in trade for imports of other, quite different products.

While much trade is inter-industry trade, especially in agricultural products and other primary products, there is also substantial intra-industry trade (IIT) —two-way trade in which a country both exports and imports the same or very similar products (product varies that are such close substitutes that they are classified within the same industry). For example, for each of perfumes and cosmetics the amount that the United States export is close to the amount that in imports.

We can quantify the relative importance of IIT in a country'trade in a product by splitting the total trade (the sum of exports plus imports) into two components. The first component is net trade, the difference between exports and imports of that product. Net trade is not intra-industry trade. Rather, net trade shows the product'importance in the country'inter-industry trade, in which some products are (net) exported and other products are (net) imported. In measurement we often use the convention that net trade is a positive value if the country is a net exporter of the product, and it is a negative value if the country is a net importer of the product

(The "positive" and "negative" are not value judgments, just ways of measuring).

Intra-industry trade is then the other component of the country'total trade in the product, the amount in which the country is both exporting and importing in the same product category. There are two equivalent ways to measure the amount of a country's intra-industry trade in a product. First, it is equal to twice the value of the smaller of exports or imports (capturing the amount of exporting of the product that is matched by the same amount of important of the product). Second, IIT is the part so total trade in the product (exports plus imports) that is not net trade. Using this latter approach,

$$\text{IIT} = (X+M) - |X-M|$$

Where X is the value of exports of the product and M is the value of imports of the product. Furthermore, we often want to compare the importance of IIT across different products or different products or different countries, we can measure the relative importance of intra-industry trade as a share of total trade in the product:

$$\text{IIT share} = \text{IIT} \div \text{Total trade} = [(X+M) - |X-M|] \div (X+M) = 1 - |X-M| \div (X+M)$$

5.2.2 What explains Intra-Industry Trade?

Why do we see so much intra-industry trade? There are several reasons. Some measured ITT probably reflects trade driven by comparative advantage. For instance, a product category may still be too broad, so that it includes different products that are produced using different production methods. Within a category, for instance, the United States may export specific products that are produced using skilled labor intensively and import other specific products that are produced using unskilled labor intensively. As another example, for some agricultural products, ITT measured over a year may reflect seasonal comparative advantages. The United States export cherries in July but imports cherries in January.

Muchintra-industry trade is driven by something other than comparative advantage, and the leading explanation focuses on the role of product differentiation—consumers view the varieties of a product offered by different firms in an industry as close but not perfect substitutes for each other. Product differentiation is rampant in perfumes and cosmetics, with strong brand names, exotic packaging, and wide-ranging claims for effectiveness and high quality. For clothes washing machines, brands from outside the United States, including Miele, Bosch, LG, Samsung, and Haier, compete with Whirlpool, Maytag, GE, and other U.S. brands, In integrated circuits there is differentiation by specific circuit design as well as by functional specification, with U.S. firms like Intel, Texas Instruments, and Micron battling with foreign firms like Toshiba, Samsung, and Infineon. The range of automobile models on offer is obviously very large. For cameras, consumers can choose from a range of brand names (including Canon, Sony, Samsung, Leica, Polaroid, and GE) and models that differ by features and quality.

Product differentiation easily can be a basis for trade. Some buyers in a country prefer varieties of the product produced in a foreign country, so they want to import the product. The foreign varieties are not necessarily cheaper than the varieties produced by local firms. Rather, each foreign variety has different characteristics, and these buyers find the foreign varieties' characteristics to be desirable. At the same time, some foreign buyers prefer varieties produced by firms in this country, and these firms are able to export to the foreign country. Even if there are no relative costs differences of the type emphasized by theories of comparative advantage, there is international trade. And much of it can be intra-industry trade, with a country exporting and importing different variants of the same basic product.

Yet, it is not only product differentiation at work in this explanation. Taken to the extreme, each of us would want to buy the unique product variant that exactly matches our personal preference. This would be different from anyone else'exact variant, so the product variant would be completely customized to our own individual taste. But we know that this is not the case for the products. Each has a limited number of variants. The customization is limited. What limits the number of variants, and the amount of customization? The answer is some form of internal scale economy, so that there is a cost advantage to producing larger amount of a specific variant.

5.3 Product Cycle Theory

Apart from differences in the relative availability of labor, capital, and natural resources (stressed by the Hechscher-Ohlin theory) and the existence of economies of scale and product differentiation, dynamic changes in technology among nations can be a separate determinant of international trade. There are examined by the technological gap and product cycle models. Since time is involved in a fundamental way in both of these models, they can be regarded as dynamic extensions of the static H-O model.

According to the technological gap, a great deal of the trade among industrialized countries is based on the introduction of new products and new production processes. As the sole producer of these products, the innovating firm and nation have a temporary monopoly in these products. Such a temporary monopoly is often based on patents and copyrights, which are granted to encourage inventions.

As the most technologically advanced nation, the United States exports a large number of new high- technology products. As they acquire the new technology, however, foreign producers eventually conquer markets abroad, and even the U.S. market for the product, because of their lower labor costs. In the meantime, U.S. producers may have introduced still newer products and production processes, and they may be able to export these products based on the new technological gap established. A shortcoming of this model, however, is that it does not explain the size of technological gaps and does not explore the reason that technological gaps arise in the first place or exactly how they are eliminated over time.

A generalization and extension of the technological gap model is the Product Cycle model developed by VernonI 1966. According to this model, when a new product is introduced, it usually requires highly skilled labor to produce. As the product matures and acquires mass acceptance, it becomes standardized; it can then be produced by mass production techniques and less skilled labor. Therefore, comparative advantage in the product shifts from the advanced nation that originally introduced it to less advanced nations, where labor is relatively cheaper. This may be accompanied by foreign direct investments from the innovating nation to nations with cheaper labor.

According to the product cycle model, a product goes through five stages: ①the introduction of the product. ②expansion of production for export. ③standardization and beginning of production abroad through imitation. ④ foreign imitators underselling the nation in third markets. ⑤foreigners underselling the innovating firms in their home market as well.

Vernon pointed out that high-income and labor-saving products are most likely to be introduced in rich nations because ① the opportunities for doing so are greatest there. ② the development of these new products requires proximity to markets so as to benefit from consumer feedback inmodifying the product. ③ there is a need to provide service. While the technological gap model emphasizes the time lag in the imitation process, the Product Cycle model stresses the standardization process. According to these models, the most highly industrialized economies are expected to export non - standardized products embodying new and more advanced technologies and import products embodying old or less advanced technologies.

A classic example of the product cycle model is provided by the experience of U.S. and Japanese radio manufacturers since World War Ⅱ. Immediately after the war, U.S. firms dominated the international market for radios, based on vacuum tubes developed in the United States. However, within a few years, Japan was able to capture a large share of the market by copying U.S. technology and utilizing cheaper labor. The United States recaptured technological leadership with the development of transistors. But, once again, in a few short years, Japan imitated the technology and was able to undersell the United States. Subsequently, The United States reacquired its ability to compete successfully with Japan by introducing printed circuits. It remains to be seen whether this latest technology will finally result in radios being labor or capital intensive and whether the United States will be able to stay in the market-or whether both the United States and Japan will eventually be displaced by still cheaper producers in such nations as Korea and Singapore.

In a 1967 study, Gruber, Mehta, and Vernon found a strong correlation between expenditures on research and development (R&D) and export performance. The authors took expenditures on research and development as a proxy for the temporary comparative advantage that firms and nations acquire in new products and new production processes. As such, these results tend to support both the technological gap and the closely related product cycle model. By turning out new products and technologies very rapidly, the United States ranks as the most competitive economy in the world.

Note that in these models trade is originally based on new technology development by the relatively abundant factors in industrialized nations (such as highly skilled labor and expenditures on research and development). Subsequently, through imitation and product standardization, less developed nations gain a comparative advantage based on their relatively cheaper labor. As such, trade can be said to be based on changes in relative factor abundance (technology) among nations over time. Therefore, the technological gap and the product cycle models can be regarded as extension of the basic H-O model into a technologically dynamic world, rather than as alternative trade models. In short, the product cycle model tries to explain dynamic comparative advantage for new products and new production processes, as opposed to the basic H-O model, which explains static comparative advantage.

5 新国际贸易理论

5.1 规模经济理论

5.1.1 规模报酬递增

在规模报酬递增的条件下，即使两国的生产和需求状况完全相同（它们有同样的生产可能性曲线和同样的无差异曲线）以致没有贸易时两国的相对商品价格也完全相同（没有比较优势和比较劣势），互利贸易也会发生。

规模报酬递增指的是产出水平增长比例高于要素投入增长比例的生产状况。例如，如果所有的投入都增加1倍，产出将增加1倍以上。由于大规模生产可以更有效地利用劳动力进行专业分工，所以规模报酬递增是有可能发生的。也就是说，当每个工人可以专门从事一项简单的重复性工作时，劳动生产率就会提高。另外，大规模的企业可以使用更加专业化和高效率的大型机器，而小企业却不能。当今世界上大约有1/3的制造行业是规模报酬递增的。

5.1.2 内部规模经济

规模经济从何而来？事实上存在两种类型的规模经济。规模经济对各个厂商来说，可以是内部性的。厂商个体的行为和决策本身会导致内部规模经济。一个大厂商可能因为种种不同的原因而有着较低的平均成本。我们举一些例子：①任何产品生产前都经常会发生前期费用。例如，设计和开发一个新的大型民用飞机的成本通常接近10亿美元。因为可以生产多架这种飞机，每架飞机的平均成本会变得更低，因为前期的固定开发成本均摊到大量飞机上。②大型装备和使用大型的、专业化的资本设备有时会很有优势。采用高速自动罐装和封口机会使得瓶装或罐装啤酒生产达到最低单位成本，但只有当它可以每分钟生产超过1 000瓶（或罐）的时候，使用这种机器才是经济的。③生产化学品的罐、桶和管道都是规模经济的来源。这种类型的投入成本在很大程度上是由表面积决定的，但其对产出的贡献由它包含的体积决定。随着尺寸的增加，体积增加的比例比表面积更大。

企业内部的规模经济可以导致一个产业偏离教材中提出的完全竞争模型，因为在规模经济的带动下，个别厂商的规模比完全竞争性行业的小厂商要大得多。但这种模式到底能偏离多远？这取决于规模经济的大小或程度。一个厂商的规模要多大，才能实现全部或大部分的规模经济？这些问题的答案对于判断供给市场的结构类型起着非常重要的作用。

如果规模经济是适度的，那么该产业中便仍有空间容纳大量的公司。如果产品是差异化的，便产生了一个较为温和的不完全竞争，我们称之为“垄断竞争”。这种市场结构的特点是：大量的厂商在某一产品不同品种的生产和销售中激烈竞争。由于各厂商的产品之间存在一定程度的差异，使其可以对自己生产的产品价格有一定程度的控制。这就与标准贸易理论中的完全竞争市场形成了对比。在完全竞争市场结构中，众多小厂商中的每一个厂商都生产相同的产品，都是价格的接受者，无法控制市场价格或者对市场价格施加影响。

如果大规模生产的规模经济收益十分巨大，则很可能导致少数厂商发展得很快从而取得规模经济的收益。巨大的规模经济收益使少数厂商垄断了全球的某一产业，于是便产生了寡头垄断。处于寡头垄断地位的大厂商知道它们可以控制或影响价格。寡头垄断中的关键问题在于大厂商之间竞争的程度。如果它们的竞争不是那么激烈，各个厂商便可能获得经济利润（或者纯利润），即超过资本投资正常收益的那部分超额利润。

5.1.3 外部规模经济

对各个厂商个体来说，规模经济也可以是外部性的。相对于单个厂商，外部规模经济是基于一个特定地理区域的整个产业的规模。随着该区域特定产业产量（当地所有该产业的厂商的全部产量）的扩大，厂商的平均成本下降。外部规模经济可以解释一些产品的生产在特定地区的集聚。外部规模经济的来源是什么？有以下几种可能性：

如果某产业的厂商在地理上的集聚能够吸引当地更多的产业需要的专业化服务以及专业化劳动力的供给，外部规模经济效应就产生了。电影制作公司在好莱坞积聚的原因之一是，好莱坞拥有一大批在电影制作各方面都非常熟练的人员和提高电影制作需要的特殊服务的诸多公司（你也可以看到外部规模经济的自我强化性——如果你想进入电影圈和电影制作圈，或提供服务给电影公司，你知道应该去哪儿）。当产品和生产技术的新知识（或其他有用的商业信息）通过厂商之间的直接接触或高技能劳动力的流动而在某一地区的厂商之间迅速传播时，也会产生外部规模经济。在硅谷，拥有高科技的计算机、软件、半导体的相关制造商之间，知识扩散非常迅速，公司人员不断流动；在纽约集聚着金融及银行业；在意大利集聚着时装、鞋类及饰品产业；在瑞士集聚着制表业，这些都是外部规模经济很好的例子。

5.2 产业内贸易理论

5.2.1 产业内贸易的理论

根据比较优势理论，如果一国参与国际贸易，通常出口其相对生产成本较低的产品，而进口其相对生产成本较高的产品，根据这一理论，我们只会在现实生活中看到产业间贸易，即一国出口某些产品是为了进口其他一些完全不同的产品。

虽然许多贸易属于产业间贸易，尤其是农产品和其他初级产品，但是也存在大量的产业内贸易（ITT），即在一个国家的每个行业内，同时进口和出口相似产品的双向贸易（产品种类之间的替代性高，以至于它们被划分到同一产业）。比如，美国对香水和化妆品这两类的出口量与进口量几乎相当。

将贸易总额（出口加进口）分成两个部分，我们就可以量化产业内贸易在一个国家的某种产品贸易中的相对重要性。第一个组成部分是净贸易，指某类产品出口价值与进口价值之差。净贸易不是产业内贸易。净贸易额衡量的是这类产品在国家的产业间贸易的重要性，表明哪些产品是（净）出口的，而哪些产品是（净）进口的。在计算中我们约定俗成，如果该产品是净出口，则净贸易额为正值；如果该产品是净进口，则净贸易额为负值（正和负不代表价值评判，只表示测量方法）。

产业内贸易是一国产品类贸易总额的另一个组成部分，在一个国家中该贸易额既

包括了同一类产品的出口，也包括了同一类产品的进口。这里有两种方法可以测定一国某种产品产业内贸易的数量。第一种方法是在某种产品的出口和进口价值中取较小数值的两倍（这种产品出口数额被其进口数额相抵的数量）；第二种方法是 IIT，IIT 是贸易总额（出口加进口）去除净贸易剩下的那一部分，其数学表达式为：$IIT = (X+M) - |X-M|$。

该式中，X 代表该产品的出口量；M 代表该产品的进口量。此外，我们经常想要比较 IIT 在不同产品或不同国家之间的重要性。显然，不同产品或不同国家的总贸易额是不一样的，因此我们可以用 IIT 占总贸易额的比重衡量产业内贸易的相对重要性，即

$$IIT比重 = IIT \div 总贸易额 = [(X+M) - |X-M|] \div (X+M) = 1 - |X-M| \div (X+M)$$

5.2.2 产业内贸易的原因

为什么能观察到如此多的产业内贸易？有多种原因。有些测算出的产业内贸易可能反映了比较优势驱动下的国际贸易。比如，如果产品类别定义得过于宽泛，它就会包含使用不同方法生产的不同产品。又如，在一个产品类别中，美国会出口那些密集使用高技能劳动力生产出来的特定产品，而进口那些密集使用低技能劳动力生产出来的其他产品。另一个例子是，对于一些农产品，测算出的产业内贸易跨越了年度，可能反映了季节性的比较优势。美国在 7 月份出口樱桃，但是在 1 月份进口樱桃。

很多产业内贸易是由比较优势以外的因素驱动的。最具有代表性的解释是产品差异化。所谓产品差异化，即消费者认为产业内不同厂商生产的同一产品看来十分相似，但是彼此之间不能完全替代。香水和化妆品行业中的产品差异化是非常明显的，如强大的品牌、充满异国情调的包装、五花八门的产品效果以及对高质量的宣传。又比如洗衣机，来自美国以外地区的品牌包括 Miele、博世、LG、三星、海尔、惠而浦、美泰克、通用电气以及其他品牌。在集成电路行业中，有具体的电路设计以及功能规范的差异化，美国企业诸如英特尔、得州仪器、美光与国外厂商如东芝、三星、英飞凌竞争。汽车行业的消费者的选择范围显然更大。在照相机行业，消费者可以从一系列的品牌（包括佳能、索尼、三星、徕卡、宝丽来和通用电气）中选择，每一种品牌都有不同的功能，其质量也有区别。

产品差异化无疑可以被认为是贸易的基础。一国的一些买家偏好外国生产的产品，他们希望进口这些产品，尽管国外产品的价格并不一定比当地企业生产的便宜。然而，每个国外产品有它的不同特征，并且这些买家发现这些国外产品的特征满足他们的需求。与此同时，一些国外买家喜欢本国企业所生产的产品，因此本国企业能够将产品出口到国外。即使没有比较优势理论所强调的相对成本差异，国际贸易也会发生。它可以是产业内贸易，即一国同时进口和出口不同种类的相同的基础产品。

然而，在这种情况下，并不是只有产品差异化这一个因素在起作用。在极短情况下，每个消费者想要购买的是完全符合个人偏好的特定产品。由于每个人的偏好是不同的，所以产品差异应当完全按照每个人的偏好来定制。但这并不符合实际情况：每类产品只有一定数量的差异，定制化是有限的。是什么限制了产品差异种类的数量与定制化的程度？答案是某种形式的内部规模经济，因此对某一特定差异化产品的大量生产会产生成本优势。

5.3 产品生命周期理论

除了劳动力、资本和自然资源的相对可用量的差异（赫克歇尔—俄林模型所强调的），以及规模经济和产品差别的存在以外，各国技术的动态变化也可以作为一个引发国际贸易的单独因素。技术差距模型和产品生命周期模型研究的就是这一问题。由于这些模型中都包含了时间因素，我们可以将其视为对静态赫克歇尔—俄林模型的动态扩展。

根据技术差距模型，工业化国家之间贸易的很大一部分都是以新产品和新工序的引进为基础的。作为这些产品的唯一生产者，发明厂商和国家在这些产品的市场上暂时处于垄断地位。这种暂时垄断地位通常是建立在为鼓励发明创造而授予的专利或版权基础之上的。

作为科技最发达的国家，美国出口大量的高新技术产品。但是，外国生产者获得新技术后，它们就能凭借其较低的劳动力成本最终占领外国市场，甚至是美国市场。与此同时，美国厂商会获得高新的产品和生产工序，由于新的技术差距，他们仍能向国外出口这些新产品。但是，这个模型也有一个缺点，就是它不能解释技术差距的大小，也没有给出技术差距产生和随着时间推移而消失的原因。

对技术差距模型的一个推广是弗农在1966年推出的产品生命周期模型。根据该模型，当一种新产品刚刚诞生时，其生产往往需要高素质的劳动力。当这种产品成熟并广为大众接受时，它就变得标准化了，可以用大规模生产技术和素质较低的劳动力进行生产。因此，生产该产品的比较优势会从最早引入它的发达国家转移到劳动力相对便宜的不发达国家。这一过程都伴随着发明国向劳动力便宜的国家的直接投资。

根据产品生命周期理论，一种产品的生命周期可以划分为5个阶段：①产品推出；②为出口扩大生产；③产品标准化并且国外通过模仿开始生产；④外国模仿着开始在第三国市场上低价销售；⑤模仿者在发明者本国市场上低价销售。

弗农还指出，高收入和劳动集约型的产品一般在富国最先投产，这是因为：①这些国家进行这种生产的机会最大；②这些新产品的发展需要接近市场以迅速从消费者处获得反馈，从而进行改进；③存在对提供服务的需求。技术差距模型强调的是模仿过程中的滞后性，而产品生命周期模型强调的是产品的标准化过程。根据这些理论，工业化程度最高的国家应当出口含有新的、更先进的技术的非标准化产品，进口含有旧的、已普遍应用的技术的标准化产品。

关于产品周期模型的一个典型例子就是第二次世界大战后美、日两国在无线电产品上的竞争。第二次世界大战结束以后，由于真空管技术在美国迅速发展，美国垄断了无线电产品的世界市场。但是，几年后，日本由于模仿了美国的技术并凭借其低价的劳动力，也占据了很大一部分市场份额。随后，美国发明了晶体管，重新在技术上领先。但是几年之后，日本再次通过模仿掌握了这一技术，又一次可以用低价和美国竞争。而美国又通过引入印刷电路在同日本的竞争中重新占了上风。生产无线电的最新技术究竟是劳动力密集型还是资本密集型，美国能否在这个市场中占有一席之地，或者美国和日本最终会不会被诸如韩国、新加坡等成本更低的生产商所代替，这一切仍然尚待分晓。

在 1967 年进行的一项研究中，格鲁伯、梅塔和弗农发现，在出口和研发费用之间存在很强的相关性。他们把研发费用当作国家或厂商在新产品或新工序上获得暂时比较优势的代表。这样一来，这些结果就倾向于支持技术差距模型和密切相关的产品生命周期模型。由于能以非常快的速度推出新产品和技术，美国是世界上最富有竞争力的经济体。

Part Two
Policy of
International Trade

6 Tariff and Non-tariff Barriers

According to the theory of free trade, comparative advantage and specialized production can achieve the most efficient allocation of the world's resources. Not only does free trade and specialization improve the welfare of the world, but also benefit the participating countries. Each country can overcome its own production capacity constraints and achieve a consumption combination that cannot be achieved in isolation.

Although free trade policy is strongly convincing, it has met with considerable resistance among companies and workers whose incomes have fallen as a result of import competition or face unemployment. Policymakers are torn between pursuing greater global efficiency in free trade and satisfying the public's desire to preserve short－term benefits such as jobs and incomes. The benefits of free trade can take many years to materialize, spreading across all corners of society, while the costs of free trade are immediate and borne by specific groups.

If the government wants its manufacturers to be protected from foreign competition, it will close its economy to self-sufficiency. Conversely, if a country does not restrict the international exchange of goods and services, it means it prefers free trade. Policy makers of other economies need to determine the extent of trade liberalization or protectionism.

This chapter will address barriers to free trade – the role of tariffs and non-tariffs in the global trading system.

6.1 Tariff

6.1.1 The meaning of Tariff

Tariff is a duty levied by the customs of a country or a separate customs territory on goods and articles entering or leaving the territory.

The positive effect of levying tariff lies in: to increase national income, to protect domestic production, and to adjust import and export trade structure. Tariffs also have negative effects: for example, if import tariffs set too high, it will stimulate smuggling activities, resulting in the loss of tariffs. If The import tariff is too high, then the protection is too high, which makes the protected industries and enterprises dependent and affects the cultivation and improvement of competitiveness. In addition, the tariff structure is not reasonable, and the protection effect on enterprises decreases, even appearing negative protection.

A tariff is an indirect tax whose burden will eventually be passed on to consumers.

6.1.2 Types of Tariff

6.1.2.1 Duties may be divided into import duties, export duties and transit duties if they are classified according to the flow of goods

Import duties can be divided into MFN duty and general duty. Normal import duties refer to MFN duties. Import duties are usually levied when foreign goods enter the customs or when they are shipped to the domestic market from places such as free ports, free trade zones or customs bonded warehouses. For export tariff, at present, most countries do not levy export tax, except some developing countries. The purpose of levying export taxes is to increase revenue or to ensure the production of the country or the supply of the market. For transit tariffs, most countries no longer levy a transit tax and only levy a small licensing fee, printing fee, visa fee and statistical fee.

6.1.2.2 According to tariff treatment, there are import surtax, price difference tax, preferential tax and generalized system of preferences

Import surtax. It means that in addition to a general import duty, additional duties are imposed for a particular purpose. It mainly has counter-vailing and anti-dumping duty.

Price difference tax is imposed on the difference between the domestic price and the import price, when the domestic price of a commodity is higher than the price of similar imported goods, in order to protect the domestic production and market.

Preferential tax is imposed to give special privilege duty or duty-free treatment for all or parts of the commodities that imports from a certain country or area. However, it does not apply to goods imported from non-preferential countries or regions.

Generalized system of preferences (GSP) is a general system of tariff concessions granted by developed industrial countries to certain products from developing countries, particularly manufactured and semi-manufactured goods. The principles of the GSP are generalized, non-discriminatory and non-reciprocal. The generalized principle means that developed countries should give general preferential treatment to manufactured and semi-manufactured goods exported by developing countries. Non-discrimination principle means that all developing countries should be free from discrimination and enjoy GSP treatment without exception. The non-reciprocal principle means that developed countries should unilaterally grant tariff preferences to developing countries instead of requiring developing countries or regions to provide reverse preferences.

6.1.2.3 According to the collection standard, there are specific tariff, AD valorem tax, mixed tax and alternative duty

Specific tariff is the tariff calculated on the basis of the weight, quantity, length and area of goods. AD valorem duty is a tariff levied based on the price of an imported commodity. A mixed tax combines both specific tariff and AD valorem duties on imported goods. Alternative duty is to choose the higher or lower tax which is among the specific tariff and AD valorem levied on the import commodities.

6.1.3 Effective Rate of Protection of Tariff

The effective rate of protection of tariff is the degree to which the tariff protects the whole economy, or certain industries, or products of the importing country. The effective rate of protection for a sector is formally defined as: ERP = (V' −V) /V×100%, where V is value added in the sector at world prices and V' value added in the presence of trade policies.

Suppose that an automobile sells on the world market for \$10,000 and that the parts out of which that automobile is made sell for \$8,000. The markets are perfectly competitive markets. In the full competition, without the import transportation, insurance and other related costs, the prices of the car and its parts in the domestic market should be the same as the prices in the international market. At this time, value added in the sector at world prices is 2,000 dollars.

To encourage the domestic auto industry, the domestic country places a 10% tariff on imported autos, allowing domestic assemblers to charge \$11,000 instead of \$10,000. At this time, value added in the sector at world prices is 3 000 dollars in the presence of trade policies.

According to the formula of effective rate of protection, the EPR of automobile is 50%.

ERP = (3,000−2,000) /2,000×100% = 50%

Now, to encourage domestic production of parts, the country imposes a 20 percent tariff on imported parts, raising the cost of parts to domestic assemblers from \$8,000 to \$9,600. Even though there is no change in the tariff on assembled automobiles, this policy makes it less advantageous to assemble domestically. After the tariff on parts, it then, while providing positive protection to parts manufacturers, provides negative effective protection to assembly at the rate of −30%.

ERP = (1,400−2,000) 2,000×100% = −30%

6.1.4 Welfare Effects of a Tariff—Small Country Case

To measure the welfare effects of tariffs, first consider " small country " case, which cannot affect world prices. In practice, many countries do not have the ability to influence the terms of trade (Figure 6.1).

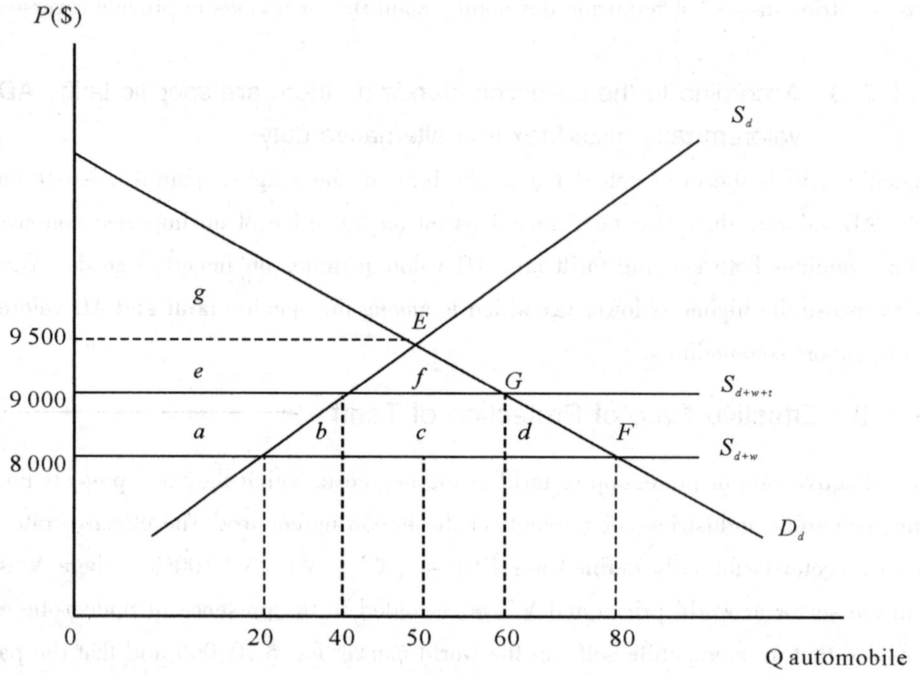

Figure 6.1 Welfare Effect of Tariff

In the figure above, before trade, the market equilibrium point of a small country is E, determined by the intersection of the domestic supply curve and the demand curve. At an equilibrium price of $9,500, the quantity demanded and supplied is 50. Now suppose that the country is an open economy. The international price of an automobile is $8,000, lower than the domestic price. Because the world market can supply an unlimited number of automobile s at a price of $8,000, the world supply curve for cars is a horizontal line (perfectly elastic). The line S_{d+w} represents the total supply of automobiles provided by domestic and foreign countries to consumers in small countries. This is the total supply curve under free trade terms.

The equilibrium in free trade is at point F. At this time, the demand for automobiles in small countries increased to 80, while the supply of domestic automobiles decreased to 20. The excess demand for automobiles was made up by 60 imported automobiles. Free trade has reduced the price of an automobile from $9,500 to $8,000. Free trade is better for consumers because they can buy more automobiles at lower prices. However, domestic producers are selling fewer automobiles than they used to, at the current prices.

In free trade, sales and profits in the domestic auto industry are falling, and unemployment rate are rising. Suppose that the management and workers of the automobile companies join forces to persuade the government to impose protective tariffs on automobile imports. Given the small country's inability to influence international market conditions, the world's auto supply curve remains unchanged and unaffected by the tariff. This means that the terms of trade of small countries have not changed. Tariffs raise the domestic price of imported goods, all of which are borne by domestic consumers.

From the figure above, we can see that before the tariff is imposed, the consumer surplus is equal to the area $a+b+c+d+c+e+f+g$. After the tariff is imposed, the consumer surplus becomes the area e+f+g, and the area a+b+c+d is reduced. This change affects the social welfare from many aspects. The tariffs bring in extra tax revenue for the government and benefit domestic auto makers. At the same time, tariffs waste resources and harm domestic consumers. As long as a country's position in international trade is negligible, import tariffs are bound to reduce its level of welfare.

6.2 Non-tariff Barriers

6.2.1 Import quota

An import quotais a direct restriction on the quantity of some good that may be imported. The restriction is usually enforced by issuing licenses to some group of individuals or firms.

6.2.2 Voluntary export quotas

Voluntary export quotasmeans that the exporting country, at the request or under the pressure of the importing country, "automatically" sets export restrictions on certain commodities to that country within a certain period of time, and prohibits the export if the quota is exceeded.

6.2.3 The import license system

The import license system refers to the system whereby the importer must first apply to the relevant state authorities for the import of commodities, and only after the importer has been examined and approved and an import license issued.

6.2.4 Export subsidy

Export subsidy refers to the cash subsidy or financial preferential treatment given by a government to an exporter when exporting a commodity, in order to reduce the export price of certain commodities and strengthen its competitiveness in the international market. There are direct subsidies and indirect subsidies.

6.2.5 Dumping of commodities

Dumping of commodities means exporting producers sell commodities at prices below normal value in foreign markets. It can be divided into accidental dumping, predatory dumping and continuous dumping.

6.2.6 Foreign exchange control

Foreign exchange controlrefers to a system whereby a government balances its international payments and maintains its own exchange rate by imposing restrictions on international settlement and foreign exchange transactions by decree. It can be divided into quantitative, cost and hybrid exchange control.

6.2.7 State monopoly of import and export

State monopoly of import and exportmeans that in foreign trade, the export of commodities is directly handled by government agencies or the import and export of commodities is monopolized by certain agencies authorized by the government.

6.2.8 Discriminatory government procurement policy

Discriminatory government procurement policyrefers to the practice of the state to enact laws and regulations, stipulating that government agencies must have priority in purchasing domestic products, thus causing discrimination against foreign products and restricting imports.

6.2.9 Various domestic taxes

In some countries, particularly in Western Europe, domestic taxation systems are widely used to restrict imports. It is a trade policy that is more flexible and easier to disguise than tariffs. Because domestic taxation isnot generally subject to trade treaties or multilateral agreements. The formulation and enforcement of domestic taxation is the purview of national and sometimes even local government agencies.

6.2.10 Minimum price and prohibition of import

The minimum price refers to the minimum price of a commodity stipulated by a government.

6.2.11 The import deposit system

When the importer imports commodities, he/she must first deposit a sum of cash in the designated bank without interest in accordance with the proportion of the import amount and the stipulated time. This increases the financial burden on importers, thus discouraging imports.

6.2.12 Product classification and customs valuation

There is a certain degree of flexibility in which tariff code the imported goods fall under, and the specific determination is decided by the customs on the spot. This increases the burden and uncertainty of import tariffs and makes it difficult to trade. At the same time, the customs authorities can arbitrarily raise the customs value of imported goods to increase the tariff burden of imported goods, to achieve the purpose of restricting the import of goods.

6.2.13 Technical barriers to trade

Technical barriers to traderefer to some compulsory or voluntary technical measures taken by a country or a regional organization for the purpose of safeguarding the basic security of the country or region, ensuring the life and health of human beings, protecting the safety of plants and animals, protecting the ecological environment, preventing fraud, and ensuring product quality. These measures have an impact on the access of goods, services and investments from other countries or regional organizations to the markets of that country or region. TBT mainly consists of five systems: technical regulations, standards and conformity assessment procedures, packaging and labelling requirements, commodity quarantine and inspection requirements, green barriers and information technology.

第二部分
国际贸易政策

6 关税与非关税

到目前为止，我们对自由贸易理论的讨论得出的结论是，比较优势和专业化生产能够实现世界资源的最有效利用。自由贸易和专业化分工不仅提高了世界福利，也使各个参与国家从中受益。每个国家都能克服自身的生产能力的限制，实现在孤立条件下无法实现的消费组合。

尽管自由贸易政策的理论依据非常充分，但在那些因进口竞争而收入下降以及面临失业的企业和工人当中，自由贸易政策却遇到了巨大的阻力。政策制定者在追求自由贸易更高的全球效率和满足公众愿望保持就业及收入等短期利益之间左右为难。自由贸易的收益可能要经过许多年才能实现，贸易收益遍及社会各个角落，而自由贸易的成本却立竿见影，并由具体的某些群体来承担（如面临进口竞争压力行业的工人）。

如果政府希望本国厂商可以免受海外竞争，它将封闭本国的经济，也就是自给自足；相反，如果一国不限制货物和服务的国际交换，这意味着它倾向于自由贸易。其他经济体则处于两个极端之间。围绕贸易政策的讨论并不是确定一个经济体应该选择自给自足还是自由贸易，更现实的情况是确定该经济体在两点之间的定位。也就是说，政策制定者需要决定的是贸易自由化或贸易保护主义的程度。

本章将阐述自由贸易的壁垒——关税和非关税在全球贸易体制中的作用。

6.1 关税

6.1.1 关税的含义

关税是一个国家或一个单独关税区的海关对进出境（国境或关境）的货物和物品所征收的一种税。

征收关税的积极作用在于：增加国家财政收入，保护本国生产，调节进出口贸易结构。但是关税也存在消极影响，如进口关税设置过高，会刺激走私活动，造成关税流失；进口关税太高，保护过分，使被保护的产业和企业产生依赖性，影响竞争力的培育和提高；关税结构不合理，对企业的保护作用下降，甚至出现负保护。

关税是一种间接税，其负担最终将转嫁到消费者身上。

6.1.2 关税的种类

6.1.2.1 如果按照商品流向分类，关税可以分成进口关税、出口关税和过境关税

进口关税主要可分为最惠国税和普通税两种。通常情况下的进口关税是指最惠国税。进口关税通常是在外国商品进入关境时征收，或是在商品从自由港、自由贸易区或海关保税仓库等地提出运往国内市场时征收。对于出口关税而言，目前大多数国家不征收出口关税，征收出口关税的主要是一些发展中国家。征收出口关税的目的，是增加财政收入或者为了保证本国的生产或本国市场的供应。对于过境关税而言，大多数国家已不征收过境关税了，仅征收少许准许费、印花费、签证费和统计费等。

6.1.2.2　如果按照关税待遇分类，有进口附加关税、差价关税、特惠关税和普遍优惠制

进口附加关税是指除了征收一般进口关税以外，还根据某种目的再加征额外的关税。它主要有反贴补关税和反倾销关税。

差价关税，又称“差额关税”，是指当某种商品的国内价格高于同类进口商品价格时，为了保护国内生产和市场，按国内价格与进口价格间的差额征收的关税。

特惠关税，又称“优惠关税”，是指对某个国家或地区进口的全部商品或部分商品，给予特别优惠的低关税或免税待遇。但它不适用于从非优惠国家或地区进口的商品。特惠关税有的是互惠的，有的是非互惠的。

普遍优惠制，简称“普惠制”，它是发展中国家在联合国贸易与发展会议上经过长期斗争，在1968年通过建立普惠制决议后取得的。它是发达工业国家对来自发展中国家的某些产品，特别是工业制成品和半制成品给予的一种普遍的关税减免优惠制度。普惠制的原则是普遍的、非歧视的和非互惠的。所谓普遍的，是指发达国家应对发展中国家出口的制成品和半制成品给予普遍的优惠待遇。所谓非歧视的，是指应使所有发展中国家都不受歧视，无例外地享受普惠制待遇。所谓非互惠的，是指发达国家应单方面给予发展中国家关税优惠，而不要求发展中国家或地区提供反向优惠。

6.1.2.3　如果按征收标准分类，有从量关税、从价关税、混合关税和选择关税

从量关税是按照商品的重量、数量、长度和面积等计量单位为标准计征的关税。从价关税是以进口商品的价格为标准计征的关税。混合关税是对进口商品采取从量关税和从价关税同时征收的方法。选择关税是对于一种进口商品同时订有从价关税和从量关税两种税率，征税时选择其中较高或较低的一种征税。

6.1.3　关税有效保护率

关税保护率就是关税对进口国整体经济或某类产业或产品的保护程度。有效保护率就是一种加工产品在国内各种保护措施下的增值量和其在自由贸易条件下增值量的差额与自由贸易条件下的增值量之比。其公式为：ERP＝（V' －V）/V×100%。

假设国际市场上汽车售价为每辆10 000美元，整套配件每套售价为8 000美元。该国对汽车及其整套配件实行完全自由贸易。在充分竞争下，可以忽略进口运输、保险等有关费用时，该国国内市场上汽车及其整套配件价格应与国际市场相同。此时，国内汽车组装生产的加工增值为2 000美元。如该国对汽车实行保护，征收10%的关税，而对其整套配件仍实行自由贸易。交纳关税以后，国内汽车价格可从10 000美元提高到11 000美元，则加工过程增值为3 000元。根据有效保护率公式可知，关税对汽车的有效保护率为50%，即ERP＝（3 000－2 000）/2 000×100%＝50%。

假如对汽车的进口征税不变，但对汽车整套配件不再实行自由贸易，而要征收20%的关税，则汽车整套配件的国内市场售价从8 000美元提高至9 600美元。那么，装配过程的增值为1 400美元（11 000美元－9 600美元），其有效保护率为－30%，即ERP＝（1 400－2 000）2 000×100%＝－30%。由此可见，由于对汽车整套散件加征关税，使汽车装配产业的保护从正保护转变为负保护。

6.1.4　关税福利效应——小国模型

为了测算关税的福利效应，我们需要考虑小国的情形，即进口只占世界市场供给

量的很小一部分的国家。小国是价格的接受者，其进口商品面临的是固定的世界价格。现实中，许多国家都不具备影响贸易条件的能力。关税的福利效应见图 6.1。

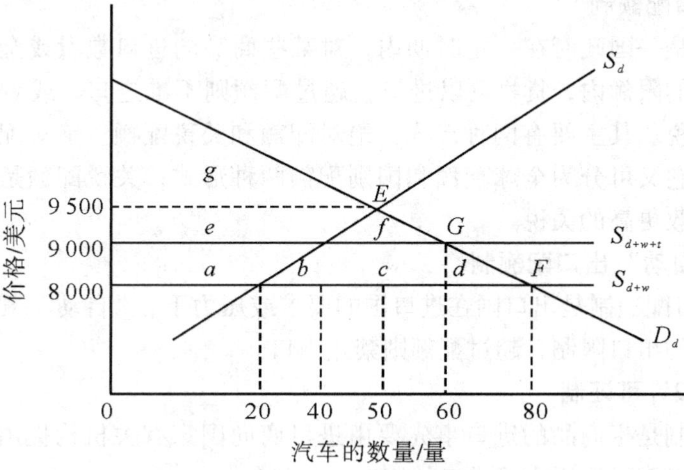

图 6.1　关税的福利效应

图 6.1 显示，在进行贸易之前，小国的市场均衡点为 E，由国内供给曲线与需求曲线的交点决定。在 9 500 美元的均衡价格水平下，产品的供给数量是 50 辆汽车，需求数量也是 50 辆汽车。现在假设该国对贸易进行开放，并且国际上的汽车价格为 8 000 美元，低于国内价格。因为世界市场可以在 8 000 美元的价格水平上提供无限数量的汽车，所以汽车的世界供给曲线为一条水平直线（完全弹性）。直线 S_{d+w} 表示国内和国外为小国的消费者提供的汽车总供给量，这是自由贸易条件下的总供给曲线。

自由贸易条件下的均衡点位于图中的 F 点。此时，小国对汽车的需求数量增加至 80 辆，而国内汽车的供给数量却减少至 20 辆，国内汽车的超额需求由进口的 60 辆汽车加以弥补。与贸易发生之前的情况相比，自由贸易使汽车价格从 9 500 美元下降到 8 000美元。因为消费者可以以更低的价格购买更多的汽车，所以自由贸易对他们更加有利。但是，在现在的低价格水平下，国内生产者的汽车销售量却比以前减少了。

在自由贸易中，国内汽车产业受到国外竞争的冲击。国内汽车产业的销售额和利润都在降低，工人的失业也不断增加。假设汽车企业的管理阶层和劳动者联合起来，说服政府对汽车进口征收保护性关税。假定小国对进口的每辆汽车征收 1 000 美元的关税，由于小国无力影响国际市场状况，世界的汽车供给曲线仍保持不变，没有受到关税的影响。这就意味着小国的贸易条件也没有发生变化。关税提高了进口商品的国内价格，这个增量全部由国内消费者承担，总供给曲线向上移动的幅度等于关税的数量。

从图 6.1 可知，在征收关税之前，消费者剩余等于面积 $a+b+c+d+c+e+f+g$；而在征收关税以后，消费者剩余变为面积 $e+f+g$，减少了面积 $a+b+c+d$，这种变化从多个方面影响了社会福利。关税为政府带来了额外的税收收入，并使国内汽车生产商受益。同时，关税也浪费了资源，并损害了国内消费者的利益。只要一国在国际贸易中的地位微不足道，进口关税就必然会降低该国的福利水平。

6.2 非关税贸易壁垒

6.2.1 进口配额制

进口配额制是一国政府在一定时期内，对某些商品的进口数量或金额事先规定一个限额，在规定的限额内，货物可以进口，超过配额则不准进口，或者可以进口但要被征收更高的关税。其主要有两种形式：绝对配额和关税配额。绝对配额是指超过限额则不准进口，它又可分为全球配额和国别配额两种形式；关税配额是指超过限额的进口商品要被征收更高的关税。

6.2.2 “自动”出口配额制

“自动”出口配额制是出口国在进口国的要求或压力下，“自动”规定某一时期内某些商品对该国的出口限制，超过配额则禁止出口。

6.2.3 进口许可证制

进口许可证制是指商品的进口事先要由进口商向国家有关机构提出申请，经过审查批准并发放进口许可证后方可进口的制度。

6.2.4 出口补贴

出口补贴是指一国政府为降低某些商品的出口价格，加强其在国际市场上的竞争能力，在出口某种商品时给予出口厂商的现金补贴或财政上的优惠待遇。出口补贴主要有直接补贴和间接补贴两种方式。

6.2.5 商品倾销

商品倾销是指出口厂商以低于正常价值的价格在国外市场出售商品，其可分为偶然性倾销、掠夺性倾销和持续性倾销等。

6.2.6 外汇管制

外汇管制指一国政府通过法令对国际结算和外汇买卖实行限制来平衡国际收支，维护本币汇率的制度。外汇管制可分为数量型、成本型和混合型外汇管制。

6.2.7 进出口的国家垄断

进出口的国家垄断是指在对外贸易中，由政府机构直接经营商品的出口或由政府授权某些机构垄断经营商品的进出口。

6.2.8 歧视性的政府采购政策

歧视性的政府采购政策是指国家制定法令，规定政府机构在采购时必须优先购买本国产品，从而导致对国外产品歧视，限制进口的做法。

6.2.9 各种国内税

一些国家，特别是西欧国家，广泛采用国内课税制度来限制进口。这是一种比关税更加灵活、更易于伪装的贸易政策和手段，因为国内课税通常不受贸易条约或多边协定的限制，国内课税的制定和执行是属于本国政府机构有时甚至是地方政府机构的权限。

6.2.10 最低限价和禁止进口

最低限价是指一国政府规定某种商品的最低价格。

6.2.11 进口押金制

进口押金制又称“进口存款制”，进口商在进口商品时，必须先按进口金额的规定比例和规定时间在指定的银行无息存放一笔现金。这就增加了进口商的资金负担，从而抑制进口。

6.2.12 产品归类和海关估价

进口商品归在哪一个税号内是具有一定的灵活性的，具体的确定由海关现场决定。这就增加了进口关税的负担和不确定性，增加了交易的困难度。同时，海关当局还可以提高进口商品的关税价格来增加进口商品的关税负担，从而达到限制商品进口的目的。

6.2.13 技术性贸易壁垒

技术性贸易壁垒是指一国或一个区域组织以维护国家或区域基本安全、保障人类的生命健康保护动植物的安全、保护生态环境、防止欺诈行为、保证产品质量等为由而采取的一些强制性或自愿性的技术性措施。这些措施对其他国家或区域组织的商品、服务和投资进入该国或该区域市场产生影响。技术性贸易壁垒主要由技术法规、标准和合格评定程序，包装和标签要求，商品检疫和检验规定，绿色壁垒以及信息技术壁垒五个体系构成。

7 Measurements of Pushing Exports

To address the debate over unfair trade, we turn first to dumping, a way in which private firms may export more than competitive supply and demand would lead us to expect. Then we explore how government push exports with outright or subtle subsidies.

7.1 Dumping

7.1.1 The definition /types of dumping

7.1.1.1 The definition of dumping

Dumping is selling exports at a pricethat is too low-less than normal value (or "fair market value" as it is often called in the United States). There are two legal definitions of normal value: ①The long-standing definition of normal value is the price charged to comparable domestic buyers in the home market (or to comparable buyers in other markets). Under this traditional definition, dumping is international price discrimination favoring buyers of exports. ②The second definition of normal value arose in the 1970s. It is cost-based-the average cost of producing the product, including overhead costs and profit. Under this second standard, dumping is selling exports at a price that is less than the full average cost of the product.

7.1.1.2 The types of dumping

Why would an exporting firm engage in dumping? Why would it sell exports at a price lower than the price it charges for its product in its home market, or lower than its average cost? There are several reasons. To judge whether dumping is good or bad, it is important to understand the full range of reason why dumping occurs.

(1) Predatory dumping

Predatory dumping occurs when a firm temporarily charges a low price in the foreign export market, with the purpose of driving its foreign competitors out of business. Once the rivals are gone, the firm will use its monopoly power to raise prices and earn high profits.

(2) Cyclical dumping

Cyclical dumping occurs during periods of recession. During the part of the cycle when demand is low, a firm tends to lower its price to limit the decline in quantity sold. For instance, in a competitive market initially in long-run equilibrium, price equals full average cost (long-run average cost) for the representative firm. If an industry recession or an economy wide recession then causes demand to decline, market price will fall below this full average cost in the short run. A firm continues to produce and sell as long as price exceeds average variable cost. If any of these sales are exports, the firm is dumping.

(3) Seasonal dumping

Seasonal dumping is intended to sell off excess inventories of a product. For instance, toward the end of a fashion seasons, U.S. clothing manufactures may decide to sell off any remaining stock of swimsuits at prices that are below full average cost. That is, they have a sale. With production costs sunk, any price above the marginal cost of making the sale is sensible. If some of these low-priced sales are to Canada, the U. S. firm is dumping. Perishable agricultural products are also good candidates for seasonal dumping. A big harvest tends to lower the market price and to provide a larger quantity available for export. Similarly, dumping can be a technique for promoting new products in new markets. This is the equivalent of an introductory sale that an exporting firm could use to establish its product in a new foreign market.

(4) Persistent dumping

Persistent dumping occurs because a firm with market power uses price discrimination between markets to increase its total profit. A firm maximizes profits by charging a lower price to foreign buyers if: It has less monopoly power (more competition) in the foreign market than it has in its home market; Buyers in the home country cannot avoid the high home prices by buying the good abroad and importing it cheaply.

When these conditions hold, the firm can make home-country buyers pay a higher price and thus earn a higher total profit. This is not predatory; it is not intended to drive any other firms out of business. And it can persist for a long time—as long as these market differences continue.

7. 1. 2 Reacting to dumping

Domestic firms competing against exports dumped intothere are likely to complain loudly to their government, charging that this is unfair. How should the importing country view dumping? What should be its government policy toward dumping?

7. 1. 2. 1 Reacting to persistent dumping

In one sense the importing country's view is easy. It should welcome dumping and thank the exporting country. After all, we do not usually argue when someone tries to sell us something at a low price. This instinct seems clearly correct for persistent dumping. Compared to the high price in the exporting country, the importing country gets the gains from additional trade at the low export price. The importing country's terms of trade are better. The benefits to consumers are larger than the losses to the import-competing producers.

However, the other two types of dumping may not be so simple.

7. 1. 2. 2 Reacting to predatory dumping

There is a sound economic reason for the importing country to view predatory dumping negatively. Although the importing country gains from low-priced imports in the short run, it will lose because of high-priced imports once the exporting firm succeeds in establishing its monopoly power.

A key question is how frequently foreign firms use predatory dumping. Predatory dumping of manufactured goods was widely alleged during the international chaos of the 1920s and 1930s. In truth, there is no clear evidence that widespread predatory dumping has been practiced, despite a rich folklore about it. Predatory dumping is likely to be rare in modern markets. An exporting firm considering predatory dumping must weigh the sure losses from low prices in the short run against the possible but uncertain profits in the more distant future. Even if the firm could drive out its current competitors in the importing country, it may expect that, once it raises prices, new firms, including new exporters from other countries, will enter as competitors. The predatory exporter would not be able to raise prices or to keep them high for very long. Recent research suggests that no more than 5 percent of all cases of alleged dumping in the United States, the European Union, Canada, Mexico, and India show even a moderate possibility for predation (and it is possible that none of these cases involves predation).

7. 1. 2. 3 Reacting to cyclical dumping

Cyclical dumping is the most complicated kind of dumping for the importing country. Most cyclical dumping is probably the normal working of well-functioning, competitive global product markets. When demand declines, the market price falls in the short run. A firm will continue to produce, sell, and even export some amount of the product, as long as the revenue earned at least covers variable cost. This is exactly what we want to happen when there is a decline in demand. Production declines somewhat in many countries as the world price falls. There is an efficient global "sharing" of the decline in demand. Once the recession ends, demand, price, and global production will recover (If instead too much production capacity continues to exist, then eventually there will need to be and efficient global sharing of capacity reduction before price can recover).

The importing country may not be completed convinced that cyclical dumping is fair just because it is usually globally efficient. When demand declines by, say, 10 percent, which countries absorb how much of global reduction in output? Is it fair that the import-country firms have to reduce their output and suffer losses? In particular, if the decline in demand is a result of a national recession in the exporting country, why is it fair that the exporting country can "export some of its unemployment"?

As usual, it is easy to answer the question of what is fair. The international sharing of recessions is one of the effects that come with the general benefits of international trade. The real problem here is the concern about producer losses. For instance, if the key concern is about unemployed workers, the country should provide suitable unemployment insurance or adjustment assistance.

7.1.3 Actual antidumping products

Our discussion suggests that dumping is often good for the country importing the dumped exports but that two types of dumping could be bad for the importing country. Predatory dumping can be bad if it is successful, but success is probably rare. Cyclical dumping can sometimes unfairly harm the importing country, but much of the time it is probably the normal working of the competitive market. The implication is that the importing-country's government policy toward dumping (its antidumping policy) should examine each case and consider benefits and costs before imposing antidumping duties or other restrictions on dumped imports. In fact, actual government policies are not at all like this.

The WTO rules permit countries to retaliate against dumping if the dumping injures domestic import-competing producers. If the government in the importing country finds both dumping and injury, then the government is permitted to impose an antidumping duty—an extra tariff equal to the discrepancy (the dumping margin) between the actual export price and the normal value.

Antidumping cases throughout the world actually were infrequent until the late 1970s, and as of 1980 only about 34 countries had antidumping laws. Then more countries adopted antidumping laws, especially since 1990, and by 2010 more than 100 countries had them.

Up to the late 1980s, the four "traditional user" of antidumping (the United States, the European Union, Canada, and Australia) accounted for over 90 percent of the cases, but then the use spread. From 1986—1990 to 2008—2012 the number of cases worldwide increased by 33 percent, and the share of the four traditional users (including Canada, with 24 cases during 2008—2012) dropped to 22 percent of total cases. India had no antidumping cases until 1992, but by 2008—2012 it was the top initiator in the world. China enacted its antidumping policies in 1997 and quickly rose to be a major initiator. Argentina and Pakistan also went from zero to top 10.

Worldwide, the products most often involved in dumping cases are chemicals, steel and other metals, plastics and rubber products, machinery, textiles, and apparel. The countries whose exporters are most frequently charged with dumping are China, South Korea, the United States, Thailand, and Indonesia. For China, in 2009, about 2 percent of its exports were subject to antidumping measures in the importing countries.

Let's look more closely at U. S 's antidumping policy. A case usually begins with a complaint from U.S. producers. The U.S. Department of Commerce examines whether dumping has actually occurred, and the U.S. International Trade Commission examines whether U.S. firms have been injured. In addition, negotiations may occur with foreign exporters. If they agree to raise prices or to limit their exports, then the case can be terminated or suspended (This type of outcome has been common in cases involving steel and chemicals).

In about 94 percent of it determinations, the Department of Commerce finds some amount of dumping—the law and the procedures are biased to make showing dumping easy. In cases in which the comparison is between the export price and the home market price, there are arcane rules about cost tests and ignoring export prices that are above the home market price. The upshot is that only low-priced exports tend to be compared to only high-priced home market sales. In cases in which export prices instead are compared to average cost, obtaining and interpreting data on the costs incurred by foreign exporters are often difficult, so the Commerce Department has leeway in determining what normal value is. Lindsey and Ikenson (2002), using actual by the Department of Commerce, concluded that in 10 of the 18 cases there actually was no dumping, and in 4 of the other 8 cases the actual dumping was less than half the amount found by the Department.

The injury standard is not strict, but injury is usually the key to the outcome of a case. In about two-thirds of the cases, the International Trade Commission finds material injury to U.S. import-competing industries.

If both dumping and injury are found, customs officials are instructed to levy an antidumping duty. More than half of the cases brought in the United States result in antidumping duties or an exporter agreement to restrain its export prices or volumes. We can see that more than half of the cases in most of the other countries shown and in the world overall result in antidumping duties or exporter agreements.

Recent research shows some clear patterns of effects from all this. Shortly after the complaint is filed, the prices of the exporters charged with dumping increase, probably to try to reduce the final dumping margin. Export quantities decrease because of the higher price and because of the uncertainty about the outcome of the case. If antidumping duties are imposed, the export quantities decrease further, by an average of 70 percent, and often to zero. The exporter also has an incentive to raise its export price. The antidumping duties are reduced or eliminated if a subsequent review by the Department of Commerce finds less or no dumping.

A study of the overall effects of imposing antidumping duties concluded that the United States suffers a loss of well-being of nearly $4 billion per year. About half of that amount is deadweight loss. The other half is the transfer to foreign exporters that raises their prices. The net loss to the United States could be lower than this because the study does not attempt to quantify the value of avoiding any harmful effects from predatory dumping (probably minimal) and cyclical dumping (hard to measure).

Under current antidumping policies in the United States and a growing number of other countries, we get the following results: ①The procedure is biased toward finding dumping. ②The injury test considers only harm to import-competing producers. There is no consideration or whether predation or some other source of harm to the country is involved. There is little or no consideration of the benefits to consumers of the low-priced imports. ③Overall, the process is biased toward imposing antidumping duties, even though this usually lowers the well-being of the importing country, antidumping duties also generally lower world welfare.

If an exporting country's government believes that an importing country's government violated the WTO's rules in deciding to impose an antidumping duty, it can complain to the WTO. By early 2014 there had been 101 such complaints, including 47 about the laws and procedures of the U.S. government. As of early 2014, panels had been convened and reached decisions in close to half of these cases. Usually, the panels found errors by the importing countries, including using inappropriate procedures, determining dumping margins (or subsidy rates) in a manner inconsistent with WTO rules, and determining injury using incomplete information or biased analysis. In some of the cases the importing countries implemented changes (like revoking the duties) to bring their practices in line with WTO rules, but in others they have not (yet). While the WTO dispute settlement procedure can provide some guard against misuse of antidumping duties, the process is too slow to minimize the effects of such misuse.

Antidumping policy starts out sounding like it is about unfair exports. But a closer examination indicates that something else is going on. Antidumping policy has become a major way for import-competing producers in a growing number of countries to gain new protection against imports, with the usual deadweight costs to the world and to the importing country. The average antidumping duties imposed against foreign exporters are generally very high, much higher than most regular tariffs, so the deadweight losses can be large. There is also the cost of arguing the cases and gathering the data to prove or disprove dumping and injury. In addition, importing-competing firms use the threat of a dumping complaint to prod exporters to raise their prices and restrain their competition-the harassment effect-even if no complaint is actually filed.

7. 1. 4 Proposals for reform

Although there are exceptions, the current practice of retaliation against dumping is usually bad for the world and for the importing country. Yet this practice is fully consistent with current WTO rules. Reform of the WTO rules is an important item on the agenda for the current Doha Round of multilateral trade negotiations. Three possibilities for reform are discussed in the following paragraphs.

7. 1. 4. 1 Antidumping actions could be limited to situations in which predatory dumping is plausible

This reform would focus on the type of dumping that is most likely to be bad for the world and for the importing country. It would also align antidumping policy with antitrust policy (as it is called in the United States; it is called competition policy, antimonopoly policy, or similar names in other countries). Pro-competition policies usually forbid any predatory action to gain monopoly power. This reform would try to limit the scope of antidumping policy. However, the procedures in a country could still be biased toward finding both dumping and something potentially predatory about it.

7. 1. 4. 2 The injury standard could be expanded to require that weight be given to consumers and users of the product

This change would shift the discussion toward injury to net national well-being, not just injury to domestic import - competing producers. Some countries, including the European Union, Canada, and Thailand, already have a "public interest test" in their antidumping regulations. This reform would try to limit the scope for antidumping actions in a general way rather than by focusing on one type of dumping.

This reform would also change an odd feature of current antidumping policy, that consumes will be substantially affected by dumping decisions but have no legal standing in the process. In fact, most antidumping actions involve intermediate goods like steel and chemicals. The buyers (like automobile firms) of these products are often well organized politically. They can be effective in opposing import protection on the intermediate products that they buy and use. Current dumping policies give import-competing producers of intermediate products an end run around this political battle. Reforming antidumping policy to include consumer interests would reopen the battle and probably reduce some of the bad use of antidumping policy.

7. 1. 4. 3 Antidumping policy could be replaced by more active use of safeguard policy, another kind of increased import protection allowed by WTO rules

Safeguard policy is the use of temporary import protection when a sudden increase in imports causes injury to domestic producers. The intent is to give some time for import-competing firms and their workers to adjust to the increased import competition.

Defenders of antidumping policy often state that antidumping policy facilitates trade liberalization because it allows protection for industries that are hurt more than expected by increasing imports. This is really an argument for safeguard policy. Safeguard policy is better because: ①There is no need to show that foreign exporters have done anything unfair. ②The interests of consumers can be considered in the process that leads to the decision of whether or not to impose a safeguard, and what form it will take if imposed. ③The focus is on adjustment by the import-competing producers. ④There is pressure to adjust because the import protection is temporary.

Safeguard actions have not been much sued in the United States. One famous case is Harley-Davidson in the 1980s. After a safeguard was imposed, Harley-Davidson came back so strongly and quickly in its battle with Japanese competitors (Suzukiand Honda) that it asked that the safeguard protection be removed earlier than scheduled. More recently, the tariffs on steel imposed by the U. S. government in 2002 was the outcome of the government's investigation of a request by American steel firms for safeguard relief. The tariffs that the U.S. government imposed in 2009 on imports of tires from China are another example. Clearly, antidumping actions such as these steel and tire tariffs can still be controversial, but at least all parties affected have a right to be heard in the debate.

7.2 Exports Subsidies

7.2.1 The definition of exports subsidies

Governments promote or subsidize exports more often than they restrict or tax exports. Some government efforts to promote exports are not controversial according to international precepts (although there are questions about how effective they are). Government agencies like Export.gov of the U.S. Department of Commerce provide foreign-market research, information on export procedures and foreign government regulations, and help with contacting buyers. Government agencies sponsor export promotion events like trade fairs and organized trips. Governments establish export processing zones that permit imports of materials and components with easier customs procedures and low or no tariffs.

Governments also provide various forms of financial assistance that benefit their exporters. An exports subsidy is controversial because it violates international norms about fair trade. Our analysis of export subsidies will conclude that export subsidies are usually bad from a world point of view. However, the international division of gains and losses turns out to be very different from what you would expect just by listening to who favors export subsidies and who complains about them. Export subsidies are bad for the countries that use them but are good for the countries that complain about them.

Governments subsidize exports in many ways, some of them deliberately subtle to escape detection. They use taxpayer's money to give low-interest loans to exporters or their foreign customers. An example is the U.S. Export-Import Bank, or Eximbank. Founded in 1930s, it has compromised its name by giving easy credit to U.S. exporters and their foreign customers but not to U.S. importers or their foreign suppliers. Governments also charge low prices on inputs (such as raw materials or domestic transport services) that go into production that will be exported. Income tax rules are also twisted to give tax relief based on the value of goods or services each firm exports.

Export subsidies are small on average, but they loom large in certain products and for certain companies. For instance, most Eximbank loans have been channeled toward a few large U.S. firms and their customers. Boeing, in particular, has been helped to extra foreign aircraft orders by cheap Eximbank credit. More broadly, the biggest export subsidies apply to agricultural products.

What are the effects on the country whose government offers the export subsidy? Let's examine the effects for a competitive industry, using our standard supply - and - demand framework. We will reach the following conclusions: ①An export subsidy expands and production of the subsidized product, In fact, the export subsidy can switch the product from being imported to being exported. ②An export subsidy lowers the price by foreign buyers, relative to the price that local consumers pay for the product. In addition, for the export subsidy to work as intended (the government subsidizes only exports, not domestic purchases), something must prevent local buyers from importing the product at the lower foreign price. ③The export subsidy reduces the net national well-being of the exporting country.

7.2.2 Exportable product, small exporting country

Figure 7.1 shows a small country, in this case a country whose exports of steel pipes do not affect the world price of $100 per pipe (standard length). With free trade the firms in the country's competitive steel-pipe industry produce 160 million pipes per year and export 90 million (=160-70). The government of this country then decides to offer to its firms an export subsidy of $20 per pipe. The revenue per pipe exported the in $120, equal to the $100 price paid by foreign buyers plus the $20 subsidy. If a pipe firm can get $120 for each pipe exported, it will not sell to any domestic buyer at a price lower than $12. Of course, this is only possible if domestic buyers cannot just buy imported pipes from the world market at $100. Sometimes must keep the export market separate from the domestic market. (This should sound familiar—it sounds like persistent dumping. In fact, receiving an export subsidy is another reason why an exporting firm would engage in dumping) (Figure 7.1).

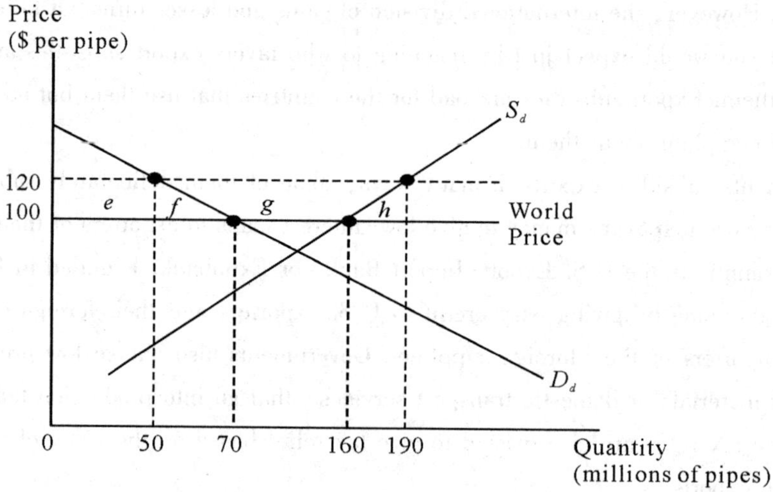

Note: With free trade at the world price of $100, this small country exports 90 million steel pipes. If the country instead offers an export subsidy of $20 per unit exported, revenue per unit exported rises to $120, and the exporting firms must receive this amount as the selling price from domestic buyers as well. Domestic production rises from 160 to 190 million, Domestic consumption falls from 70 to 50 million, and the country exports 140 million pipes. Domestic producers gain surplus equal to area *e+f+g*, domestic consumers lose surplus equal to area *e+f*. and the cost to the government of paying the export subsidy is area *f+g+h*. The net loss in national well-being because of the export subsidy is areas f plus area h.

Figure 7.1 Export Subsidy, Small Country, Exportable Product

What are the other effects of the export subsidy in this case? If revenue per unit rises to \$ 120 (for both export and local sales), the quantity produced increases to \$ 190 million. If the domestic price increases to \$ 120, local quantity demanded decreases to 50 million. Quantity exported increases to 140 million (= 190−50).

Who are the winners and losers in the exporting country? Producers gain surplus equal to area $e+f+g$. Consumers lose surplus equal to area $e+f$. The cost to the government of paying the export subsidy is area $f+g+h$, equal to the export subsidy of \$ 20 per pipe times the 140 million pipes exported with the subsidy.

The export subsidy has increased exports and production of this product, but is it good for the exporting country? Using our one-dollar, one-vote metric, the answer is no. After we cancel out the matching gainsand losses, the net loss in national well-being is areas f and h. Area f is consumption effect of the export subsidy, the lost consumer surplus for those consumers squeezed out of the market when the domestic price rises above the world price. Area h is production effect of the export subsidy, the loss due to encouraging domestic production that has a resource cost greater than the world price (the world standard for efficient production). These two triangles are on the opposite sides of the graph, because this is an exportable product rather than an importable product. The loss of national well-being for this small exporting country is also a loss for the world.

7.2.3 Exportable product, large exporting country

We have just seen that a small exporting country harms itself by offering an export subsidy to its competitive exporting industry. Perhaps the result is different if the exporting country is large enough to affect the world price. Not so-in fact, it may be worse.

Figure 7.2 shows this case. With free trade the world price is \$ 100 per pipe. When the exporting-country government offers the export subsidy of \$ 20 per pipe, exporting firms want to export more to get more of the subsidy. To get foreign consumers to buy more of the exported product, the exporting firms must lower the export price. And, just as in the small-country case, domestic buyers in the exporting country must end up paying \$ 20 more than the export price (assuming that they cannot import from the rest of the world at the new world price).

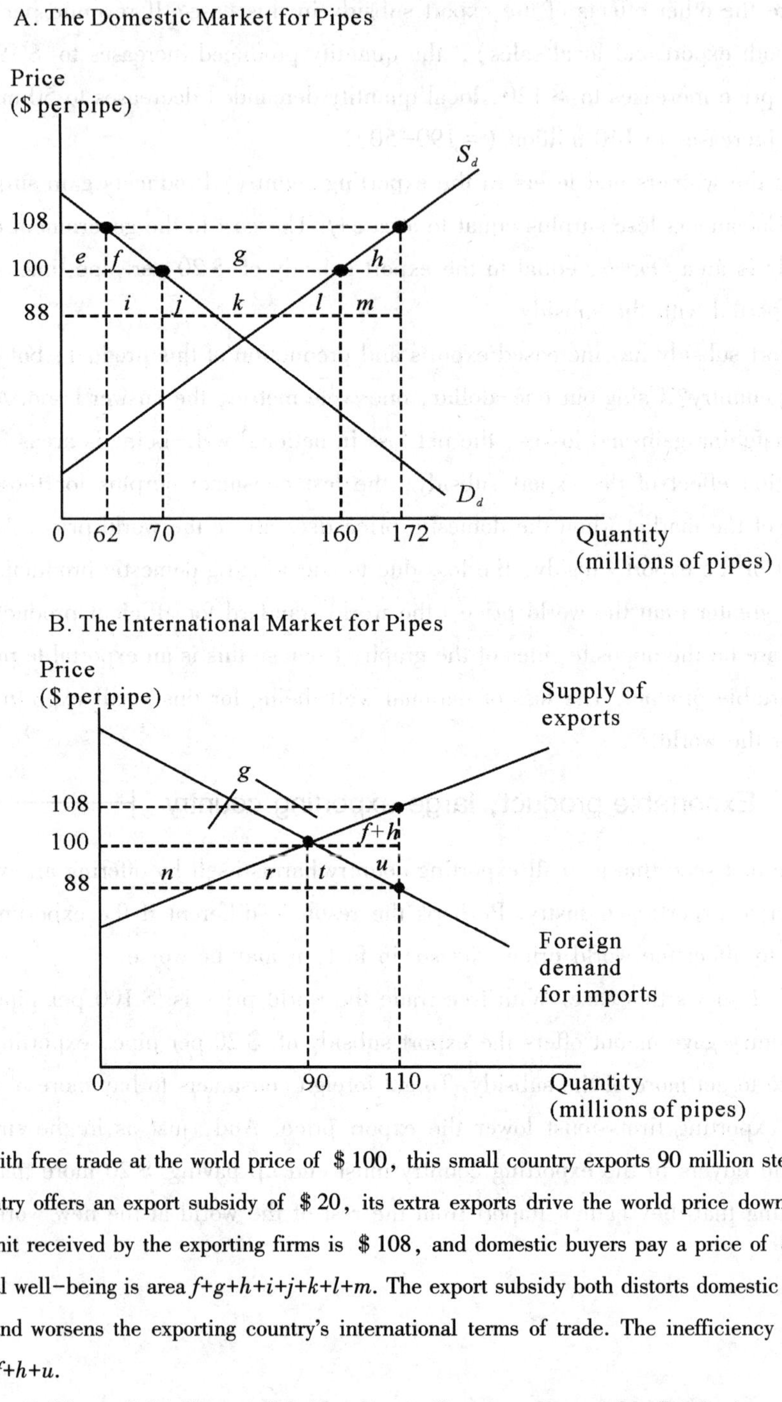

Note: With free trade at the world price of $100, this small country exports 90 million steel pipes. If instead the country offers an export subsidy of $20, its extra exports drive the world price down to $88. The revenue per unit received by the exporting firms is $108, and domestic buyers pay a price of $108. The net loss in national well-being is area *f+g+h+i+j+k+l+m*. The export subsidy both distorts domestic production and consumption and worsens the exporting country's international terms of trade. The inefficiency created for the world is area *f+h+u*.

Figure 7.2 **Export Subsidy, Large Country, Exportable Product**

We can see the resulting equilibrium more easily in panel B of Figure 7.2. The export subsidy created a wedge of $20 between the price that foreign importers pay and the revenue per unit that exporters receive. This $20 wedge "fits" (vertically) at the quantity traded of 110 million pipes. The new world price is $88, the price paid by the importers. The revenue per unit to the exporting firms, and the new price in the exporting country, is $108.

Panel A of Figure 7.2 shows what is happening in the exporting country. At $108 per pipe, production in the exporting country increases from 160 million to 172 million, and domestic consumption decreases from 70 to 62 million. Quantity exported increases from 90 to 110 million.

As in the small-country case, the export subsidy has increased domestic productionand exports of pipes. What are the effects on well-being in the exporting country? Producer surplus increases by area $e+f+g$. Consumers surplus falls by area $e+f$. The export subsidy costs the government $20 times the 110 million units exported. This government cost of $2.2 billion is area $f+g+h+i+j+k+l+m$ in panel A or B. This net loss has three parts: ①The consumption effect (area f). ②The production effect (area h). ③The loss due to the decline in the exporting country's international terms of trade (area $i+j+k+l+m$ = area $n+r+t+u$).

The export subsidy gives a good bargain to foreign buyers. However, their gain is a loss to the exporting country from selling at a lower world pricc.

We can also use panel B to seethe effect on world well-being. Area $n+r+t$ is increased surplus for the importing country. The net loss to the world is the triangular area $f+h+u$. This is the loss from too much trading of steel pipes.

7.2.4 Switching an importable product into an exportable product

"If you throw enough money at something, it will happen." This adage applies to export subsidies. They can turn an importable product into one that is exported. Let's see how.

To keep things from getting too complicated, we will examine the small-country case shown in Figure 7.3. With free trade at the world price of $2 per kilogram, the country would import 80 million kilos of butter (=120−40). The government now offers an export subsidy of $2 per kilo and prevents domestic consumers from importing cheap foreign butter. The revenue per kilo exported now rises to $4, and domestic production increases to 90 million kilos. At the higher domestic price of $4 per kilo, domestic consumers reduce their butter purchases to 60 million kilos. With the export subsidy, the country is now an exporter of 30 million kilos.

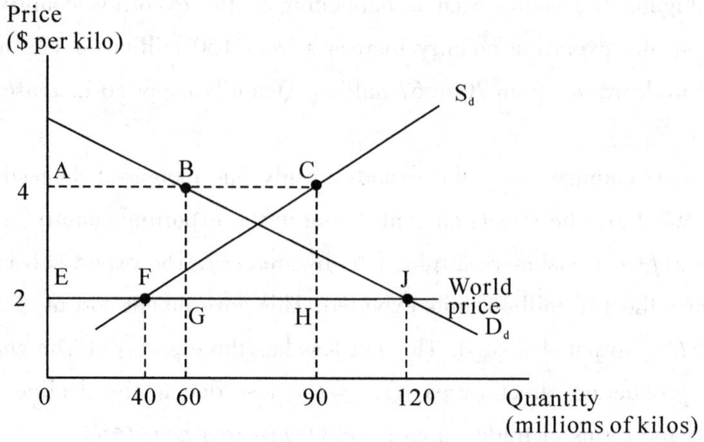

Note: With free trade and no export subsidy, this small country imports 80 million kilos of butter. If instead the country's government offers an export subsidy of $2 per kilo, the revenue per unit received by producers doubles to $4. The country becomes an exporter of 30 million kilos of butter. The net loss of national well-being is the sum of a production deadweight loss of area FCH and a consumption deadweight loss of area BJG.

Figure 7.3 An Export Subsidy Turns an Importable Product into an Export

The export subsidy switches an importable product into an exportable product. Domestic producers gain surplus of area ACFE. Domestic consumers lose surplus of area ABJE. The cost of the export subsidy tothe government is area BCHG. The net loss of national well-being looks a bit peculiar because the triangles of the consumption effect and the production effect overlap each other. The net national loss (and the net loss to the world) is area BJG plus area CHF.

This example of usingexport subsidies to create exportable is not far-fetched! At this point you might want to the conclusions stated at the beginning of this section. You should see that these conclusions apply to all three of our case. If the market is competitive, an export subsidy is bad for the exporting country.

7.2.5 WTO rules on subsidies

As a result of the agreements reached in the Tokyo Round and Uruguay Round of trade negotiations, the WTO now has a clear set of rules for subsidies that may benefit exports. The WTO rules divide subsidies into two types: ①Subsidies linked directly to exporting are prohibited, except export subsidies used by the lowest-income developing countries. Example: A firm receives a tax break based on the amount that it exports. ②Subsidies that are not linked directly to exporting but still have an impact on exports are actionable. Example: Low-priced electricity is provided to assist production by local firms in an industry, and some of this production is exported.

If an importing country's government believes that a foreign country is using a prohibited subsidy or an actionable subsidy that is harming its industry, the importing country can follow one of two procedures: ①File a complaint with the WTO and use its dispute settlement procedure. ②Use a national procedure similar to that used for dumping (used more than).

If the importing country can show the existence of a prohibited or actionable subsidy and harm to its industry, it is permitted to impose a countervailing duty, a tariff use to offset the price or cost advantage created by the subsidy to foreign exports.

7. 2. 6 Should the importing country impose countervailing duties?

How should the importing country respond to subsidized exports? Should the country simply enjoy the bargain? Or should the importing-country government heed the complaints from import-competing producers about unfair competition and impose a countervailing duty on the subsidized exports?

If the exporting country is large enough to affect world prices, then the export subsidy lowers the price that the importing country pays for these exports. As we saw in Figure 7. 2 B, the importing country overall is better off, but the import-competing industry is harmed. By WTO rules, the importing-country government is permitted to impose a countervailing duty. What happens if it does so?

To keep things from getting too complicated, Let us use an extreme version of the large-country case examined in Figure 7. 2. In this version, all of the export subsidies are passed forward to the buyers of imports in the foreign country. That is, the price charged to importers falls by the full amount of the export subsidy. Still, be warned: Even this simplified case can be confusing. We will focus on two different measures of well-being, one for the importing country and one for the world. We will make comparisons among three different situations: ①free trade. ② export subsidy with no countervailing duty. ③ export subsidy plus countervailing duty.

Figure 7. 4 shows the Canadian and international market for cold-rolled steel. With free trade, Canada imports 50 million tons per year from Brazil at the free-trade price of \$300 per ton. Then, the Brazilian government offers a subsidy of \$50 per ton exported. If all of this is passed on to buyers, the export price declines to \$250 per ton. Canadian imports increase to 80 million tons, Canadian production declines to 130 million tons, and Canadian producer surplus declines by area v. Canadian consumption increase to 210 million tons, and Canadian consumer surplus increases by area $v+w+y+z$. The net Canadian gain from the Brazilian export subsidy is area $w+y+z$. Still, Canadian producers are harmed, and they complain about the unfair competition.

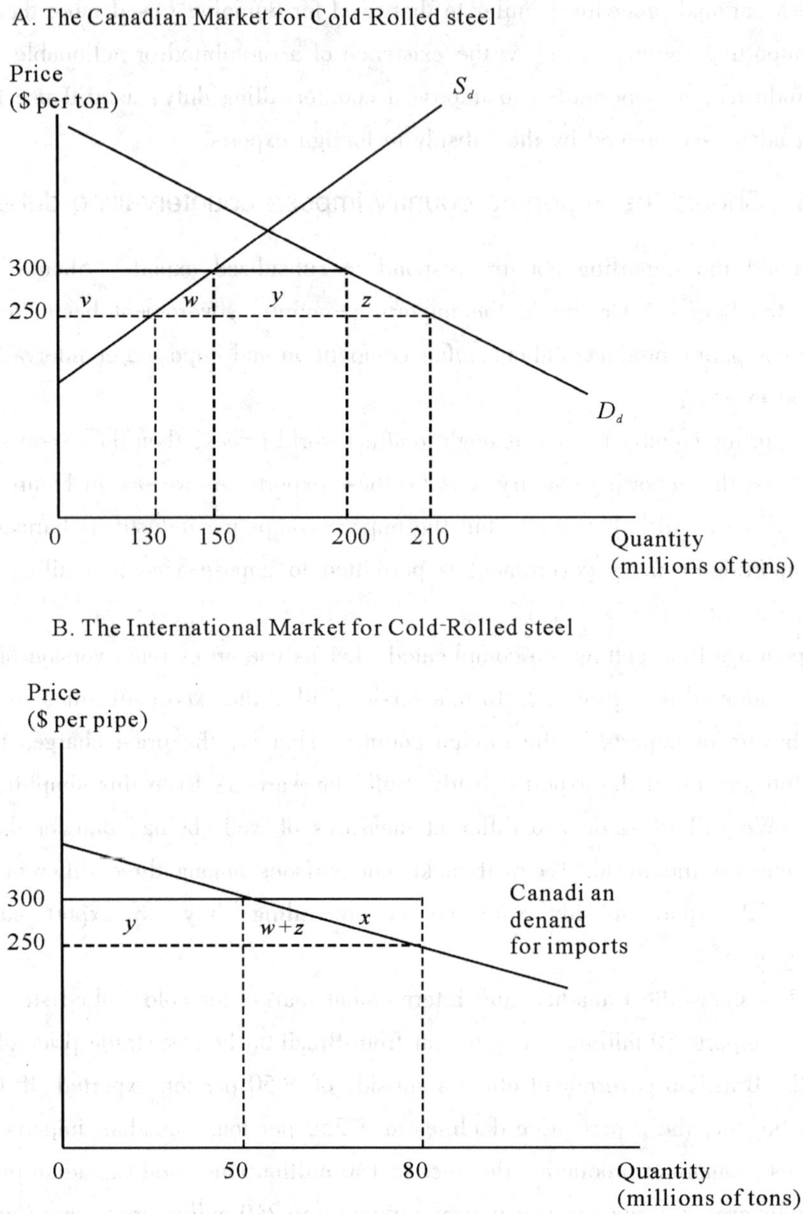

Note: The diagram shows the effect of ① a Brazilian export subsidy on steel to Canadaand; ② a Canadian countervailing duty on imports of subsidized steel exports from Brazil. An odd pattern results — Each policy in turn brings a net loss to the country adopting it, yet for the world as a whole the Canadian countervailing duty undoes the harm done by the Brazilian export subsidy.

Figure 7.4 A Foreign Export Subsidy and a Countervailing Duty

For the world, this is too much steel trade. Steel tons that each cost \$300 of Brazilian resources to produce are valued at less than \$300 per ton by Canadian buyers (as shown ton-by-ton the Canadian demand-for-import curve).

What happens if the Canadian government imposes countervailing duty of \$50 per ton of imported steel? The duty-inclusive price of imports rises back to \$300. In this subsidy-plus-countervailing-duty situation, the world returns to the same price \$300 and volume of trade (50 million tons) as with free trade. This makes good sense for world efficiency because the deadweight loss of excessive trade (area x inFigure 7.4 B) is eliminated. For the world, the countervailing duty is a successful use of specificity rule. In this case the world's problem is excessive exports in steel, and the countervailing duty directly affects exactly the problem activity.

Conclusions about the effects of the countervailing duty on Canada's well-being depend on what we compare to. In comparison to the situation with the export subsidy and no countervailing duty, Canada is worse off for imposing the countervailing duty. A countervailing duty in this case is bad for the country imposing it but good for the whole world. We can use Figure 7.4 A to see the effect on the importing country of imposing the countervailing duty, given that an export subsidy exists. The duty-inclusive price rises to \$300. Canadian producers gain area v, Canadian consumer lose area $v+w+y+z$, and the Canadian government collects area y as revenue from the countervailing duty. The net national loss to Canada of imposing countervailing duty is area w+z (the standard result for imposing a tariff).

Let us look at a second valid comparison, the comparison between free trade and the combination of the export subsidy and countervailing duty. In both of these situations, the price in Canada is the same (\$300), as are all quantities. The only difference is that the Canadian government is collecting revenue (area y) in the subsidy-and-duty situation. Who is effectively paying the countervailing duty? The Brazilian government! It paysthe export subsidy to the Brazilian firms, who pass it on to import buyers in Canada through the lower export price. The Canadian import buyers then send it to the Canadian government when they pay the countervailing duty. The well-being of Canada is higher than it would be with free trade because the Brazilian government is now effectively paying Canadian taxes.

Because export subsidies are bad for the world as a whole, and retaliating against them is good for the world as a whole, WTO rules are wise to allow importing countries to impose ex countervailing duties. However, it turns out that subsidy complaints and countervailing duties. During 2008-2012 only 101 subsidy cases were initiated in the world, and in mid-2013 there only 93 countervailing actions in effect.

The United States has been the largest user of countervailing duties, with 37 of these new cases and 52 of the countervailing duties in force. The European Union and Canada also make some use of countervailing duties. China, the United States, and India are the countries most frequently charged with subsidizing exports. Steel products are the most frequently involved. Countervailing duties also tend to be lower than antidumping duties. For instance, for the United States the average countervailing duty is about 10 percent.

While countervailing duties are often good for the world, they can also be misused in the same way that antidumping duties are misused. Importing-competing producers have an incentive to complain about possible foreign subsidies to exports, in an effort to gain protection against these exports. Many activities of a government could have some element of subsidy in them. In anti-subsidy cases, it is often possible for the complaining firms to establish that some kind of foreign subsidy exists that might benefit exports, perhaps with some help from a government process biased toward helping the import-competing domestic firms. Then, these firms can gain the protection of countervailing duties if they can show that they have been injured by the "subsidized" exports.

The softwood lumber dispute between the United States and Canada is an example of a controversial anti-subsidy case. In early 2001 a VER limiting Canadian exports expired. U.S. lumber firms immediately renewed their complaint that Canadian lumber firms benefit from a subsidy because the Canadian government does not charge high enough fees for logging on government lands. The Canadian government contended that its fees were appropriate, so there was no subsidy. The U.S. government found otherwise. The U.S. Commerce Department concluded that the low fee was a subsidy of 19 percent and the Canadian lumber exporters also were dumping by an additional 8 percent on average. The U.S. International Trade Commission found injury to U.S. firms from the lumber imports that grew rapidly after the VER expired. U.S. lumber producers clearly gained surplus from the combined average duty of 27 percent against Canadian lumber. U.S. consumers lost. Most obviously, the cost of building a typical new home rose by over $1 000. Most new-home buyers could pay this, so they suffered a straight loss of money. The deadweight loss consumption effect occurred for the estimated 300, 000 American families that could not afford the higher house prices. Most of them had modest incomes, and they reluctantly remained in less desirable housing.

If the Canadian logging fee was a subsidy because it was too low, then world well-being was enhanced by the U.S. countervailing duty. However, if the Canadian fee was appropriate and not a subsidy, thenthe countervailing duty (and perhaps the antidumping duty) was simple import protection, with a net loss for the world. It is not an easy call for the referee of world efficiency.

7.2.7 Strategic export subsidies could be good

In the previous section we assumed competitive supply and demand, and we reached the conclusion that an export subsidy harmed the exporting country. For some industries this competitive assumption is wrong. Suppose instead that the real-world market in question features the clash of two giant firms, each of which could supply the whole market. The economics of an export subsidy looks very different if international competition in the industry consists of an oligopolistic duel between two firms for the global market. In this battle of giants, an export subsidy can be either good or bad, both for the exporting country and for the world.

To see the possibility of a good subsidy, let us imagine a simplified case inspired by the continuing real-world competition between Boeing of the United States and Europe's Airbus. Suppose that it becomes technologically possible for them to build a new kind of passenger plane, perhaps a superjumbo jet. To keep a clear focus on the key points, let us say that there is no inherent difference between Airbus and Boeing in the cost of making the new plane. Still, aircraft manufacture can benefit from scale economies—as a firm expands its planned output, the cost of making another unit drops as output rises. Either firm is capable of supplying the whole world market at a low cost. If only one firm captures the whole world market, it will reap some monopoly profits. If both firms produce, they will vie for sales and drive the price down to their marginal costs. In this rivalry case, they make no operating profits.

These simple examples bring out the two key points about an export subsidy or similar type of subsidy in a global duel between two exporting giants: ①The subsidy might be a good thing for the exporting country. ②The case for giving the subsidy is fragile, depending on too many conditions to be a reliable policy.

In our example, we saw one condition that matters. If another national government also offers its firm strategic policy assistance, it is possible that both countries lose well-being. Another condition that matters is the possibility that there is no prize for the game. For instance, there may not be enough consumer demand for the new product, so economic profits will be negative instead of positive, even if there is only one producer. How would the government separate the false pleas of some if its firms for strategic help from the valid ones? While there is a theoretical case for the national benefit of strategic trade policy, we may be skeptical that a national government could actually use it effectively.

7 促进出口的措施

为了论述不公平贸易问题，本章主要讨论倾销，这是企业出口量远远大于公平竞争条件下供给和需求共同决定的出口数量的一种方式。在此之后，我们将探讨政府如何通过直接或者间接补贴来促进出口。

7.1 倾销

7.1.1 倾销的含义和分类

7.1.1.1 倾销的含义

倾销是指远低于正常价值（或者美国人常说的“公平市场价值”）出口商品的行为。正常价值有两个官方定义：①长久以来，正常价值被定义为国内消费者在国内市场所支付的具有可比性的价格。根据这一传统定义，倾销是一种有利于出口品购买者的国际价格歧视。②正常价值的第二种定义源于20世纪70年代。它以成本为基础，这里的成本是指包括期间费用和利润在内的产品的平均生产成本。根据第二种定义，倾销是指以低于全部平均成本的价格出口产品的行为。

7.1.1.2 倾销的分类

为什么出口商会进行倾销呢？为什么要以低于其商品的国内售价或者低于平均成本的价格来出口商品呢？有多种原因。为了判别倾销的好坏，了解全部有关倾销产生的原因是非常必要的。

（1）掠夺性倾销

掠夺性倾销是指厂商暂时以低价向国外市场出口商品，其目的是将其国外竞争者逐出市场。一旦竞争对手被迫退出，该厂商将利用垄断力量抬高价格，获取暴利。

（2）周期性倾销

周期性倾销发生于经济衰退期。在经济周期需求较弱阶段，厂商往往以降价来减少销量的下滑。例如，在一个长期均衡的竞争市场中，代表性厂商的价格等于全部平均成本（长期平均成本）。如果产业衰退或者整个经济衰退导致需求下降，市场价格将在短期低于区别平均成本。只要价格高于平均变动成本，这个厂商就会继续生产下去。如果这些产品是销往国外的，那么这个厂商就是在进行倾销。

（3）季节性倾销

季节性倾销的目的在于将库存商品清空。例如，在一个畅销季节接近尾声时，美国服装厂商决定以低于全部平均成本的价格出售所有余下的泳衣存货，进行大甩卖。由于沉没成本的存在，任何高于这些甩卖产品边际成本的价格都是可行的。如果这些低价产品部分卖给加拿大，那么美国厂商就在进行倾销。易腐烂的农产品也是季节性倾销的主要产品。一场大丰收将会降低市场价格，并且为出口提供大量的产品。同样，倾销也可作为一种在新市场推销新产品的手段，它与出口厂商试图在海外市场立足而进行新产品倾销相当。

(4) 持久性倾销

持久性倾销的发生主要是因为具有市场控制力的厂商在不同市场之间实行价格歧视，以增加总利润。厂商可以通过低价向国外销售商品，获得利润最大化的条件为：厂商在国外市场的垄断力量比其在国内市场要小（在国外面临更多的竞争），且国内购买者不能通过国外市场购买、低价进口来规避国内的高价。

当具备这些条件，厂商就可以使国内购买者支付一个更高的价格，进而获得一个更大的总利润。这并不是掠夺性的，因为它并不是为了驱逐任何其他厂商。而且只要市场差别继续存在，它就可以持续存在较长时间。

7.1.2 对倾销的反应

遭到外国出口倾销竞争的本国政府大声抱怨，认为这是不公平的。那么进口国应该如何看待倾销？政府又应当对倾销采取何种政策？

7.1.2.1 对持久性倾销的反应

从某种角度分析，进口国的态度应当非常明朗。它应该欢迎倾销并且感谢出口国。毕竟，当有人试图以低价向我们销售产品时，我们通常不会去同他争论。这种直觉对于持久性倾销来说是对的。相比出口国国内的高价，进口国可以从低价格额外获利。若进口国的贸易条件变得更好了，消费者收益则大于进口竞争性企业的损失。

但是，另外两种倾销并非如此简单。

7.1.2.2 对掠夺性倾销的反应

一个关键问题是外国厂商是否经常进行掠夺性倾销。在 20 世纪 20 年代至 30 年代的全球经济混乱时期，据说有过大量工业制成品掠夺性倾销的情况。但是，事实上并没有明确证据表明真的存在过大范围的掠夺性倾销。掠夺性倾销在目前的市场中似乎也是很少见的。一个想要进行掠夺性倾销的厂商必须考虑短期实行低价带来的确定性损失和长期的不确定性盈利。即便是厂商能够在进口国家市场上将现有的竞争者驱逐出去，但是可以预见的是，一旦它提高价格，新厂商包括其他国家的新出口商，就会以竞争者姿态进入该市场。因此，掠夺性出口商不能提高价格或者很难维持较长时间的高价。我们在最近的调查中发现，在美国、欧盟、加拿大、墨西哥和印度的倾销案件中，只有不超过 5%的案件可能属于掠夺性倾销（还有可能所有的案件都不属于掠夺性倾销）。

7.1.2.3 对周期性倾销的反应

周期性倾销对于进口国来说是一种最复杂的倾销。大多数周期性倾销是功能完善的竞争性全球市场的正常经营活动。当需求下降，市场价格在短期就会下降。只要获得的收益能够抵消变动成本，厂商就会继续生产、销售甚至出口部分数量的产品。这也是需求下降时人们意料之中的。一旦衰退期结束，需求、价格和全球产量将会复苏；相反，如果仍有大量产能过剩，那么最终在价格复苏前需要一个有效的产量削减的全球分担机制。

仅是全球有效还不足以使进口国完全相信周期性倾销是公平的。当需求下降，如下降 10%时，各国应该承担多少全球产出的减少？让进口国厂商减少产出并承担损失公平吗？尤其是当需求下降是因为出口国经济衰退所致，那么为什么这些出口国家“出口部分失业”就是公平的？

通常，回答“什么是公平的”这个问题不是一件容易的事情。全球共同承担经济衰退是国际贸易利益带来的影响之一，而这里的真正问题是生产者损失。例如，如果需要解决的是失业问题，那么国家就应当提供适当的失业保险和就业帮助。

7.1.3 实际的反倾销政策

在我们的讨论中，倾销一般会给进口国带来好处，只有两类倾销对进口国有害。掠夺性倾销如果成功了，对进口国是有害的，尽管其成功的可能性很小。周期性倾销有时会不公平地伤害进口国，但在大多数情况下它属于竞争性市场中企业的正常运营活动。我们从中得到的启示是：进口国在对他国的倾销制定相关政策（反倾销政策）时，应当具体情况具体分析。在征收反倾销税或者其他限制倾销产品进口的措施前，政府应当考虑收益和成本。但事实上，各国制定政策时并非如此。

根据世界贸易组织的规定，如果倾销对进口国国内进口竞争企业的厂商造成伤害，那么允许进口国对倾销采取报复措施。如果进口国政府发现倾销及其导致的损害，那么政府可以征收反倾销税——等于实际出口价格和正常价值之间的差额（倾销幅度）。

在20世纪70年代之前，全球范围内的反倾销案件实际上都是较少的。20世纪80年代仅有34个国家颁布了反倾销法规。但是，从90年代起，更多的国家制定了反倾销法规。到2010年，至少有100个国家有类似法规。

直到20世纪80年代后期，反倾销法宝的“四大传统使用者”（美国、欧盟、加拿大、澳大利亚）涉及了90%以上的反倾销案件，但是随后反倾销的使用被推广开来。1986—1990年到2008—2012年世界范围内的倾销案件增加了35%，并且四大传统使用者（其中加拿大在2008—2012年发起了24个案件）所占份额下降到了22%。印度在1992年之前没有一例反倾销案件，但在2008—2012年它却居反倾销案件十大发起者之首。1997年，中国实行了反倾销政策，很快成为一个主要的发起者。阿根廷和巴基斯坦也从零案件跃居前十位。

全球最常遭到反倾销指控的产品是化学制品、钢材和其他金属制品、塑料和橡胶制品、机械、纺织品和服装。最频繁遭到反倾销指控的出口国是中国、韩国、美国、泰国和印度尼西亚。2009年，2%的中国出口品遭遇到来自进口国的反倾销措施。

我们更详细地考察了美国的反倾销政策。某个反倾销案件通常始于美国国内生产商提起诉讼。然后美国商务部调查倾销是否真实发生，美国国际贸易委员调查美国厂商是否因此受到损害。此外，还可与外国出口商进行谈判。如果它们同意提高价格或者限制出口，那么这个案件就会被暂停或终止（以这种结局告终的案件普遍出现于钢材和化工产品的案件中）。

美国商务部通常会将94%的诉讼案件裁定为倾销，且美国的法律程序也偏向于做出倾销的裁决。在比较出口价格和国内市场价格之时，美国商务部不仅对成本的测算设置一些不为人知的规则，还故意忽略那些高于国内市场价格的出口价格。其结果是将低出口价与国内市场的高价进行比较。在出口价格与平均成本比较的案件中，获得和解释出口产品的成本数据通常会很困难，所以美国商务部在决定正常价值的时候有很大的自由度。林德塞和艾肯森利用18个反倾销案件中的实际数据，检验美国商务部使用方法的偏向性。他们得出的结论是在18个案件中有10个实际上不存在倾销，而在另外8个案件中有4个，其实际的倾销量不到美国商务部确认数量的一半。

损害的评判标准并不严格，但损害通常是认定倾销案件的关键所在。在大约 2/3 的反倾销案件中，美国国际贸易委员都会发现倾销对美国进口竞争产业具有实质性损害。

一旦确认了倾销和损害，海关官员就会被授权征收反倾销税。在美国所提出的诉讼案件中，有一半以上的案件处理结果为征收反倾销税，或者由出口商签署协议同意限制出口产品的价格和数量。可以发现有一半以上的案件无论是从其中的国家（地区）或者全球来看，都导致了反倾销税或者是出口商协议。

近期的研究清晰地显示了一些反倾销案件处理过程的效应模式。在诉讼提出后的短期内，被指控为倾销的产品价格便有所上升，这大概是为了减少最终倾销的幅度。由于价格上升和对案件结果的不确定性，出口量也随之减少。如果产品被征收反倾销税，那么出口量会下降更多，平均下降 70%，而且通常会下降至零。出口商也有动机去提高其出口价格。因为如果美国商务部在后期审查中发现倾销减少或者不存在倾销了，那么反倾销也会随之减少或者取消。

对征收反倾销税的总体效应的近期研究得出：美国每年遭受近 40 亿美元的福利损失，大约有一半的无谓损失。另外一部分损失转嫁给了外国出口商，它们的出口价格被提高。美国的净损失可能会比这个少，因为这项研究并没有量化因避免任何由掠夺性倾销（可能很少）和周期性倾销（难以测算）产生的影响而带来的价值损失。

就当前美国以及其他国家日益增多的反倾销政策来看，我们能够得出以下结论：①诉讼程序偏向于裁定倾销。②损害调查仅考虑低价进口品对国内生产竞争者的损害，并未考虑国家遭受到的掠夺性倾销或者其他形式的损害；也几乎或根本就未考虑低价进口品给消费者带来的福利。③这个过程偏向于征收反倾销税，即使这通常会降低进口国家的社会福利。反倾销也会降低全世界的福利。

如果出口国认为进口国政府在征收反倾销税时违背了世界贸易组织规则，那么它可以向世界贸易组织提起诉讼。截至 2014 年年初，已有 101 起这样的诉讼，其中有 47 起针对的是美国政府的法律和程序。2014 年年初，世界贸易组织专门委员会已经对 101 诉讼中的一半诉讼进行了传唤和裁决。专门委员会通常裁定进口国过错，包括使用不恰当程序，使用与世界贸易组织规则相悖的方法判定倾销幅度（或者补贴比率），以及使用不完整信息或者有偏差数据判定损害程度等。在某些案件中，一些进口国服从裁定，如撤销反倾销税，但也有国家依然我行我素。即便是世界贸易组织的争端解决机制能防范一些对反倾销税的滥用，也会因这个过程过于长，无法将滥用的伤害降到最低。

反倾销政策起初看起来是针对不公平的出口，但是仔细研究则会发现其他的内容。反倾销政策已经成为越来越多的国家进口竞争部门生产者获得新的贸易保护的一种重要途径，并给全球和进口国带来无谓损失。对外国出口商征收的平均关税税率远远高于正常关税税率，这样带来的无谓损失也会很大，这还不包括案件辩护的成本和收集资料、证明存在或不存在倾销和损害的成本。此外，进口竞争性产业的厂商利用反倾销诉讼的威胁迫使出口商提高产品价格和限制竞争，这被称为“威慑效应”，尽管它们可能不会真正提起诉讼。

7.1.4 改革建议

虽然存在例外，但是当前针对倾销的报复措施往往对全球和进口国都有害。可是这些行为完全符合世界贸易组织规则，所以启动世界贸易组织规则的改革是多哈回合全球多边贸易谈判的重要议题。在下面的段落中，我们将讨论三种可能的改革方案。

7.1.4.1 反倾销诉讼可能被限于有可能存在掠夺性倾销的案件中使用

这类改革着眼于最有可能对全球和进口国造成伤害的倾销类型。同时，改革也会将反倾销政策和反托拉斯政策（反托拉斯是美国的提法，在其他国家也可称为“竞争政策”“反垄断政策”或者相似的名称）相结合。支持竞争政策通常禁止通过掠夺性行为获得垄断力量。这种改革会尽可能限制反倾销政策的运用。但是，一国的法律仍然倾向于认定倾销行为及其某种程度的掠夺性。

7.1.4.2 损害的标准应当扩展，应该增加产品消费者和使用者的感受

这种改变将讨论转向对国家净福利的损害，而不只是对进口竞争性产业生产者的损害。一些国家（包括欧盟国家、加拿大和泰国）已经在它们的反倾销规则中加入了“公共利益检测”环节。这种改革从总体上限制反倾销行为的范围而不是仅着眼于某种限制。

这类改革还会修正现行反倾销政策中的一些奇特现象，如消费者会因为反倾销裁决受到很大的冲击，但在裁决过程中没有任何法律地位。事实上，大多数反倾销行为把诸如钢铁和化工品这类中间产品也包括在内。这些产品的购买者（如汽车公司）通常是组织良好的政治团体，在反对它们所购买和使用的中间品的进口保护政策上具有一定的影响力。但现行反倾销政策的实施，已经关闭了进口竞争的中间产品生产者涉足这一政治斗争的最后机会。对于改革中的反倾销政策来说，如果将消费者利益包括进来，那么整个战役将重新开局，而且也有可能减少反倾销政策的滥用。

7.1.4.3 反倾销政策可能被更为积极的保障措施所替代

保障措施是世界贸易组织允许地对不断增加的进口采取贸易保护的措施。当突然激增的进口对国内生产者造成损害的时候，进口国可以使用暂时性的进口贸易保护措施，其目的是给进口竞争厂商及其工人一段缓冲时间来应对激增的进口竞争。

反倾销政策的支持者通常认为，反倾销政策有助于贸易自由化，因为它允许保护那些受到不断增加的进口损害的产业，那些产业受到的损害比预期的还要大。但实际上这却是支持保障措施的一个真正的论据。实施保障措施比反倾销税要好，是因为：①没有必要证明外国厂商是否不公平竞争；②在实施过程中可能顾及了消费者利益，并依次决定是否实施保障措施，以及如果实施，将采取何种具体形式；③重点放在进口竞争产品生产者如何调整上；④之所以有压力去调整完全是因为进口保护只是暂时的。

保障措施并没有在美国得到大规模实施。一个有名的案例是20世纪80年代的哈雷—戴维森案。在保障措施实施之后，哈雷—戴维森重新变得强大，很快便能与日本竞争者（铃木和本田）抗衡，并要求提前废除保障措施。更近一点的案例是2002年美国政府对进口钢铁所征收的关税。2009年，美国对从中国进口的轮胎征收高额关税是另外一个例子。很显然，尽管对钢铁和轮胎实施的保障措施仍然饱受争议，但至少所有利益相关方面有权进行申诉。

7.2 出口补贴

7.2.1 出口补贴的含义

各国政府鼓励出口、补贴出口产品比它们限制或者对出口产品征税更为频繁。有些国家根据国际规则鼓励出口倒是不会引起争议，但问题是它们那么做是否有效。如美国商务部出口司提供海外市场调查、出口程序和国外政府法规等信息，并且帮助联系海外客户。政府机构还会发起如贸易展销会和组织考察团等出口促进活动。也有的政府建立出口加工区，对加工区的原材料和零部件给予便捷的通关程序，并提供低税率或者零关税。

政府还提供一些有利于出口的各种形式的财政支持，如出口补贴。出口补贴存在争议主要是因为它违背了公平贸易的国际准则。我们在分析了出口补贴后，会发现从全球来看出口补贴通常不是好的政策。但是，全球范围内的政策受益者和受害者的划分，与我们仅倾听补贴政策支持方和受害方的观点后的预期完全相反。出口补贴对于那些使用它的国家来说是不利的，而对于那些抱怨它的国家则有利！

政府对出口的补贴形式多样，其中有些还刻意隐晦、不为人知。比如，用纳税人的钱向出口商或者它们的国外客户提供低息贷款。美国进出口银行便是一例。该行成立于20世纪30年代，它向美国出口商以及它们的外国消费者而不是美国的进口者及其外国供应商提供优惠贷款。这显得有点名不副实。政府还可以对出口产品的投入品（如原材料或者国内运输服务）定很低的价格，而且所得税也会根据每个企业出口产品或者服务的价值给予相应的免除。

出口补贴的数额平均而言都很小，但是对于某种特定商品或者某特定公司来说却显得很多。例如，美国进出口银行的大多数贷款都发给了少数大型的美国公司和它们的客户。尤其是波音公司，如果获得一些大的外国飞机订单就能得到该行的诸多优惠。最多的出口补贴被给予了农产品。

这些由政府提供的补贴对国家有什么影响？我们用标准的需求和供给框架来分析它对竞争性产业的影响，会得到以下结论：①出口补贴扩大了补贴产品的产量和出口量。事实上，出口补贴可将一种产品由进口转变为出口。②相对于当地消费者所支付的价格而言，出口补贴会降低国外购买者的支付价格。此外，由于出口补贴是有意为之（政府只对出口补贴而不对国内购买者进行补贴），所以必须采取措施，防止本国购买者以降低了的国外价格进口该产品。③出口补贴降低了出口国的国家净福利。

7.2.2 小国情况下可出口产品

图7.1显示的是小国情况，其钢管的出口并不能影响100美元/根（标准长度）的国际市场价格。在自由贸易时，这个国家竞争性的钢管企业每年生产16 000万根钢管，并且每年出口9 000万根（16 000-7 000）钢管。政府现在决定给予这些厂商每根20美元的出口补贴。那么企业每出口一根钢管可得到120美元的收入，其中，国外购买者支付100美元，国家出口补贴20美元。如果企业可以从每根出口的钢管中获得120美元，它将不会以低于120美元的价格在国内销售。当然，只有当国内购买者不能从国际市场上以每根100美元的价格购回钢材才有可能。因此，必须要有某种因素能保持出口市场与国内市场的分离。这听起来应该很熟悉，就像是持久性倾销。事实上，接受出口补贴是出口企业进行倾销的另一个原因。小国的出口补贴效应见图7-1。

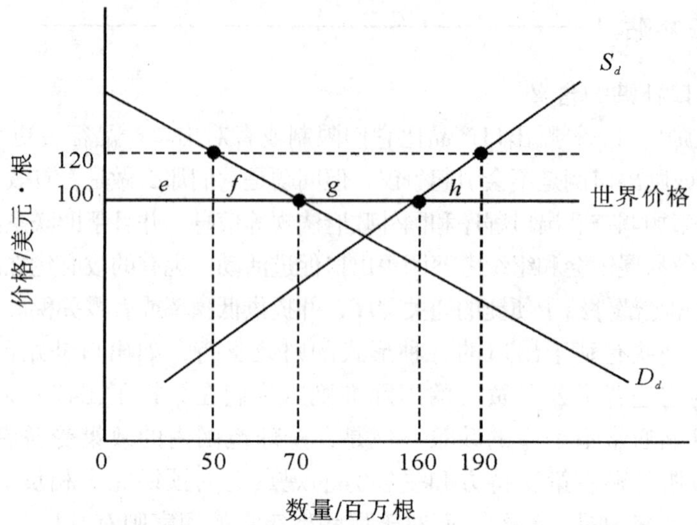

注：在自由贸易时，世界价格是100美元，这个小国出口9 000万根钢管。如果该国政府对每根出口钢管给予20美元的补贴，每根钢管的出口收入上涨至120美元，而且出口厂商在国内市场上销售必须也要获得同样的收入。这样，国内产量从16 000万根钢管上升到19 000万根钢管，国内消费从7 000万根钢管下降到5 000万根钢管，出口14 000万根钢管；国内生产者获得面积为$e+f+g$的生产者剩余，国内消费者减少面积为$e+f$的消费者剩余，政府支付出口补贴的成本是面积$f+g+h$。由于出口补贴造成的国民福利净损失是面积$f+h$。

图7.1　小国的出口补贴效应

在这个案例中，出口补贴还有什么其他影响吗？如果美国钢管的收益上涨到120美元（对于出口和本地销售而言），那么钢管产量会上升到19 000万根。如果国内价格上涨到120美元，本国需求量就会下降到5 000万根，而出口量会上升到14 000万根（19 000–5 000）。

在出口国中，谁是受益者，谁是受害者？国内生产者获得面积为$e+f+g$的生产者剩余。消费者损失了面积为$e+f$的消费者剩余。政府支付的出口补贴的成本为面积$f+g+h$，等于每根钢管的出口补贴20美元乘以出口数量14 000万根钢管。

出口补贴增加了产品的出口量和产量，但是对出口国有益吗？利用一元一票来衡量，答案是否定的。在收益和损失相互抵消后，面积$f+h$是国民净福利损失。其中面积f是出口补贴的消费效应，即当国内价格上升超过了世界价格时，国内那些消费者被挤出市场所造成的消费者剩余的损失。面积h是出口补贴的生产效应，即由于这种生产的资源成本高于世界市场价格（生产效率的世界标准），因此鼓励国内增加生产反而导致损失。因为这是可出口产品而不是可进口产品，所以这两个三角形在图上的位置相反。出口小国的福利损失同样也是世界福利的损失。

7.2.3　大国情况下可出口产品

我们刚分析了一个出口小国对本国出口竞争性行业实行出口补贴会使本国福利遭受损失，而当出口国大到可以影响世界市场价格时，也许结果会有所不同。但事实上，情况可能会更糟。

如图7.2所示，在自由贸易下，钢管的世界市场价格为100美元/根。当出口国提供每根 20 美元的出口补贴后，出口厂商便会增加出口量以获得更多的补贴。为了让外国消费者购买更多的出口品，出口厂商必须降低它们的出口价格。而且，正如在小国例子中，出口国的国内购买者支付的价格必须比出口价格高 20 美元（假定它们不能以新的世界市场价格从其他国家进口该产品）。从图 7.2 中的图 B 我们可以更容易看到最终的均衡结果。出口补贴在一个每单位产品在外国进口商支付的价格和进口商得到的收入之间插入了 20 美元的楔子。这 20 美元的差额（垂直距离）正好导致贸易量为 11 000万根。新的世界市场价格为 88 美元，这也是进口商所支付的价格。而出口企业获得的单位收入以及出口国国内新的价格是 108 美元。大国的出口补贴效应见图 7.2。

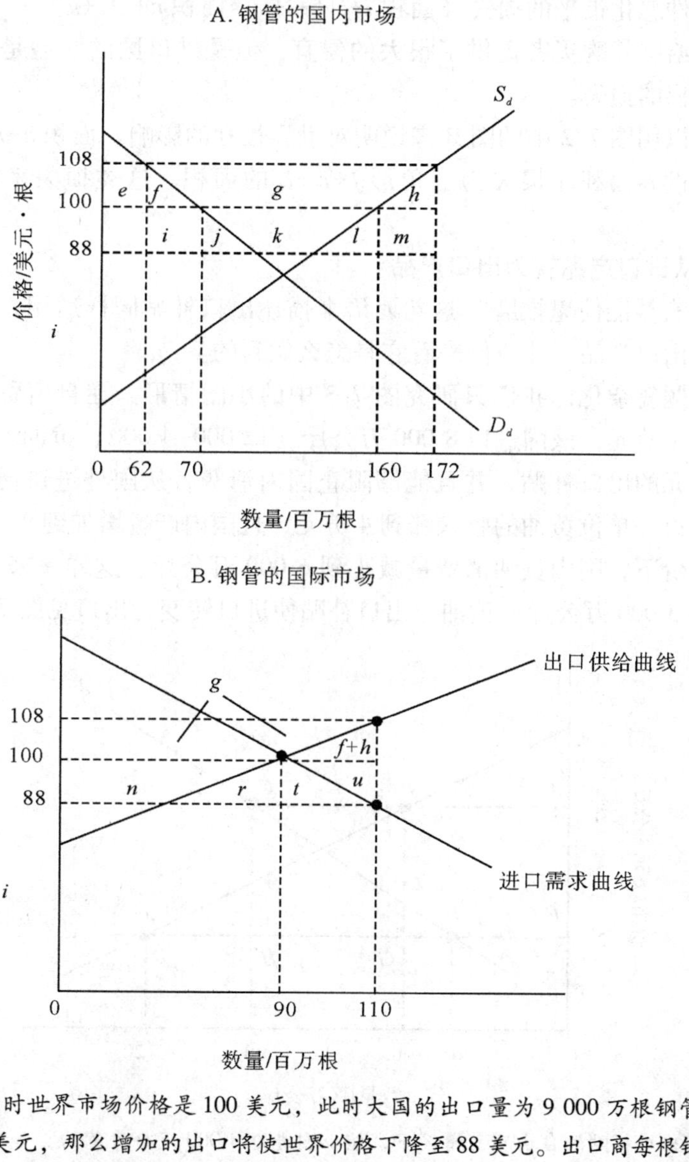

注：在自由贸易时世界市场价格是 100 美元，此时大国的出口量为 9 000 万根钢管。如果该国给予的出口补贴为 20 美元，那么增加的出口将使世界价格下降至 88 美元。出口商每根钢管得到的出口收入是 108 美元，而且国内购买者也需支付价格 108 美元。该出口国国民福利净损失是面积 $f+g+h+i+j+k+l+m$。出口补贴不仅扭曲了国内生产和消费，同时还恶化了出口国家的贸易条件。整个世界的效率损失是 $f+h+u$。

图 7.2　大国的出口补贴效应

图 7.2 中的图 A 表明了出口国正在发生的一切。在价格为每根钢管 108 美元时，出口国的产量从 16 000 万根钢管增加到 17 200 万根钢管，国内消费量从 7 000 万根钢管减少到 6 200 万根钢管，出口数量从 9 000 万根钢管增加到 11 000 万根钢管。

和小国情况一样，出口补贴增加了国内钢管产量和出口量。这对出口国的福利有什么影响？生产者剩余增加了面积 $e+f+g$。消费者剩余减少了面积 $e+f$。政府出口补贴的成本是 20 美元乘以出口数量 11 000 万根，即 22 亿美元。图 A 中的面积 $f+g+h+i+j+k+l+m$（或者图 B 中的面积 $f+g+h+n+r+t+u$）。出口国家的净损失包括图 A 和图 B 中的部分，这种净损失包括三个部分：①消费效应（面积 f）；②生产效应（面积 h）；③由于出口国国家贸易条件恶化带来的损失（面积 $i+j+k+l+m$ = 面积 $n+r+t+u$）。

出口补贴给国外购买者提供了很大的便宜，但是进口国的收益是出口国以低于世界价格出口销售的损失。

我们还可以用图 7.2 中的图 B 来说明对世界福利的影响。面积 $n+r+t$ 是进口国增加的福利剩余。世界福利净损失为三角形 $f+h+u$ 的面积。这类损失来源于过多的钢管贸易。

7.2.4 从进口产品转为出口产品

我们用“有钱能使鬼推磨”这句谚语来描述出口补贴同样适用，因为它可以使一种进口产品转出口产品。让我们来看它是怎么做到的。

为避免问题复杂化，我们只研究图 7.3 中的小国情形。在自由贸易下，黄油世界价格为每公斤 2 美元，该国进口 8 000 万公斤（12 000−4 000）黄油。政府现在给予黄油每公斤 2 美元的出口补贴，并且能够阻止国内消费者从国外进口便宜的黄油。那么该国厂商出口每一单位黄油的收入涨到 4 美元，且国内产量增加到 9 000 万公斤。在国内 4 美元的高价下，国内黄油消费量减小到 6 000 万公斤。这样一来，在政府补贴下，该国现在出口 3 000 万公斤的黄油。出口补贴使进口转变为出口见图 7.3。

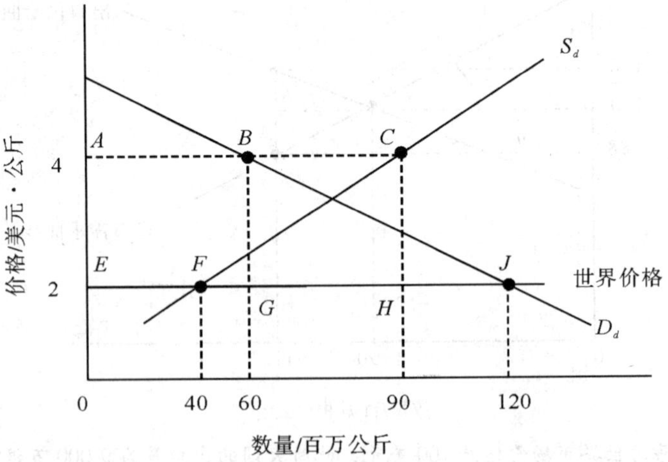

注：在没有出口补贴的自由贸易情况下，该小国进口 8 000 万公斤黄油。如果该国政府提供每公斤黄油 2 美元的出口补贴，那么生产者每公斤的收益将增至 4 美元，这个国家就摇身变成了出口 3 000万公斤的黄油出口国。国民福利净损失是生产扭曲损失面积 FCH 与消费扭曲损失面积 BJG 之和。

图 7.3 出口补贴使进口转变为出口

出口补贴使一种进口品转变为出口品。国内生产者获得面积为ACFE的剩余。但是国内消费者损失了面积ABJE的剩余。政府提供的出口补贴成本是面积BCHG。国民福利净损失看起来有点特别，因为消费效应和生产效应的三角形是部分交叠的。国民福利净损失（和世界福利净损失）为面积BJG和面积CHF之和。

利用出口补贴使进口产品变成出口产品，并不是天方夜谭。这时候我们可能会想到本章开始时提出的结论，会发现这些结论适用于所有这三种情况。如果市场是竞争性的，那么出口补贴对出口国是有百害而无一利的。

7.2.5 世界贸易组织关于补贴的规则

作为东京回合和乌拉圭回合贸易谈判的成果之一，世界贸易组织具有一套明确的可能有益于出口补贴的规则。这些世界贸易组织规则把补贴分为两类：①除了允许最低收入国家使用出口补贴外，其他直接与出口相关的补贴是禁止的，如企业根据出口量得到的税收减免；②不与出口直接相关，但是仍然对出口产生影响的补贴是可以被提起诉讼的，如提供低价电力用以帮助当地企业生产，且这些企业生产的部分产品是用来出口的。

如果进口国政府认定某一外国正在使用禁止性补贴或者可诉性补贴，且其正在损害进口国产业，那么该进口国可以选择下面两种程序中的一种：①向世界贸易组织提起诉讼使用争端解决机制；②使用类似于针对他国倾销的国家应对程序（这一程序使用得更为频繁）。

如果进口国能够证明存在禁止性或可诉性补贴，且这些补贴对本国产业造成伤害，那么它就有权征收反补贴税，用来抵销出口补贴带来的价格或者成本优势。

7.2.6 进口国是否应该征收反补贴税

进口国对出口补贴应当采取何种反击？是简单轻松地享受便宜的进口商品？还是接受进口竞争产业的生产者控诉出口国不公平竞争，并对补贴产品征收反补贴税？

如果出口国大到足以影响世界价格，那么大国的出口补贴会使进口国对其进口产品支付更低的价格。正如图7.2中的图B所示，进口国整体福利改善了，但是其进口竞争产业却遭受了损害。根据世界贸易组织规则，允许进口国政府征收反补贴税。如果这么做了，那将会发生什么？

为了避免问题复杂化，我们分析图7.2中的大国这样的极端情况。在这种情况下，所有的出口补贴被转移给国外市场的进口品购买者。也就是说，进口国少支付的价格等于出口补贴额。但是，需要注意的是：即使这种简化的情况也有可能会使人混淆。我们将分析集中在福利的两种不同测量方法上，一种从进口国角度，另一种从世界角度。我们将在三种不同的情况下进行比较：①自由贸易；②出口补贴但不征收反补贴税；③出口补贴加上反补贴税。

图7.4分别显示了加拿大和国际的冷轧钢筋市场。在自由贸易下，加拿大每年从巴西以每吨300美元的价格进口5 000万吨冷轧钢筋。然后，巴西政府给每吨冷轧钢筋提供50美元的出口补贴。如果这些全部转移给购买者，那么出口产品价格将下降至每吨250美元。加拿大进口量将增加到8 000万吨。加拿大国内产量下降至13 000万吨，并且加拿大生产者剩余减少面积v。加拿大消费量增加到21 000万吨，同时加拿大的消费者剩余增加了面积$v+w+y+z$。加拿大从巴西出口补贴中得到的净收益为面积

$w+y+z$。加拿大国内生产者遭受了损害，所以它们抱怨受到了不公平竞争。外国补贴和反补贴税见图 7.4。

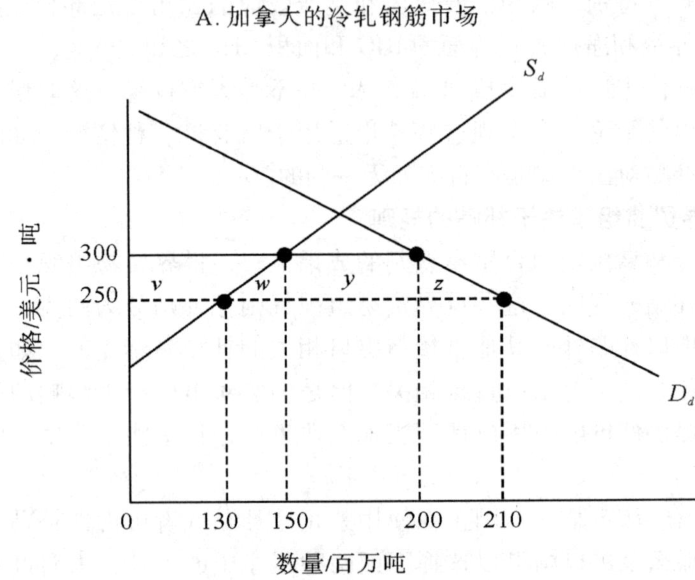

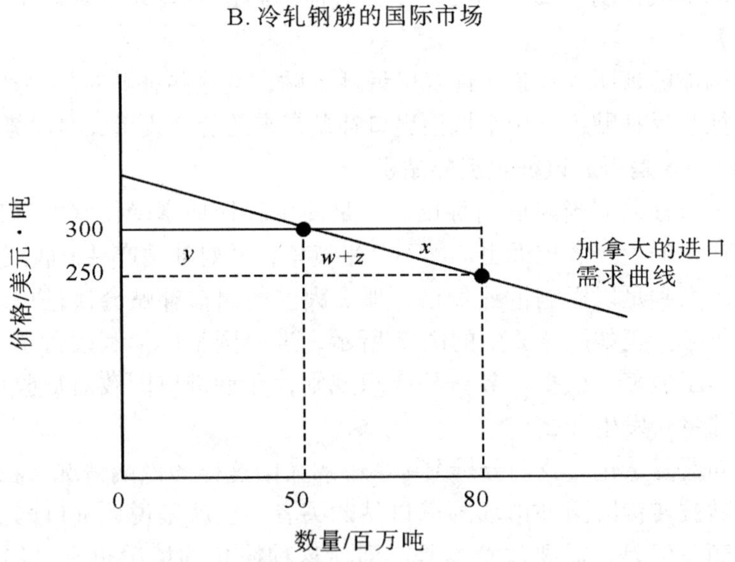

注：图中内容表明①巴西钢材出口补贴对于加拿大的影响；②加拿大反补贴税对受到出口补贴的巴西钢材的影响。奇怪的结果是，每项政策最终都给政策实施带来净损失，但是对于全球整体而言，加拿大的反补贴税消除了巴西出口补贴造成的损害。

图 7.4 外国补贴和反补贴税

对于世界来说，存在过度的钢铁贸易。在巴西花费 300 美元的资源才能产 1 吨钢材，但加拿大的购买者支付的价格却远低于每吨 300 美元（正如加拿大每吨钢材的进口需求曲线所示）。

如果加拿大政府对每吨进口钢材征收 50 美元的反补贴税，那么情况会如何？含关税的进口产品价格回归到 300 美元。在这种既有补贴又有反补贴税的情况下，全球重新回到自由贸易下的300美元的价格和贸易量（5 000万吨）。这对于全球效益是有意义的，因为由于过度贸易所导致的无谓损失（图7.4中图B的面积x）被消除了。对于全球来说，反补贴税是对症规则的成功应用。在这个案例中，世界的问题是过度地出口钢材，反补贴税正好是对症下药。

关于反补贴税对加拿大国民福利的影响的结论取决于如何比较。在有出口补贴的情况下，加拿大征收反补贴税将使国民福利变得更糟。在这种情况下，反补贴税对于其实施国是有害的，而对于世界而言是有益的。图7.4中的图A表明了在存在出口补贴时，征收反补贴税对进口国的影响。含税价涨至300美元，加拿大生产者获得面积v的收益，消费者损失面积$v+w+y+z$，加拿大政府得到的反补贴税收入为面积y。加拿大由于征收反补贴税的国民福利净损失为面积$w+z$（征税的标准结果）。

再来分析另一个对比，即自由贸易和出口补贴加反补贴税之间的对比。在这两种情况中，加拿大国内的价格都是一样的（300美元），销售的数量也是一样的。唯一不同的是加拿大政府在出口补贴加反补贴税情况下得到了税收收入（面积y）。是谁实际支付了反补贴税？是巴西政府！它支付给巴西厂商的出口补贴通过较低的出口价格被转移给加拿大的购买者。当加拿大的进口购买者支付反补贴税时，又将它转移给了加拿大政府。此时，加拿大的福利要比自由贸易时更高，因为巴西政府实际上支付了加拿大的税负。

因为出口补贴对全球整体而言是不利的，而对出口补贴采取报复措施对全球来说却是有益的，所以世界贸易组织规则非常明智地允许进口国家征收反补贴税。但是，实际结果却是补贴诉讼和反补贴税使用频率远低于倾销诉讼和反倾销税的使用频率。2005—2009年，全球仅有69起补贴案件。截至2010年中期，只有66起反补贴措施生效。

美国是使用反补贴税最多的国家，涉及32起新反补贴案件和43起正在实施的反补贴税。欧盟和加拿大也使用了反补贴税。中国、美国、印度是遭受出口补贴指控最频繁的国家。钢铁产品是频繁受到出口补贴指控的产品。反补贴税正逐渐低于反倾销税。例如，美国平均的反补贴税税率仅为10%。虽然反补贴税对于全球来说有益，但是与反倾销税一样，反补贴税也存在滥用的情况。进口竞争性产品生产者有动机指控有可能受到出口补贴的国外产品，获得保护同这些产品竞争。同时，政府的很多行为都存在补贴因素。在反补贴案件中，也许在政府的偏袒和帮助下，那些有抱怨的进口竞争性企业很有可能确信某种外国产品存在鼓励出口的补贴。如果它们能够证明受到出口补贴产品的损害，那么这些厂商就能够从征收反补贴税中获得保护。

美国和加拿大之间的关于软木材的纠纷就是一个有争议的反补贴案件。在2001年年初，一项限制加拿大软木材出口的VER（自愿出口限制）到期了。美国木材企业立即重新提起诉讼，控诉加拿大木材企业从补贴中获益，因为加拿大政府没有对政府工地上的伐木征收足够高的费用。加拿大政府认为它们收的费用是合理的，所以不存在补贴。美国政府却不这么认为。美国商务部认定这种偏低的费用相当于19%的补贴，同时认定加拿大木材出口平均还有额外的8%的倾销。美国国际贸易委员会发现在VER期满后，激增的进口对美国木材企业造成损害。很显然，美国木材商从对加拿大木材征收的27%的平均组合税中获得了收益。而美国消费者遭受了损失。建造一栋传统的新房的成本上涨了1 000美元。对于大多数可以支付得起的新房购买者，遭受的是纯粹的货币损失。对于大概30万个无法支付更高房价的美国家庭而言，就会形成消费效应的无谓损失。他们中大多数都是中等收入家庭，而且不愿意继续居住在破旧的房子中。

如果加拿大的伐木费用因为太低而被认为是补贴，那么世界福利将因美国的反补贴税而提高。但是，如果加拿大的伐木费用是合理的，并且不被认为是补贴，那么反补贴税（也许是反倾销税）就是简单的进口贸易保护，对世界来说是一种净损失。

7.2.7 战略性出口补贴可能是有益的

在前面的章节中，我们假定在完全竞争市场中，出口补贴会对出口国造成伤害。对于一些行业，这种完全竞争市场假设是不成立的。假设在现实生活中的市场上只有两个巨型企业相互竞争，且每个企业都可以为整个市场提供足够的产品。如果这个行业是由两个能够垄断世界市场的寡头企业之间的国际竞争形成的，那么出口补贴的经济效应与前面的分析将会存在巨大差异。在这个寡头竞争中，出口补贴对出口国和世界既可能是有益的也可能是有害的。

为了说明有益的出口补贴，我们可以设想一个简化的例子，这个设想受到了美国的波音公司和欧洲的空客公司在现实中相互持续竞争的启发。假设两家公司在技术上都可能生产某种新的民用飞机，如超大型喷气式飞机。为了突出重点，我们假设空客公司和波音公司以同样的成本生产这种新品。飞机制造业可以从规模经济中获利——随着厂商产量的扩张，单位制造成本会随着产量的增加而下降。任何一家公司都能够以一个低成本供给整个全球市场。如果只有一家公司占领全球市场，那么它将获得垄断利益。如果两家公司都生产，那么它们为了销量而竞争，并把价格压低至边际成本。在这种状况下，它们不能获得经营利润。

这些简单的例子揭示了两家公司在全球竞争下，提供出口补贴及类似形式的补贴的两个结论：①补贴可能对出口国有益；②提供补贴的结果非常不确定，取决于太多的外部条件。

在我们的例子中，还可以看到一种重要情况：如果其他国家的政府也给它的企业提供战略性政策支持，那么很有可能连这个国家都遭受福利损失。而另外一种重要情况则是可能存在没有收益的博弈。例如，新产品没有足够的消费需求，那么即便只有一个厂商生产，经济利润有可能为负。政府将如何辨别企业要求实行战略性保护措施的申请？虽然在理论上存在战略性贸易政策的国家利润，但是人们可能会怀疑，中央政府是否真正有效地使用这种政策。

8 The Political Economy of Protectionism

8.1 Arguments of the Political Economy of Protectionism

In this section, we analyze the various arguments for protection. These range from clearly fallacious propositions to arguments that can stand up, with some qualification, to close economic scrutiny.

(1) One fallacious argument is that restrictions are needed to protect domestic labor against cheap foreign labor. This argument is not valid because even if domestic wages are higher than wages abroad, domestic labor costs can still be lower if the productivity of labor is sufficiently higher domestically than abroad. If not, expensive-labor nations can still specialize in the production and export capital-and technology-intensive commodities.

(2) Other fallacious argument for protection is scientific tariff. This is the tariff rate that would make the price of imports equal to domestic prices and allow domestic producers to meet foreign competition. However, this would eliminate international price differences and trade in commodities subject to such scientific tariff.

(3) Two questionable arguments are that protection is needed ① to reduce domestic unemployment and ② to cure a deficit in the nation's balance of payments (i.e., the excess of the nation's expenditures abroad over its foreign earnings). Protection would reduce domestic unemployment and a balance-of-payments deficit by leading to the substitution of imports with domestic production. However, these are beggar-thy-neighbor measures that come at the expense of other nations, which are likely to retaliate and cause all nations to lose in the end. Domestic unemployment and a deficit in a nation's balance of payments should be corrected with appropriate domestic monetary, fiscal, and trade policies rather than with trade restrictions.

(4) One qualified argument for protection is the infant-industry argument to allow a nation to develop an industry in which it has a potential comparative advantage. Temporary trade

protection is then justified to establish and protect the domestic industry during its infancy until it can grow and meet foreign competition. For this argument to be valid, however, protection must be temporary, and the return in the grow-up industry must be sufficiently high to also offset the higher prices paid by domestic consumers of the commodity during the period of infancy.

Several important qualifications must be made with regard to the infant-industry argument for protection. First, this argumentis more justified for developing nations (where capital markets may not function properly) than for industrial nations. Second, it is usually difficult to remove. Third, and most important, what trade protection (say, in the form of an import tariff) can do, an equivalent production subsidy to the infant industry can do better. The reason is that a purely domestic distortion should be overcome with a purely domestic policy (such as a direct production subsidy to the infant industry) rather than with a trade policy that also distorts relative prices and domestic consumption. A production subsidy is also a more than a more direct form of aid that is easier to remove than an important tariff. One practical difficulty is that a subsidy requires revenues rather than generating them as, for example, an import tariff does.

The same general principle also holds for other types of domestic distortion. For example, suppose that an industry generates an external economy (i. e., a benefit to society at large, say, by training workers who then leave to work in other industries). There is then likely to be underinvestment in the industry (because the industry does not receive the full benefit from its investments). One way to encourage the industry and confer greater external economies on society would be to restrict imports. But this also increases the price of the product to domestic consumers, A better policy would, again, be to provide a direct subsidy to the industry. Similarly, a direct tax would also be better than a tariff to discourage activities (such as automobile travel) that give rise to external diseconomies (pollution) because the tax does not distort relative prices and consumption.

(5) Trade restrictions are often advocated to protect domestic industries important for national defense. But even in this case, direct production subsidies are generally better than tariff protection. The closest we come to a truly valid economic argument for protection is the optimum tariff. That is, if a nation is large enough to affect its terms of trade, the nation can exploit its market power and improve its terms of trade and welfare with an optimum tariff. However, as we have seen, this is a beggarthy-neighbor policy and other nations are likely to retaliate and lead to losses all around.

It is clear that by increasing the commodity price, trade protection benefits producers and harms consumers (and usually the nation as a whole). However, since producers are few and stand to gain agreat deal from protection, they have a strong incentive to lobby the government to adopt protectionist measures. On the other hand, since the losses are diffused among many consumers, each of whom loses very little from the protection, they are not likely to effectively organize to resist protectionist measures. Thus, there is a basis in favor of protectionism. For example, the U.S. sugar quota raises individual expenditures on sugar by about \$1.50 per person per year in the United States. But with a U.S. population of 285 million people, the quota generates more than \$400 million in rents to the few thousand sugar producers in the country.

In industrial countries, protection is more likely to be provided to labor-intensive industries employing unskilled, low-wage workers who would have great difficulty in finding alternative employment if they lost their present jobs. Some empirical support has also been found for the pressure-group or interest-group theory, which postulates that industries that are highly organized (such as the automobile industry) receive more trade protection than less organized industries. Industries that produce consumer products are also able to generally obtain more protection than industries producing intermediate products because the latter can exercisecountervailing power and block protection by the latter, which would increase input prices and lead to higher consumer prices.

8.2 Strategic Trade and Industrial Policies

Strategic trade policy is a relatively recent development advanced in favor of an activist trade policy and protectionism. According to this argument, a nation can create a comparative advantage (through temporary trade protection, subsidies, tax benefits, and cooperative government-industry programs) in such fields as semiconductors, computers, telecommunications, and other industries that are deemed crucial to future growth in the nation. These high-technology industries are subject to high risks, require large-scale production to achieve economies of scale, and give rise to extensive external economies when successful. Strategic trade policy suggests that by encouraging such industries, the nation can reap the large external economies that result from them and enhance its future growth prospects. This is similar to the infant-industry argument in developing nations, except that it is advanced for industrial nations to acquire a comparative advantage in some crucial high-tech industry.

Examples of strategic trade and industrial policy are provided by semiconductors in the 1970s and 1980s in Japan and by the development of the Concorde (the supersonic aircraft) and Airbus in Europe in the 1970s, Semiconductors in Japan are usually given as the textbook case of successful strategic trade and industrial policy. The market for Semiconductors (such as computer chips) was dominated by the United States in the 1970s. Starting in the mid-1970s, Japan's powerful Ministry of Trade and Industry (MITI) targeted the development of this industry by financing research and development, granting tax advantages for investments in the industry, and fostering government-industry cooperation, while protecting the domestic market from foreign (especially U.S.) competition.

These policies are credited for Japan's success in nearly wrestling control of the semiconductors market from the United States in the mid-1980s. Most economists remain skeptical, however, and attribute Japan's stunning performance in this field primary to other forces, such as greater educational emphasis on science and mathematics, higher rates of investment, and a willingness to take a long-run view of investments rather than stressing quarterly profits, as in the United States. In Europe, the Concorde was a technological feat but a commercial disaster, and Airbus Industries would not have survived without heavy government subsidies.

There are also serious difficulties in carrying strategic trade and industrial policies. First, it is extremely difficult to pick winners (i.e., choose the industries that will provide large external economies in the future) and devise appropriate policies to successfully nurture them. Second, since most leading nations undertake strategic trade policies at the same time, their efforts are largely neutralized, so that the potential benefits to each may be small. Third, when a country does achieve substantial success with a strategic trade policy, this comes at the expense of othercountries (i.e., it is a beggar-thy-neighbor policy), which are likely to retaliate, Faced with all these practical difficulties, even supporters of strategic trade policy grudgingly acknowledge that free trade is still the best policy, after all. That is, free trade may be suboptimal in theory, but it is optimal in practice.

While generally opposed to industrial targeting and strategic trade policies domestically, the United States did retaliate against countries that adopted these policies to the detriment of U.S. economic interests. An example was the semiconductor agreement that the United States negotiated with Japan in 1991 discussed earlier. On a broader scale, the United States and Japan engaged in negotiations (called the Structural Impediments Initiative, or SII) during the mid-1990s aimed, among other things, at opening the entire Japanese distribution system more widely to U.S. firms. During the 1990s, the United States also demanded a sharp reduction in subsidies granted to Airbus Industries by the governments of France, Germany, England, and Spain, to agriculture by the European Union, and since the turn of the new century on subsidies for Airbus's development of its new super jumbo aircraft. Furthermore, the United States has requested that other countries, such as Brazil, China, and India, remove excessive restrictions against specific U.S. exports and demanded protection for its intellectual property (such as patented materials) from unauthorized and uncompensated use.

8.3 History of U.S. Commercial Policy

This section surveys the history of U.S. commercial policy. It starts by examining *the Trade Agreements Act of* 1934 and then discussing the importance of the General Agreement on Tariffs and Trade (GATT). Next we examine the 1962 Trade Expansion Act and the results of the Kennedy Round of trade negotiations. Subsequently, we discuss *the Trade Reform Act of* 1974 and the outcome of the Tokyo Round of trade negotiations. Finally, we examine the 1984 and the 1988 Trade Acts.

8.3.1 The Trade Agreements Act of 1934.

During the early 1930s, world trade in general and U.S. exports in particular fell sharply because of ① greatly reduced economic activity throughout the world as a result of the Great Depression and ② passage in 1930 of the Smoot-Hawley Act, under which the average import duty in the United States reached the all-time high of 59 percent in 1932. The aim was to stimulate domestic employment, but it provoked retaliation by other countries, and this led 1929 to the collapse of world trade (American imports in 1932 were only 31 percent of their level, and exports fell even more).

To reverse the trend toward sharply reduced world trade, the U.S. Congress passed the Trade Agreements Act of 1934, which authorized the President to negotiate mutual tariff reductions by as much as 50 percent of the rates set under the Smoot-Hawley Tariff Act. Tariff reductions were to be based on the most-favored-nation-principle, which extended to all trade partners any reciprocal tariff reduction negotiated by the United States with any of its trade partners. This bilateral trade approach, however, faced the serious shortcoming that tariff reductions were negotiated, for the most part, only in commodities that dominated bilateral trade.

8.3.2 The General Agreement on Tariffs and Trade (GATT)

The General Agreement on Tariffs and Trade (GATT) was an international organization, created in 1947 and headquartered in Geneva (Switzerland), devoted to the promotion of freer trade through multilateral trade negotiations. GATT rested on ① the principle of nondiscrimination, or the unconditional acceptance of the most-favored-nation principle; ② the elimination of nontariff trade barriers (such as quotas), except for agricultural products and for nations in balance-of-payments difficulties and ③ consultation among nations in solving trade disputes within the GATT framework. By 1993, a total of 123 members (including the United States and all major members, with the exception of the members of the former Soviet Union and China) were signatories of the GATT and covered over 90 percent of world trade.

Initial success in lowering tariffs under GATT auspices were limited by the protectionist measures adopted by the U.S. Congress during the 1950s. These were ① the peril-point provisions, which prevented the president from negotiating any tariff reduction that would cause serious damage to a domestic industry; ② the escape clause, which allowed any domestic industry that claimed injury from imports to petition the International Trade Commission (the U.S. Tariff Commission until 1975) to recommend to the president to revoke any negotiated tariff reduction. A rising share of imports in an industry was sufficient to prove injury and; ③ the nation security clause, which prevented tariff reductions (even if already negotiated) when they would hurt industries important for national defense.

8.3.3 The 1962 Trade Expansion Act and the Kennedy Round

The Trade Expansion Act of 1962 replaced the product-by-product approach of the Trade Agreements Act, authorized the president tonegotiate across-the-board tariff reductions of up to 50 percent of their 1962 level, and provided Trade Adjustment Assistance (TAA) to displaced workers (in the form of retraining and moving assistance) and to firms (in the form of tax relief, low-cost loans, and technical help) injured by tariff reductions. Under the authority of this act, the United States negotiated the **Kennedy Round** of multilateral trade negotiation in 1967, which lowered average tariff rates on industrial products to less than 10 percent in industrial nations.

8.3.4 The Trade Reform Act of 1974 and the Tokyo Round

The Trade Reform Act authorized the president to negotiate ① tariff reductions of up to 60 percent and removal tariffs of 5 percent or less than and ② a code of conduct for nations in applying nontariff trade barriers to reduce their restrictive effect. The act also liberalized the criteria for adjustment assistance. Under theauthority of the act, the United States participated in the multilateral tariff negotiations known as the Tokyo Round, which were concluded in 1979 and resulted in average tariff reductions (phased over an eight-year period, starting in 1980) of 31 percent for the United States, 27 percent for the European Union (EU), and 28 percent for Japan.

8.3.5 The Trade and Tariff Act of 1984

This had three major provisions: ①It authorized the president to negotiate international agreements for the protection of intellectual property rights and to lower barriers to trade in services, high-technology products, and direct investments. ②It extended the Generalized System of Preferences (GSP), which granted preferential access to the exports of developing members to the United States. ③It provided authority for negotiation in the Uruguay Round that started in 1986.

8.3.6 The Omnibus Trade and Competitiveness Act of 1988

This called on the U.S. Special Trade Representative (USTR) to set a rigorous schedule for negotiating reductions in trade barriers with members that heavily restricted U.S. exports and required retaliation if negotiations failed.

8.4 The Uruguay Round

In December 1993, The Uruguay Round, the eighth and most ambitious round of multilateral trade negotiations in history in which 123 members participated, was competed after seven years of tortuous negotiations. Disagreements between the United States and the European Union (EU), especially France, on reducing agricultural subsidies delayed its conclusion for three years. The aim of the Uruguay Round was to check the proliferation of the new protectionism and reverse its trend; negotiate international rules for the protection of intellectual property rights; and improve the dispute settlement mechanism by ensuring more timely decisions and compliance with GATT rulings. The agreement was signed by the United States, and most other members on April 15, 1994, and took effect on July 1, 1995. The major provisions of the accord were the following:

(1) Tariffs. Tariffs on industrial products are to be reduced from an average of4.7 percent to 3 percent, and the share of goods with zero tariffs is to increase from 20-22 percent to 40-45 percent; tariffs were removed altogether on pharmaceuticals, construction equipment, medical equipment, paper products, and steel.

(2) Quotas. Nations are to replace quotas on agricultural imports and imports of textiles and apparel with less restrictive tariffs by the end of 1999, for agricultural, and the end of 2004 for textiles and apparel; tariffs on agricultural products are to be reduced by 24 percent in development members and by 36 percent in developed members; tariffs on textiles are to be cut by 25 percent.

(3) Antidumping. The agreement provides for tougher and quicker action to resolve disputes resulting from the use of antidumping laws, but it does not ban their use.

(4) Subsidies. The volume of subsidized agricultural exports is to be reduced by 21 percent over a six-year period; government subsidies for industrial research are limited to 50 percent ofapplied research costs.

(5) Safeguards. Members may temporarily raise tariffs or other restrictions against an import surge that severely harms a domestic industry, but it bars members from administering health and safety standards unless based on scientific evidence and not simply to restrict trade. For example, a member can only keep out beef imports from cattle raised with growth hormones by showing that the beef so produced is unsafe for human consumption.

(6) Intellectual property. The agreement provides for 20-year protection of patents, trademarks, and copyrights, but it allows a 10-year phase-in period for patent protection in pharmaceuticals for developing members.

(7) Services. The United States failed to secure access to the markets of Japan, Korea, and many developing members for its banks and security firms, and did not succeed in having France and the European Union lift restrictions on the showing of American films and TV programs in Europe.

(8) Other industry provisions. The United States and Europe agreed to continue talking about further limiting government subsidies to civil aircraft makers, opening up the distance telephone market, and limiting European subsidies to steelmakers; the United States also indicated that it intended to continue negotiating the further opening of the Japanese computer chip market.

(9) Trade-related investment measures. The agreement phases out the requirement that foreign investors (such as automakers) buy supplies locally or exports as much as they import.

(10) World Trade Organization. The agreement also called for the replacement of the General Agreement on Tariffs and Trade (GATT) secretariat with the World Trade Organization (WTO) in Geneva with authority not only in trade in industrial products but also in agricultural

products and services. Trade disputes are also to be settled by a vote of two-thirds or three-quarters of the members rather than unanimously as under GATT (which meant that the guilty member could block any action against it).

When fully implemented by 2005, the Uruguay Round is estimated to increase world trade by about 20 percent (with one-quarter of the increase in trade in manufactures and the rest in agriculture) and generate total gains in world income of \$349 billion (\$164 billion from liberalizing trade in agriculture, \$130 billion from manufactures and \$55 billion from services), with developing members receiving 42 percent of the total gains (mostly from liberalization of trade in manufactures), which is roughly double their share of world GDP.

During 1996 and 1997, multilateral agreements to open up trade in telecommunications, financial services, and information technology (that were not reached at the Uruguay Round) were concluded. Over time, these agreements could provide larger gains in trade volumes than the entire Uruguay Round treaty. In 1999, the European Union reached a free trade agreement with Mexico (which became effective in July 2000) to end all tariffs on their bilateral trade by 2007. In December 2001, China was admitted as the 144th member of the WTO and in 2003 Armenia, Macedonia, Cambodia, and Nepal joined, thus raising total membership to 148.

In August 2002, Congress granted President Bush trade promotion authority, formerly known as fast track, to negotiate broad trade agreements that allowed no amendments, but only an up-or-down vote by Congress to ratify or reject the agreement. The purpose of this legislation was to assure foreign governments that Congress would act expeditiously on any agreement that they negotiated with the U.S. government. The legislation also required the president to consider environmental protection, labor rights, and antidumping laws in his negotiations, and it provided up to \$1.2 billion a year in health insurance and other benefits to workers who lost their jobs, and added farmers and ranchers to the list of those eligible. In December 2002, the United States reached a free trade agreement with Chile and in April 2003 with Singapore. In February and March 2004, the United States negotiated free trade agreements with Australia, Morocco, and six Central American countries (Costa Rica, EI Salvador, Guatemala, Honduras, Nicaragua, and Santo Domingo). Congress, however, must approve these agreements.

8.5 Outstanding Trade Problems and the Doha Round

Despite the great benefits resulting from the successful completion of the Uruguay Round, many serious trade problems remain. One problem is the serious trade disputes between the United States and the European Union on the tax breaks, on the subsidies that the European Union grants for the development of the super jumbo aircraft by Airbus, and on the European Union's ban U.S. exports of hormone-raised beef and genetically modified (biotech) food. In fall 2003, the United States also severely restricted China's rapidly growing exports of knit fabrics and other textile products. In March 2001, the United States had also imposed a 30 percent import tariff on some steel products imported from the European Union, Japan, and other countries or regions, but removed it in December 2003 when Europe threatened heavy WTO-sanctioned retaliation.

The second problem is that subsidies and tariffs on agricultural products remain very high; antidumping measures and safeguards are still possible and frequently abused, and so the potential for serious trade disputes remains.

A third trade problem is the tendency for the world to break up into three major trading blocs: the European Union (EU), the North America Free Trade Area (NAFTA), and a (much less defined) Asian bloc. Although these trading blocs could be regarded as building blocks of a free trading system, they can also become stumbling blocks and lead to more bilateral deals, protectionism, and inter-bloc trade conflicts.

The fourth problem is the call by some developed members, such as the United States and France, for the establishment of labor and environmental standards. These are supposed to ensure a leveling of working conditions between developed and developing members and avoid social dumping by the latter (i.e., developing members competing unfairly by denying their worker's basic rights and decent wages and working conditions). The danger is that the movement to establish labor and environmental standards can easily be captured by protectionistic forces. The same is true for environmental standards. Trade-related competition polices (such as subsidies and regulations) as well as trade-relative investment measures (TRIMs) also need to be dealt more adequately than they have been in the Uruguay Round.

An attempt was made to launch a Millennium Round of trade negotiations at the WTO Trade Conference held in Seattle in December 1999. The attempt labor because ① developing countries were adamantly opposed to putting labor and environmental standards on the agenda for the new round; ② the European Union and Japan objected to the U.S. desire to put on the agenda the complete liberalization of trade in agricultural products; ③ the United States objected to discussing competition and investment policies that the European Union wanted. All this came up in the face of large demonstrations organized by a strong anti-globalization movement, which blamed globalization for many human and environmental problems worldwide and for sacrificing human and environmental well-being to the corporate profits.

In November 2001, the Doha Round was successfully launched in Doha, Qatar, to be concluded by the end of 2004. The agenda includes the further liberalization of production and trade in agriculture, industrial products, and services; further tighten rules for antidumping measures and safeguards, and dealing with investment and competition policies. In particular, developing members are reluctant to make concessions because they feel that the Uruguay Round failed to deliver a great deal of what it promised them. Developing members insist making the Doha Round a true development round. However, at the ministerial conference in Cancun, Mexico, in September 2003, members were unable to agree on the agenda for the Round primarily because of disagreements between developing and developed members on the agricultural subsidies in developed members. In July 2006, Doha Round was failed after five-years' negotiation. Until the beginning of 2011, all efforts to conclude the Doha Round were failed.

8 保护主义的政治经济学

8.1 保护主义的政治经济学的各种观点

本节将分析关于保护主义的不同观点，从显然谬误的提法到在一定限定条件下证明能够站住脚的观点均包括在内。

（1）一个错误观点认为“需要贸易限制来保护国内劳动力不受国外廉价劳动力的冲击”。这种观点的错误在于即使国内工资比国外高，如果劳动力的生产力远高于国外，国内劳动力成本也可以降下来。即便不是这样，拥有昂贵劳动力的国家也可以专门生产并出口资本和技术密集型产品。

（2）另一个关于保护主义的错误观点是“科学的关税”。这种观点认为应征收进口商品的价格等于国内价格的关税，从而允许国内生产者对付国外竞争。然而，这会消除采用这种“科学的”关税的商品的国际价格差和贸易。

（3）两国有问题的观点是需要通过保护来减少国内的失业和消除国际收支赤字（一国在海外的支出超过其海外收入）。通过引导国内产品取代进口，保护措施会减少国内失业和收支赤字。然而，这是“以邻为壑”的观点，因为它们是以其他国家的损失为基础的，很可能导致其他国家以牙还牙，最终两败俱伤。国内失业和收支赤字可以用适当的货币、财政和贸易政策而不是贸易限制来弥补。

（4）一种相对合理的关于保护的观点是“幼稚产业观点”，它认为一个国家应当保护其具有潜在比较优势的产业，以促进其发展。对幼稚工业进行暂时的贸易保护，直至它能对付外国竞争，具有经济规模并形成长期的竞争优势为止，那时就可以取消保护了。然而，这一观点成立的前提是，此项工业成熟后的回报率必须足够高，足以抵消在其“幼稚期间”国内消费者为该产品支付的高价格。

要使保护幼稚产业的观点合理，有以下几条重要的限制条件：第一，这种观点在发展中国家（资本市场还不能正常发挥功能）比在工业化国家更适用；第二，很难确定哪项产业或潜在的产业符合这些要求，经验表明，一旦给予保护就很难取消；第三，也是最重要的，相比贸易保护（以进口关税的形式）所能做的，采用对幼稚产业给予等价的生产补贴能做得更好。其原因在于，单纯的国内价格扭曲应当用单纯的国内政策（如对幼稚产业直接的生产补贴）来解决，而不是采用扭曲相对价格和国内消费的贸易政策。与进口关税相比，生产补贴是更直接的帮助形式，也更容易取消。

同样的普遍原则也适用于其他类型的国内扭曲。例如，如果某一产业出现了外部经济（让整个社会受益，如经过培训的员工到其他部门工作），该产业就会投资不足（因为它没有从其投资中得到全部的好处）。一种促进该产业发展并协调所产生的对社会更大的外部经济的办法是限制进口，但它会提高国内消费者购买该产品的价格。因此，一种更好的政策是对该产业给予直接的补贴。类似地，一项直接税收可以比关税更好地限制会导致外部不经济（如污染）的行为（如汽车旅行），因为这种税收没有扭曲相对价格和消费。

（5）一般主张对国防至关重要的国内产业也应通过贸易限制加以保护。但即便是国防工业，一般来说，直接的生产补贴也比关税保护好。关于保护，最接近真正正确的经济观点是“最佳关税”。也就是说，如果一个国家大到可以影响它的贸易条件的话，它就可以运用最佳关税来开发市场潜力并改进贸易条件和福利。然而，正如我们已经知道，这是一个“以邻为壑”的政策，其他国家也可能以牙还牙，最终将导致两败俱伤。

显然，提高商品价格，贸易保护会使生产者受益而使消费者受损（通常也损害了整个国家）。然而，既然生产者人数很少并坚持从保护中大量获利，他们就有很强烈的动机游说政府采取保护手段。此外，既然损失被众多的消费者分担了，每个消费者因为贸易保护所受的损失很少，不可能有效地组织起来抵制保护手段。这样一来，就形成了一个喜欢保护主义的倾向。例如，对糖的进口实行配额，使美国每年每人在糖上的花费只增加了 1.5 美元，但在美国 2.85 亿人口的基础上，限额对美国数千家糖厂来说，则产生了 40 亿美元的租金。

发达国家更倾向于保护劳动密集型产业，以帮助其雇佣无技术、低工资的那些如果失去当前工作很难再找到工作的工人。人们已经发现的一些经验证据支持“压力集团”和“利益集团”理论，这个理论假定高度组织的产业（如汽车产业）比低度组织的产业得到了更多的贸易保护。一种产业如果只由几家公司组成，便容易组织起来。另外，生产消费品的产业一般能比生产作为其他产业原料的中间产品的产业得到更多的保护，因为后者会运用反补贴权力阻碍保护，这会提高其原料的价格并导致更高的消费者价格。

8.2 战略贸易与产业政策

战略贸易政策是近期提出的一个支持积极贸易政策和保护主义的观点。根据这种观点，一个国家可以（通过暂时的贸易保护、补贴、税收优惠和政府与产业部门的合作计划）在诸如半导体、计算机、远程通信和其他被认为对该国至关重要的领域创造出比较优势。这些高科技产业有很高的风险，要求大规模生产以形成规模经济，当其成功时便可带来外部经济。战略性的贸易政策认为，通过鼓励这样的产业，国家可以从中得到很大的外部经济，从而加强未来增长的前景。该观点与发展中国家的幼稚工业的观点很相似，只不过它是为发达国家提出的，帮助其在重要的高科技产业中获得比较优势。

战略性的贸易和产业政策的例证可在 20 世纪 70 年代和 80 年代日本的半导体工业、20 世纪 70 年代欧洲空中客车的开发中找到。日本的半导体工业通常被用作成功的案例，编入战略性的贸易和产业政策的教科书。20 世纪 70 年代，半导体市场（如电脑芯片）由美国控制。自 20 世纪 70 年代中期开始，日本强有力的通产省[①]瞄准了这项产业的发展，它提供研究与开发资金，为这项产业的投资提供税收优惠，促成政府与工业部门的合作，还注意保护国内市场不受国外（特别是美国）的竞争冲击。

20 世纪 80 年代中期，日本成功地从美国手中夺得半导体市场的控制权应归功于这

① 通产省是日本政府干预经济的综合性职能机构。

些政策。然而，大部分经济学家对此保持怀疑，他们认为日本在此领域的惊人表现主要应归功于其他因素，如对科学和数学的重点教育、更高的投资率、用长远目光看待投资而不是像美国那样重视短期利润。在欧洲，协和飞机是一大技术成果，但却是一次商业灾难，而空中客车企业如果没有持续而大量的政府补贴便难以生存。

战略性的贸易和产业政策在实行上还有重重的困难。第一，很难选择赢家（也就是选择将来能提供大量外部经济的产业）并设计合适的政策来成功地培育它们。第二，由于大部分发达国家同时实行战略性的贸易政策，他们努力的效果会相互抵消，从而各国的潜在收益会很小。第三，当一个国家采用战略性的贸易政策取得实际的成功时，这是以其他国家的损失为代价的（是“以邻为壑”的），这样其他国家很可能会报复。面对所有这些实际困难，即便是战略性贸易政策的支持者也不得不承认“自由贸易仍然是最好的政策”。也就是说，自由贸易在理论上可能是次优的，但在实践中仍是最优的。

在美国国内普遍反对实施扶持目标产业和战略贸易政策的同时，美国也采取措施报复那些采用战略贸易政策并损害美国经济利益的国家。一个例子是前面讨论过的1991年的美日半导体协议。20世纪90年代中期，美国和日本在一个更广泛的范围内（就所谓结构性初始障碍）进行谈判，除了其他一些目标外，主要目标是要求对美国公司更广泛地开放整个日本的分销系统。在整个90年代，美国也要求迅速减少由法国、德国、英国和西班牙政府给空中客车工业的补贴以及由欧盟给予的农业补贴。而在21世纪开始时，美国还要求减少对空中客车开发新的超大型客机的补贴。此外，美国还要求其他国家如巴西、中国和印度不要专门针对美国的出口做过度的限制，并保护其知识产权（如专利材料），使之不被无授权和无补偿地使用。

8.3　美国的商业政策史

本节将研究美国的商业政策史。我们的考察自《1934年贸易协定法》开始，然后讨论关税与贸易总协定（GATT）的重要性，接下来考察《1962年扩大贸易法》和贸易谈判的肯尼迪回合的结果，之后讨论《1974年贸易改革法》和贸易谈判的东京回合的结果。最后，我们还研究了1984年和1988年的贸易法。

8.3.1　《1934年贸易协定法》

20世纪30年代早期，整个世界和美国的出口迅速下降，这是因为：①由大危机引起的世界范围的经济活动的大幅度减少；②1930年美国国会通过了《斯穆特—汗利法》。据此，美国的平均进口关税于1932年达到历史最高的59%。税法的目的是刺激国内就业，但它引起了其他国家的报复，结果造成了世界贸易的崩溃（美国1932年进口量仅为1929年的31%，出口下降得更多）。

为了扭转世界贸易锐减的趋势，美国国会通过了《1934年贸易协定法》，授权总统与其他国家谈判，互相减少根据《斯穆特—汗利法》设置的关税的50%。关税削减是以最惠国原则为基础的，这使美国的所有贸易伙伴都可以分享美国与任何一个贸易伙伴达成的关税互减的好处。美国也可以从贸易最惠伙伴国与其他任何一国签署的双边减税协议中获益。然而，这种双边贸易的方式面临严重的缺点，因为大部分减税只针对在双边贸易中具有重要地位的商品。

8.3.2 关税与贸易总协定（GATT）

关税与贸易总协定（GATT）是一个国际性组织，成立于1947年，总部设在日内瓦（瑞士）。成立该组织的目的是通过多边贸易谈判促进自由贸易。关贸总协定遵循三个基本原则：①非歧视原则，即无条件接受以上提及的最惠国原则；②消除非关税贸易壁垒（如配额），关于农产品的及因一国国际收支平衡困难造成的非关税贸易壁垒除外；③在关贸总协定框架内协商解决国家间的贸易纠纷。到1993年，关贸总协定的签约成员已有超过123个国家和地区（包括美国和所有主要国家和地区，除了苏联各国和中国），超过90%的国际贸易是根据关贸总协定的规则进行的。

在关贸总协定的主导下最初关税的成功降低因为20世纪50年代美国国会采取的保护主义措施而遭到阻碍。这些措施包括：①危险点条款。该条款具有防止总统签署任何会导致对一种境内产业造成严重破坏的关税减让协议的作用。②豁免条款。它允许任何受到进口损害的境内产业向国际贸易调查委员会（1975年前为美国关税调查委员会）申述，该委员会将建议总统废除已谈成的关税减让协议。一种产业日益增长的进口份额足以证明它已造成损害。③安全条款。当有关的关税减让协议（即使已谈成）会伤害对安全至关重要的产业时，该条款要求中止这一协议。

8.3.3 《1962年扩大贸易法》与肯尼迪回合

《1962年扩大贸易》取代了贸易协定法中从一种产品到另一种产品的谈判方式，授权总统可进行跨国界的关税减让谈判，最多可达成在1962年水平上再减让50%关税的协议，并且对那些由于关税减让而受损害的工人（通过再培训和帮助迁徙的形式）和企业（以减免税收、低息贷款和技术援助等形式的帮助）提供了贸易调整援助（TAA）。根据这一法案的授权，1967年美国发起了更广泛的多边贸易谈判即肯尼迪回合，最终使发达国家对工业品征收的平均关税低于10%。

8.3.4 《1974年贸易改革法》与东京回合

《1974年贸易改革法》授权总统：①通过谈判可减让关税最多达60%，并有权取消现行5%或更低的关税；②谈判减让非关税贸易壁垒。这项法案还放宽了获得调整援助的标准。根据法案的授权，美国参加了著名的东京回合的多边关税谈判。该谈判于1979年结束，最终造成的关税减让（从1980年开始，分八年分阶段减让关税）美国平均为31%，欧盟平均为27%，日本平均为28%。

8.3.5 《1984年贸易和关税法》

《1984年贸易和关税法》包括3个主要条款：①授权总统谈判并签约以保护知识产权，并降低服务业、高技术产品和直接投资的贸易壁垒；②扩展了普惠制，发展中成员可以经该途径向美国出口；③授权参与1986年开始的乌拉圭回合贸易谈判。

8.3.6 《1988年贸易与竞争法》

《1988年贸易与竞争法》要求美国特别贸易代表（USTR）制订了一个严格的计划与那些严重限制美国进口的成员进行消除这些贸易壁垒的谈判，如果谈判失败则要进行报复。

8.4 乌拉圭回合

1993年12月，乌拉圭回合，即历史上第8次也是最雄心勃勃的由123个国家和地区参加的多边贸易谈判经过7年曲折的谈判终于结束了。由于美国与欧共体尤其是与法国之间关于减少农业补贴方面的分歧，谈判的结束推迟了3年。乌拉圭回合的目的是建立规则以阻止新保护主义的激增并扭转这一趋势；将服务、农业和外部投资引入谈判；谈判制定国际规则以保护知识产权；通过更及时的决策和遵循关贸总协定的规则以改进调解争议的机制。1994年4月15日，乌拉圭回合的协议由美国和多数参加国签字，于1995年7月1日生效。该协议的主要条款涉及关税、配额、反倾销、补贴、安全等内容。

8.4.1 关税

在关税方面，该协议对工业品的关税从平均4.7%减让到3%；零关税货物的比例从20%~25%增加到40%~45%；取消了医药、建筑设备、医用设备、纸制品和钢铁的关税。

8.4.2 配额

在配额方面，该协议决定有关成员将在10年内以较少限制的关税代替对农业进口和纺织品及服装（根据多种纤维协议）进口的配额；发展中成员的农产品关税减少24%，发达成员减少36%；纺织品的关税减让25%。

8.4.3 反倾销

在反倾销方面，该协议提供了更有力、更迅速的行动，以解决由于运用反倾销法引起的争端，但协议并不禁止它们的运用。

8.4.4 补贴

在补贴方面，该协议决定农业出口补贴的数量将在6年内减让21%；政府对产业研究的补贴限制在应用型科学研究费用的50%以内。

8.4.5 安全

在安全方面，该协议决定其成员可以暂时地提高关税或使用其他限制来阻止严重损害国内产业的进口狂潮，但禁止国家制定健康与安全标准，除非基于科学证据，不许限制贸易。例如，某成员只有通过显示用荷尔蒙刺激生长的办法生产的牛肉对人类消费不安全，才能禁止用这种方式生产的牛肉的进口。

8.4.6 知识产权

在知识产权方面，该协议为专利、商标和版权提供了20年的保护期，但它允许发展中成员的药品专利有10年的分阶段保护期。

8.4.7 服务

在服务方面，美国未能为其银行和保险公司打开通向日本、韩国和许多发展中成员的有效进入途径，未能使法国和欧共体放松在欧洲放映美国电影和电视节目的限制。

8.4.8 其他产业条款

在其他产业条款方面，美国和欧共体同意就进一步限制政府对民营飞机制造业的补贴、开放长途电话市场和限制欧洲补贴钢铁厂商做深入的讨论。美国也表示乐于就进一步开放日本电脑芯片市场进行谈判。

8.4.9 与贸易相联系的投资手段

在与贸易相联系的投资手段方面，该协议要求外地投资者（如汽车制造厂商）逐步购买当地原料或增加进口，其数量应与进口数量相当。

8.4.10 世界贸易组织

在世界贸易组织方面，该协议还号召以位于日内瓦的世界贸易组织取代关贸总协定的秘书处，并授权它除工业品贸易外还负责农产品和服务方面的贸易。贸易争端由2/3多数的投票或3/4多数的投票来处理，而不是根据关贸总协定的一致通过原则（这意味着有错的成员可以阻挠反对它的行动）。

据估计，到2005年乌拉圭回合结束时，乌拉圭回合协议的执行使得全球贸易增长了约20%（1/4的增长在工业品贸易上，剩下的是农产品的增长），并且使得全球的收入增加了3 490亿美元（1 640亿美元来自农产品的自由贸易，1 300亿美元来自工业品的贸易，550亿美元来自服务贸易），发展中成员受益42%（大多来自工业品的自由贸易），这个比例几乎是发展中成员在世界各国和地区GDP中所占比重的两倍。

1996年和1997年，世界贸易组织达成了关于放开通信、金融和信息技术贸易的多边协议（这些协议在乌拉圭回合中未能达成）。随着时间的推移，这些协议将比整个乌拉圭回合条款在贸易额上提供更大的收益。1999年，欧盟和墨西哥达成了一项自由贸易协议（2000年7月生效），规定2007年以前取消所有双边贸易关税。2001年12月，中国被接纳为世界贸易组织第144个成员，亚美尼亚、马其顿共和国、柬埔寨和尼泊尔在2003年加入了WTO，至此成员增加到148个。

2002年8月，美国国会批准了总统的贸易促进权，即原先的快车道，它规定大范围的贸易协议谈判不必再通过修正案，只需最后经国会投票决定批准还是拒绝。这一法案的目的是向外国政府保证，国会对它们和美国政府谈判的任何协议将迅速做出反应。该法案还要求总统在谈判中考虑环境保护、劳工权利和反倾销法，每年向失业工人提供12亿美元的健康保险和其他福利，农民和农场主也包括在内。2002年12月，美国和智利达成一项自由贸易协议；2003年，美国和新加坡达成一项自由贸易协议；2004年2月和3月，美国与澳大利亚、摩洛哥和六个中美洲国家协商了自由贸易协议（哥斯达黎加、萨尔瓦多共和国、危地马拉、洪都拉斯、尼加拉瓜和多米尼克）。然而，这些协议都需要国会批准。

8.5 突出的贸易问题与多哈回合

尽管乌拉圭回合的成功带来了巨大的利益，但许多严重的贸易问题依然存在。

第一个问题就是美国和欧盟之间在关税减让方面、在欧盟允许对超大型飞机空客的发展上提供的补贴方面、在欧盟对美国的激素牛肉和转基因（生物科技）食品实行的禁令方面存在的严重贸易争端。2003年秋天，美国也严厉地限制中国针织布料和其他纺织品快速增长的出口。2001年3月，美国也对来自欧盟、日本和其他国家的钢铁产品征收30%的进口关税，但是因为欧盟威胁拟通过WTO采取严厉的制裁报复才得以取消。

第二个问题是农产品的补贴和关税仍然非常高；反倾销措施和对国家安全的保护仍可能发生并常常滥用，因此仍然存在爆发潜在的激烈贸易争端的可能。

第三个问题是存在世界分裂成三大贸易板块的趋势，即欧盟、北美自由贸易区和（尚未定义的）亚洲板块。虽然这些贸易板块被认为可能是通向自由贸易体系的一步，但它们也可能导致更多的双边贸易、保护主义和板块间的贸易冲突，成为通向自由贸易道路的绊脚石。

第四个问题是一些发达国家（如美国和法国）呼吁建立劳工和环境标准。这些标准是为了保障发达国家和发展中国家有相同的工作条件，以免后者的社会倾销（发展中成员通过否认工人的基本权利、恰当的工资及工作条件来进行不正当竞争）。但建立劳工和环境标准的运动很容易被贸易保护力量所主导。环境标准的情形也是这样。此外，它们还需要比乌拉圭回合更充分地处理与贸易相关的竞争政策（如补贴和管制）以及与贸易相关的投资措施（TRIMs）。

1999年12月在西雅图召开的世贸组织贸易会议上，人们试图策划举办一个“千年回合”的贸易谈判。但是该策划没有成功，因为：①发展中成员坚决反对将劳工和环境标准列入新的回合的议程；②欧盟和日本反对美国将农产品贸易的完全自由化列入议程的意向；③美国反对讨论欧盟所希望的竞争和投资政策。所有这些最终面对的是反全球化运动组织发起的大规模游行，它们责怪全球化带来了全球性的人类和环境问题，并认为全球化将人类和环境的福利牺牲给了跨国公司。

2001年11月，在卡塔尔的多哈最终成功地开始了多哈回合，原本预计在2004年年底结束。多哈回合的议程包括：农产品、工业产品和服务的生产与贸易的进一步自由化；进一步加强反倾销措施和国家安全的规定，以及投资和竞争的政策。特别是，发展中成员不愿意做出让步，因为他们觉得乌拉圭回合对它们承诺的许多条件都没有兑现。发展中成员坚持要让多哈回合成为真正的“发展回合”。然而，2003年9月，在墨西哥的坎昆召开的部长会议，许多成员都不同意将多哈回合纳入议程，主要因为：就发达成员农业补贴方面而言，发展中成员和发达成员之间出现了不一致。2006年7月，经过5年时间的谈判，多哈回合几乎以失败而告终。直到2011年年初，所有试图结束多哈回合的努力也均告失败。

9 Economic Integration

9.1 Definition of Economic Integration

The theory of economic integration refers to the commercial policy of discriminatively reducing or eliminating trade barriers (e. g. restrictions on international trade, payments, and factor mobility) only among the nations joining together. This results in the uniting of two or more economies in a regional trading agreement.

9.2 Forms of Economic Integration

9.2.1 Preferential trade arrangements

Preferential trade arrangements provide lower barrier on trade among participating members than on trade with nonmembers. This is the loosest form of economic integration. The best example of a preferential trade arrangement is the *British Commonwealth Preference Scheme*, established in 1932 by the United Kingdom with its members and some former members of the British Empire.

9.2.2 Free trade area

A free trade area is the form of economic integration wherein all barriers are removed on trade among members, but each member retains its own barriers to trade with nonmembers. The best examples are the *European Free Trade Association* (EFTA), formed by the United Kingdom, Austria, Denmark, Norway, Portugal, Sweden, and Switzerland in 1960s; the *North American Free Trade Agreement* (NAFTA), formed by the United States, Canada, and Mexico in 1993; and the *Southern Common Market* (*Mercosur*) formed by Argentina, Brazil, Paraguay, and Uruguay in 1991.

9.2.3 Customs union

A customs union allows no tariffs or other barriers on trade among members (as in a free trade area). In addition it coordinates trade policies (such as the setting of common tariff rates) towards nonmembers. The most famous example is the *European Union* (EU), or *European Common Market*, formed in 1957 by West Germany, France, Italy, Belgium, the Netherlands and Luxembourg.

9.2.4 Common market

A common market goes one step further than a customs union by also allowing the free movement of labor and capital among member nations. The EU achieved the status of a common market in 1993.

9.2.5 Economic union

An economic union goes another step further by harmonizing or even unifying the monetary and fiscal policies of member states. This is the highest form of economic integration. An example is *Benelux*, the economic union of Belgium, the Netherlands, and Luxembourg, formed after World War II (now part of the EU). An example of a complete economic and monetary union is the United States.

A recent development that can be analyzed with the same concepts used to analyze customs unions is **duty-free zones** or **free economic zones**. These are areas set up to attract foreign investments by allowing the importation of raw materials and intermediate products duty free.

9.3 The Effects in Customs Unions

9.3.1 Static effects in customs unions

In a customs union, the static effects include: Trade creation and trade diversion.

The static effects of lowering tariff barriers among members of a trade bloc are illustrated in the following example. Assume a world composed of three countries: Luxembourg, Germany and the United States. Consider Luxembourg and Germany decide to form a customs union, and the United States is a nonmember. The decision to form a customs union requires that Luxembourg and Germany abolish all tariff restrictions between themselves while maintaining a common tariff policy against the United States.

Referring to Figure 9.1, assume the supply and demand curves of Luxembourg to be S_L

and D_L. Also assume that the market of Luxembourg is way smaller than that of Germany and the United States. This assumption means Luxembourg cannot influence foreign prices so that the foreign supply curve of grains is perfectly elastic. Let Germany's supply price be \$3.25 per bushel and that of the United States, \$3 per bushel. The United States is assumed to be the more efficient supplier (Figure 9.1).

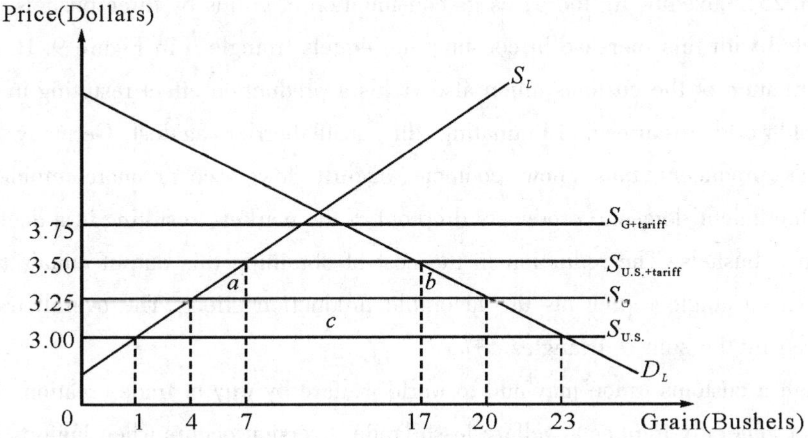

Note: The formation of a customs union leads to a welfare increasing trade creation effect and a welfare decreasing trade diversion effect. The overall effect of the customs union on the welfare of its members, as well as on the world as a whole, depends on the relative strength of these two opposing forces.

Figure 9.1 Static Welfare Effects of a Customs Union

Before the formation of the customs union, Luxembourg finds that under conditions of free trade, it purchases all of its import grains from the United States. Germany does not participate in the market because its supply price exceeds that of the United States. In free-trade equilibrium, Luxembourg's consumption equals 23 bushels, among which production equals 1 bushel, and imports equal 22 bushels. If Luxembourg levies a tariff of \$0.50 cents on each bushel imported from the United States (or Germany), then imports will fall from 22 bushels to 10 bushels.

Suppose as part of economic integration, Luxembourg and Germany form a customs union. Luxembourg's import tariff against Germany is dropped, but maintained the same on imports from the nonmember United States. By removing the tariff, Germany now becomes the low price supplier. Luxembourg purchases all of its imports, totaling 16 bushels, from Germany at \$3.25 per bushel while importing nothing from the United States.

The movement toward freer trade under a customs union affects world welfare in two opposing ways: a welfare increasing **trade creation effect** and a welfare reducing **trade diversion effect**. The overall consequence of a customs union on the welfare of its members, as well as on the world as a whole, depends on the relative strengths of these two opposing forces.

Trade creation occurs when a domestic production of one customs union member is replaced by another member's lower cost imports. The welfare of the member countries is increased by trade creation because it leads to increased production specialization according to the principle of comparative advantage. The trade creation effect consists of a *consumption effect* and a *production effect*.

Before the formation of the customs union and under its own tariff umbrella, Luxembourg imports grains from the United States at a price of \$3.50 per bushel. Luxembourg's entry into the customs union results in its dropping all tariffs against Germany. Facing a lower import price of \$3.25, Luxembourg increases its consumption of grains by three bushels. The welfare gain associated with this increase in consumption equals triangle b in Figure 9.1.

The formation of the customs union also yields a production effect resulting in a more efficient use of world resources. Eliminating the tariff barrier against Germany means that Luxembourg's producers must now compete against lower cost, more efficient German producers. Inefficient domestic producers drop out of the market, resulting in a decline in home output of three bushels. The reduction in the cost of obtaining this output equals triangle a in the figure. This triangle represents the favorable production effect. The overall trade creation effect is given by the sum of triangles $a+b$.

Although a customs union may add to world welfare by way of trade creation, its trade diversion effect generally implies a welfare loss. Trade diversion occurs when imports from a low-cost supplier outside the union are replaced by purchases from a higher cost supplier within the union. This diversion suggests that world production is reorganized less efficiently. In Figure 9.1, the total volume of trade increases under the customs union, but part of this trade (ten bushels) has been diverted from a low-cost supplier, the United States, to a high-cost supplier, Germany. The increase in the cost of obtaining these ten bushels of imported grains equals area c. This is the welfare loss to Luxembourg, as well as to the world as a whole. Out static analysis concludes that the formation of a customs union will increase the welfare of its members, as well as the rest of the world, if the positive trade creation effect more than offsets the negative trade diversion effect. Referring to the figure, this occurs if $a+b$ is greater than c.

This analysis illustrates that the success of a customs union depends on the factors contributing to trade creation and diversion. Several factors that bear on the relative size of these effects can be identified. One factor is the types of nations that tend to benefit from a customs union. Nations whose pre-union economies are quite competitive are likely to benefit from trade creation because the formation of the union offers greater opportunity for specialization in production. Also, the larger the size and the greater the number of nations in the union, the greater the gains are likely to be, because there is a greater possibility that the world's low-cost producers will be union members. In the extreme case in which the union consists of the entire world, there exists only trade creation, not trade diversion. In addition, the scope for trade diversion is smaller when the customs union's common external tariff is lower rather than higher. Because a lower tariff allows greater trade to take place member and nonmember nations, there will be less replacement of cheaper imports from nonmember nations by relatively high-cost imports from partner nations.

9.3.2 Dynamic benefits from customs unions

The nations forming a customs union are likely to receive several important *dynamic* benefits.

The greatest dynamic benefit from the formation of a customs union is the increased competition that is likely to result in. That is, in the absence of a customs union, producers, especially monopolies and oligopolists, are likely to grow sluggish and complacent behind trade barriers. But when a customs union is formed and trade barriers among member nations are eliminated, producers in each nation must become more efficient to meet the competition of other producers within the union, merge, or go out of business. All of these efforts will cut costs of production to the benefit of consumers. A customs union must, however, be careful (by passing and enforcing antitrust legislation) that larger and more efficient firms will no restrict competition.

A second possible dynamic benefit from the formation of a customs union is economies of large-scale production. However, it must be pointed out that even a small nation that is not a member of any customs union can overcome the smallness of its domestic market and achieve substantial economies of scale in production by exporting to the rest of the world. For example, it was found that plants in many major industries in such relatively small nations as Belgium and The Netherlands were already of comparable size to U.S. plants before they joined the EU and thus already enjoyed substantial economies of scale by producing for the domestic market and for export. Nevertheless, significant additional economic benefits were achieved after the formation of the EU by reducing the range of differentiated products manufactured in each plant and increasing production runs.

Another possible benefit is the stimulus to investment to take advantage of the enlarged market and to meet the increased competition. The formation of a customs union is also likely to spur outsiders to set up production facilities within the customs union to avoid the (discriminatory) trade barriers imposed on nonunion products. These are the so-called **tariff factories**. The massive investments that U.S. firms made in Europe in 1955 and again in 1986 can be explained by their desire of not being excluded from this rapidly growing market.

Finally, in a customs union that is also a common market. The free communitywide movement of labor and capital is likely to result in better utilization of the economic resources of the entire community.

9.4 Examples of Economic Integration

9.4.1 The European Union

The European Union (EU), once called the European Common Market, was founded by the Treaty of Rome, signed in March 1957 by West Germany, France, Italy, Belgium, the Netherlands, and Luxembourg, and came into being on January 1, 1958. The common external tariff was set at the average of the 1957 tariffs of the six nations. Free trade in industrial goods within the EU and a common price for agricultural products were achieved in 1968, and restrictions on the free movement of labor and capital were reduced by 1970. Membership increased to 15 after the United Kingdom, Denmark, and Ireland joined in 1973, Greece in 1981, Spain and Portugal in 1986, and Austria, Finland, and Sweden in 1995. On January 1, 1993, the EU removed all remaining restriction on the free flow of goods, services and resources (including labor) among its members, thus becoming a single unified market. The expanded Union represents the largest trading bloc in the world.

The formation of the EU significantly expanded trade in industrial goods with nonmembers. This was due to ① the very rapid growth of the EU, which increased its demand for imports of industrial products from outside the union, and ② the reduction to very low levels of the average tariff on imports of industrial products as a result of the Kennedy and Tokyo Rounds (initiated by the United States, which feared trade diversion). Besides, the formation of the EU resulted in trade diversion in agricultural commodities, particularly in temperate products, such as grains from the United States.

The development of a common agricultural policy (CAP) was particularly troublesome for the EU. The final outcome sacrificed consumers' interests to those of EU farmers in general, and French farmers in particular, by setting relatively high farm prices. The EU imposes tariffs (called variable import levies) so as always to make the price of imported agricultural products equal to the high common agricultural prices set by EU. The high farm support price level has also led to huge agricultural surpluses within the EU, high storage costs and reduced exports, and this policy was responsible for some of the sharpest trade disputes between Ell and the United States at the Uruguay Round.

At the Lomé Convention in 1975, the EU eliminated most trade barriers on imports from 46 developing nations in Africa, the Caribbean, and the Pacific region that were former colonies of EU countries. The treaty was renewed every five years, and the number of associate states (AS) rose to 71. Earlier in 1971, the EU had granted generalized tariff preferences to imports of manufactured and semi - manufactured products from developing nations. But textiles, steel, consumer electronics, shoes and many other products of great importance to developing nations were excluded. Preferences were extended to trade in tropical products in the Tokyo Round in 1979. However, since these preferences fell short of the complete elimination of trade barriers granted to former colonies, a bitter controversy arose because of the alleged trade diversion. Quotas and tariffs on developing countries' exports were gradually reduced as a result of the Uruguay Round completed in 1994. In February 2000, Lomé IV expired and was replaced by a new agreement, the Cotonou Agreement, signed in Cotonou, Benin, in June 2000. The new agreement had the same general purpose as the Lomé Convention. The EU replaced the Cotonou Agreement in 2008 with "new partnership agreements (NPAs) based on reciprocity" with the 79 countries involved, broken into six regional groups.

In fact, the dynamic benefits resulting from the formation of the EU were estimated to be much larger than the static welfare benefits. Perhaps the greatest benefit has been political, resulting in unifying into a single economic community. Nations such as Germany and France, that were once bitter enemies is a case in point. For the European Union, the road to full economic union is pawed with thorns, because a whole group of totally divided countries have to agree on a resolution. The United States has been of two minds on European unity, supportive yet wary of losing influence. In 1986, the EU amended the *Treaty of Rome* with the Single European Act, which provided for the removal of all remaining barriers to the free flow of goods, services and resources among members. This was actually achieved with the *EU* 1992 *Program*, which turned the EU into a single unified market at the beginning of 1993. This led to the pouring in of foreign direct investments into the EU out of fear of increased protectionism against outsiders.

9.4.2 The North America Free Trade Area

The North America Free Trade Area went from impossibility to reality in a few years during the late 1980s and early 1990s. The first step was the Canada-U.S. Free Trade Area (CUSFTA). The second step was bringing Mexico into the picture. Starting from 1985, the Mexican government had become increasingly determined to break down its own barriers to a freer, more privatized, more efficient Mexican economy. In 1990, the U.S. government and the Mexican government began negotiations on a trade agreement, and Canada joined the talks in 1991. The agreement was completed in 1992, and NAFTA, which replaced CUSFTA, came into existence on January 1, 1994.

As for the effects of NAFTA, there is broad agreement that NAFTA led to a substantial increase in total trade among the three members, especially in the years up to the early 2000s. The standard view is that trade creation was larger than trade diversion. In this standard view, all three NAFTA countries have gained benefits from NAFTA's trade expansion, with a gain in well-being to Mexico estimated at close to 2 percent of its GDP, a gain to Canada of close to 1 percent of its GDP, and a gain to the United States of perhaps 0.1 percent of its (very large) GDP.

NAFTA may also bring gains from increased competition in the larger area-wide market and from the increased ability for firms to achieve scale economies in this larger market. Studies of the effects on Canadian manufacturing industries during the first 10 years of free trade with the United States do show some large positive effects. Increased competition led to the demise of high-cost Canadian factories and the opening of low-cost ones. Average factory sizes did not become much bigger, which seems to question the role of increased scale economies. But there is evidence that fewer different products are being produced in these plants, so the scale economies are probably occurring through longer production runs of the smaller number of products. As a result of all this, productivity in Canadian manufacturing increased, with about 14 percent more than it would have without the free-trade area.

NAFTA has created benefits for Mexico because it has made Mexico a more attractive place for business investments by foreign firms. Firms within NAFTA look more favorably on locating production in Mexico to serve the entire NAFTA market (specially to serve the large U. S. market). The total amount invested by foreign businesses in their Mexican operations grew from $41 billion in 1993 to $403 billion in 2012. It is estimated that the investments would have been 40 percent lower without NAFTA.

As trade within NAFTA has grown, there has not been the massive shift of jobs toward Mexico that opponents in the United States predicted would result from NAFTA. While U.S. imports from Mexico grew faster than U.S. exports to Mexico during 1993-2013, U.S. exports to Mexico still grew faster than U.S. exports to other countries. Any effects from NAFTA on the number of jobs in the United States are very small compared to the typical rates of overall job loss and job creation in the U.S. economy.

The large increases in NAFTA trade do have effects on workers in the United States, but they are the subtler effects caused by shifting demands for different types of workers. Freer trade absolutely hurts import-competing groups. NAFTA allows Mexico to better exploit its comparative advantage based on less-skilled labor in such products as apparel, field crops (e.g., tomatoes), and furniture and in such activities as product assembly. On the other hand, Mexico buys more U.S. financial services, chemicals, plastics, and high-tech equipment. The expansion of U.S. trade with Mexico spurred by NAFTA is pushing in the same direction as U. S. trade expansion with other developing countries, putting some downward pressure on the wages of less-skilled workers in the United States and increasing the incomes of more-skilled U. S. workers. In Mexico, too, there have been income losses, for instance, to small farmer growing corn (maize) who cannot readily shift to more lucrative crops. And there are income gains to others. For instance, in agriculture, NAFTA has facilitated large increases in Mexican exports of fruits and vegetables to the United States.

One other seemingly technical feature of NAFTA has received a surprising amount of attention. Because each member of a free-trade area maintains its own barriers against imports from outside the area, a member country must still police its borders, to tax or prohibit imports that might otherwise avoid its higher external barrier by entering through a lower-barrier partner country. Its customs official must enforce rules of origin that determine which products have been produced within the free-trade area, so that they are treaded freely within the area, and which products have not been produced with the area. These rules guard against a firm's ruse of doing minimal processing within the area and then claiming that the outside product is locally produced.

9.4.3 Asia-Pacific Economic Cooperation

APEC is an organization promoting economic development, economic cooperation, trade and investment liberalization in the Asia-Pacific region. Its output value accounts for more than

50% of the world's gross national product, import and export volume is 41% of the total trade volume worldwide, and it has over 45% of the global population.

APEC members include Asian countries and regions as well as countries in the Americas. They also include sub-regional economic integration organizations such as North American Free Trade Area, Association of South East Asian Nations and Australia-New Zealand Free Trade Zone.

9.4.3.1 The history of APEC

APEC was formally established in Canberra, Australia in November 1989 and a total of 12 members in the Asia-Pacific region participated in the first ministerial conference. Its fundamental purpose is to promote economic growth and prosperity in the region. Besides, the main policy-making bodies of it are the annual informal leaders' meeting and ministerial meetings of its members, with a secretariat and a committee on trade and investment.

At the second ministerial conference in Singapore, 1990, APEC was formally recognized as an informal forum for high-level economic representatives of its members.

The establishment of the secretariat at the fourth ministerial conference in Bangkok in 1992, which explicitly adopted "open regionalism" as the organizational principle, marked a key step towards the systemization of APEC.

The Bogor Declaration issued in 1994 set the course and direction for economic cooperation in the region, which is promoting economic growth in the region by reducing tariff and non-tariff barriers.

The Osaka Action Agenda, issued in 1995, identified trade and investment liberalization and facilitation as well as economic and technological cooperation as the two pillars of economic cooperation in the region.

The 1998 APEC Agenda for Science and Technology Industry Cooperation into the 21st Century provided a blueprint for economic and technological cooperation among APEC members.

The 1999 Auckland conference explored the possibility of monetary cooperation and the establishment of a sub-regional free trade area.

With the recovery of economic and financial crisis, APEC resumed deliberations on a comprehensive response to the challenges of globalization at its eighth informal leaders' meeting in 2001.

In 2002, the Los Cabos conference formulated policies and measures on economic growth and development of the new economy.

The 2003 meeting focused on how to reduce the wealth gap between developed and developing members and promote the development of middle and small-sized enterprises.

The 2004 conference emphasized the continued deepening of APEC trade and investment liberalization.

The 2005 Busan conference stressed the importance of accelerating the negotiations on the Doha development agenda of WTO, approving the "Busan roadmap", creating a transparent and secure business environment and bridging regional gaps.

9.4.3.2 The Functioning of APEC

Compared with other regional economic blocs, APEC has two distinct characteristics. First, it is an open regional organization, open not only to each other but also to other countries and regions outside the organization. In addition, it is a voluntary cooperative organization.

In view of the great differences in economic development levels, institutions, cultures and religions among APEC members, they follow the principle of flexible and gradual progress in the integration process. However, members should stop taking any measures that may lead to the escalation of trade protectionism.

In the three decades since its establishment, APEC has made great progress in economic and trade cooperation. So far, its average tariff rate is lower than the world average level and continues to decline. Extensive consultations and information exchange among members have improved policy transparency and promoted trade and investment liberalization in new economic sectors such as e-commerce and the digital economy. The overall framework of economic and technical cooperation has been established and the organizational mechanism has been improved.

But overall, there are still many problems in the operation of APEC. As a large regional organization spanning both sides of the Pacific Ocean, its members differ greatly in economic system, level of development, political system and ideology. Moreover, it also includes a number of sub-regional organizations. The complex relationship of cooperation interests results in the fierce conflict and difficult cooperation process.

9 经济一体化

9.1 经济一体化定义

经济一体化理论指的是加入同盟的国家有区别的减少或消除贸易壁垒（如对国际贸易、支付和要素流动取消限制）的商业政策。因此，这往往会使两个或更多的经济体通过区域贸易协定的形式联合起来。

9.2 经济一体化形式

9.2.1 特惠贸易协定

特惠贸易协定是参加协定的成员国之间在进行贸易时互相提供比与非成员国进行贸易时更低的贸易壁垒。这是经济一体化最松散的形式。特惠贸易协定最好的例子是由英联邦及成员国以及一些大英帝国以前的成员国建立与 1932 年的英联邦优惠计划。

9.2.2 自由贸易区

在自由贸易区这种经济一体化形式中，各成员国之间消除了所有的贸易壁垒，但是每个成员国对非成员国保留了壁垒。最典型的例子是英国、奥地利、丹麦、挪威、葡萄牙、瑞典、瑞士于 1960 年形成的欧洲自由贸易联盟（EFTA），1993 年美国、加拿大、墨西哥之间达成的北美自由贸易协定（NAFTA），以及 1991 年由阿根廷、巴西、巴拉圭和乌拉圭组建的南美洲共同市场（Mercosur）。

9.2.3 关税同盟

关税同盟允许进行贸易的各成员国之间就像在自由贸易区内一样没有关税或其他壁垒。另外，它还对非成员国的贸易政策起协调作用（如设定共同税率）。最著名的例子是欧盟，或称“欧洲共同市场”，它是 1957 年由联邦德国、法国、意大利、比利时、荷兰和卢森堡组成的。

9.2.4 共同市场

共同市场比关税同盟更进一步，它也允许参加国之间资本和劳动力自由流动。欧盟于 1993 年年初初步实现了共同市场。

9.2.5 经济联盟

经济联盟比共同市场又进一步，它协调甚至统一成员国之间的货币和参政政策。这是经济一体化的最高级形式。例子之一就是由比利时、荷兰、卢森堡在第二次世界大战结束后形成的荷比卢经济联盟（现为欧盟的一部分）。一个完整的经济和货币联盟的例子就是美国。

近来出现的免税区或自由经济区可以使用与分析关税同盟时用到的相同概念进行分析。这些区域通过允许原材料和中间产品免税的形式来吸引国外投资。

9.3 关税同盟中的效应

9.3.1 关税同盟的静态效应

在关税同盟中，静态效应包括贸易创造和贸易转移效应。

为了说明贸易集团成员国相互降低关税壁垒所带来的静态福利效应，假设世界上只有卢森堡、德国和美国三个国家。卢森堡和德国决定成立关税同盟，而美国是非成员国。组建关税同盟要求卢森堡和德国取消他们彼此之间的所有关税限制，并对美国采取统一的关税政策。关税同盟的静态福利效应见图 9.1。

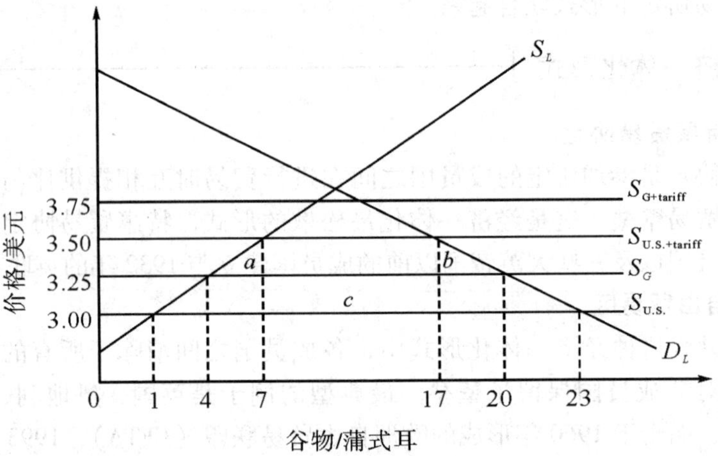

注：关税同盟的静态福利效应包括两方面，即增加福利的贸易创造效应和减少福利的贸易转移效应。两种效应的相对强弱决定了关税同盟对成员国和世界福利的总影响。

图 9.1 关税同盟的静态福利效应

如图 9.1 所示，S_L和 D_L分别代表卢森堡对谷物的供给曲线和需求曲线。假设卢森堡的市场规模远远小于德国和美国，这意味着它不能影响国外价格，因此谷物的国外供给曲线是完全弹性的。令德国的谷物供给价格为每蒲式耳 3.25 美元，美国相应的价格为每蒲式耳 3 美元。注意，这里假设美国在供给谷物方面更有效率。

在组成关税同盟之前，在自由贸易条件下，卢森堡从美国进口所需的谷物。德国没有加入这一市场，因为它的供给价格高于美国。当自由贸易达到均衡时，卢森堡的谷物消费量为 23 蒲式耳，其中的 1 蒲式耳由本国生产，其余的 22 蒲式耳来自进口。如果卢森堡对从美国（或德国）进口的每蒲式耳谷物征收 0.5 美分的关税，进口量将从 22 蒲式耳下降到 10 蒲式耳。

假设作为经济一体化的一部分，卢森堡和德国组成关税同盟。卢森堡削减了对德国征收的进口关税，而且对非成员国美国所征收的关税保持不变。关税的这种变动使德国成为有效率的供应者，此时，卢森堡以每蒲式耳 3.25 美元的价格从德国进口 16 蒲式耳谷物，而从美国的进口量则减少到 0 蒲式耳。

关税同盟内部的这种贸易自由化从两个相反的方向影响世界福利：一是增加福利的贸易创造效应；二是减少福利的贸易转移效应。两种效应的相对强弱决定了关税同盟对成员国和整个世界福利的总体影响。

当一成员国的部分国内产出被来自其他成员国的低成本进口所取代时，就发生了贸易创造效应。由于贸易创造提高了成员国之间按照比较优势理论进行专业化分工的程度，因此能够增加成员国的福利。贸易创造效应包括消费效应和生产效应两部分。

在组成关税同盟之前，在关税的保护下，卢森堡以每蒲式耳 3.50 美元的价格从美国进口谷物。加入关税同盟使得该国降低了对德国的所有关税，进口价格下跌至 3.25 美元，卢森堡的谷物消费量增加了 3 蒲式耳。在图 9.1 中，由于消费增加所增加的福利相当于三角形 b 的面积。

关税同盟能够提高世界资源的使用效率，因此还产生了生产效应。取消对德国的关税壁垒意味着卢森堡的生产者必须面临来自成本更低、效率更高的德国生产者的竞争，无效率的国内生产者将会退出市场，国内产量下降了 3 蒲式耳，降低的成本等于图中三角形 a 的面积，这是正向的生产效应。三角形 $a+b$ 的面积之和代表总的贸易创造效应。

尽管关税同盟可以通过贸易创造增加福利，但贸易转移效应却通常意味着福利的损失。当关税同盟外的低成本供应商的出口被同盟内部的高成本供应商所取代时，就发生了贸易转移效应，生产在世界范围内的这种重组是缺乏效率的。在图 9.1 中，虽然关税同盟中的贸易总量增加了，但一部分贸易（10 蒲式耳）从低成本供应商（美国）转移到了高成本供应商（德国）那里。进口这 10 蒲式耳谷物所增加的成本等于面积 c，这不仅是卢森堡的福利损失，也是整个世界的福利损失。通过静态分析，我们可以得出结论：如果正的贸易创造效应可以抵消负的贸易转移效应，那么组建关税同盟不仅会提高成员国的福利，也会使世界其他国家获益。在图形中，如果 $a+b > c$，上述情况就会发生。

这一分析说明，关税同盟的成功与否取决于决定贸易创造效应和贸易转移效应的各种因素。能够影响这两个效应相对大小的因素有很多种，其中一个是希望从关税同盟中获益的国家的类型。那些在组建同盟前经济就非常具有竞争力的国家最有可能从贸易创造中获利，因为同盟的形成使它们有更多机会从事专业化生产。同盟中的国家规模越大，国家的数目越多，世界的低成本生产国参与同盟的可能性就越高，所以获得收益的机会也越大。如果整个世界组成一个关税同盟，那么就只有贸易创造效应，没有贸易转移效应了。此外，当关税同盟调低对外的共同关税时，贸易转移的范围也将缩小，因为对外关税较低，成员国与非成员国之间的贸易量就会增大，非成员国的廉价进口商品被成本相对较高的成员国进口商品所取代的可能性就会降低。

9.3.2 关税同盟的动态效应

组成关税同盟还有可能得到一些重要的动态效应。其中，最大的动态效益是可能出现的竞争的加剧，也就是说，在没有关税同盟的条件下，生产者（特别是那些垄断者和寡头垄断者）在贸易壁垒保护下很可能变得懒惰和自满。但是当关税同盟建立且同盟国之间的贸易壁垒消除后，各国的生产者必须提高效率以对付同盟国内其他生产者的竞争、合并，避免出局。水平渐高的竞争也可能刺激新技术的发展和利用。所有这些努力都将减少生产成本而有利于消费者的福利。当然，关税同盟必须注意（靠通过并强制实行反垄断法），规模更大、效率更高的企业不会限制竞争。

建立关税同盟可能产生的第二个利益是由于市场扩大带来的规模经济。然而必须指出，甚至不属于任何一个关税同盟的小国也能通过向世界其他国家出口商品而克服国内市场的狭小以取得规模经济的产量。例如，像比利时和荷兰这样相对较小的国家，在加入欧盟之前许多主要工业部门的工厂规模已经可以与美国的规模相比，已经能通过为国内市场生产及提供出口而享有规模经济的好处。然而，在成立欧盟之后，对成员国的每个工厂来说，由于能够做到减少各工厂范围内所制造产品的差别和提高生产的运转，因而取得了巨大的经济效益。

此外，还有一个可能获得的利益是利用市场扩大的优势来刺激投资和应付越来越激烈的竞争。进一步说，关税同盟的建立有可能刺激非成员国在关税同盟的成员国内建立生产设施，以避免加强在非同盟国产品上的（歧视性）贸易壁垒。这就是所谓的"关税工厂"。美国公司于1955年后第一次以及1986年第二次在欧洲的巨额投资，就是因为不愿被这种迅速增长的市场排除在外。

最后，就关税同盟内部来说，其本身也是一个共同市场，在其范围内的劳动力和资本的自由流动，可以使经济资源得到更好地利用。

9.4 经济一体化的例子

9.4.1 欧盟

欧盟，曾被称为"欧洲共同市场"，是由联邦德国、法国、意大利、比利时、荷兰、卢森堡于1957年3月签订《罗马条约》，1958年1月1日正式成立的。它以这六国1957年的平均关税确立了共同的对外关税，1968年工业品在成员国之间实行自由贸易并达成农产品的统一价格；1970年减少了对劳动力和资本自由流动的限制。英国、丹麦、爱尔兰于1973年加入后，成员国增加到15个，希腊于1981年加入，西班牙和葡萄牙于1986年加入，奥地利、芬兰和瑞典于1995年加入。1993年1月1日，欧盟取消了所有成员国之间产品、服务和资源（包括劳动力）自由流动的限制，成为一个单一的统一市场。发展壮大后的欧盟代表世界上最大的贸易集团。

欧盟的建立有效地扩大了与非成员国的工业品贸易。这是因为：①欧盟的迅速成长增加了从联盟外国家进口工业产品的需要；②肯尼迪与东京回合（由美国因害怕贸易转移而发起）将进口工业品的平均关税降到了一个很低的水平。另外，欧盟的建立引起农产品的贸易转移，特别是温带农作物，如从美国进口的谷物。

共同农业政策（CAP）的发展对欧盟来说尤其麻烦，相对高昂的农产品价格的制定，其结果是维护了欧盟农民，特别是因法国农民的福利而牺牲了消费者的福利。欧盟征收的关税（所谓的可变进口税额）使得进口的农产品价格总是等于欧盟制定的高价。支持农业的高价格也导致欧盟内部的巨量农业剩余、高额贮藏成本和削减出口。这项农业政策是造成欧盟同美国在乌拉圭回合中最尖锐的贸易争端的主要因素之一。

在1975年的洛美会议上，欧盟取消了从非洲、加勒比海、太平洋地区的46个前殖民地发展中国家进口的大部分贸易壁垒。条约每5年重新修订一次，并把相关国家增加到71个。早在1971年，欧盟就对从发展中国家进口的制成品和半制成品给予普遍关税特惠，但是纺织品、钢铁、家用电器、鞋和其他许多对发展中国家来说意义重大的产品被排除在外。在1979年的东京回合中特惠扩展到热带产品贸易，然而这些特惠并没有完全取消前殖民者的贸易壁垒，因贸易转移一事又引起一场更为激烈的争论。作为1994年结束的乌拉圭回合的成果，对发展中国家出口的配额限制和关税在逐渐减少。2000年2月，洛美四次会议修订的条约到期，并被2000年6月在贝宁的科托努签署的科托努协议取代，新协议的基本目标与洛美会议相同。欧盟在2008年用基于互惠的新伙伴关系协定取代科托努协定。新协定涉及79个国家，被分成6个地区。

其实，因欧盟建立而产生的动态效应比静态福利效应大得多。最大的收获可能在政治方面，如曾经是敌人的德国和法国，如今却结合成了统一的经济实体。对欧盟来说，通向全面经济联盟之路铺满荆棘，因为一大群完全分离的国家必须达成一致性决议。美国在欧盟问题上有两种意向：既支持联盟但又害怕丢失影响。1986年，欧盟用单一欧洲法令修改罗马协定，取消了成员国之间所有产品、服务和资源自由流动的障碍。这最终在1992年的欧盟计划中获得成功，使得欧盟于1993年年初能够成为一个统一市场。这也使国外直接投资大量涌入，因为投资者害怕反对外部世界的保护主义重新抬头。

9.4.2 北美自由贸易区

北美自由贸易区从不可能到成为现实，仅用了从20世纪80年代末到90年代初的几年时间。第一步是加拿大—美国自由贸易区（EUSFTA），第二步是墨西哥的加入。从1985年开始，墨西哥政府不断废除贸易壁垒以实现更加自由、私有化程度更高以及更加有效的墨西哥经济。1990年，美国政府和墨西哥政府开始就贸易协定进行谈判，加拿大于1991年加入该谈判。协议于1992年达成，北美自由贸易区替代了加拿大—美国自由贸易区，于1994年1月1日正式成立。

至于北美自由贸易区带来的影响，被众人广泛认可的是一直到21世纪初，北美自由贸易区大大促进了三国间的贸易总量；贸易创造的收益大于贸易转移的损失。因此，三个国家都从北美自由贸易区不断扩大的贸易中获得收益。其中墨西哥的收益约为其GDP的2%，加拿大的收益约为其GDP的1%，美国的收益约为其GDP（数额巨大）的0.1%。

北美自由贸易区也可能通过一个更大、更为广阔的市场和厂商不断提高的生产能力实现规模经济而获益。我们对加拿大制造业在自由贸易区建立后的第一个10年所产生的影响的研究，确实显现出部分积极的影响。随着竞争越来越激烈，高成本的加拿大工厂纷纷倒闭，低成本工厂不断建立。工厂的平均规模并未发生太大变化，这似乎在质疑规模经济的作用。但是有证据表明在这些工厂中生产的产品种类变少了，所以规模经济可能发生在生产更少种类的产品的更长的生产链中。所有这些带来的结果是加拿大制造业的生产率提高，比没建立自由贸易区时提高了14个百分点。

北美自由贸易区也为墨西哥创造了收益，因为它使墨西哥成为对外商投资更具吸引力的地方。自由贸易区内的厂商更乐意在墨西哥建立生产基地，以服务整个北美自由贸易区市场（尤其是服务美国市场）。在墨西哥投资的外资量从1993年的410亿美元增加到2012年的4 030亿美元。据估计，如果没有建立北美自由贸易区，这些投资将减少40%。

随着北美自由贸易区内贸易的增加，并未出现如同美国反对者们预测的由于北美自由贸易区的成立，大量的工作机会转移至墨西哥的现象。1993—2013年，美国从墨西哥的进口增长速度大于美国向墨西哥出口的速度，且美国出口到墨西哥的增长速度快于美国出口到别国的增长速度。与美国经济中的工作岗位的损失率和创造率相比，自由贸易区的建立对美国工作机会的影响可以忽略不计。

北美自由贸易区内大量增加的贸易确实对美国工人带来了影响，但是这些影响都较为隐蔽，是由于对不同种类工人的需求变化所引起的。在这样的情况下，更自由的贸易对进口竞争产业是有绝对伤害的。北美自由贸易区鼓励墨西哥在低技能劳动如服装生产、农作物（如西红柿）种植、家具和产品组装方面更好地利用它的比较优势。此外，墨西哥购买了更多的美国金融服务、化学品、塑料和高科技设备。这种北美自由贸易区推动的美国与墨西哥之间贸易的扩张，与美国和其他发展中国家的贸易扩张方向相同，都会促使美国的低技能工人收入下降，而增加高技术工人的收入。同样，在墨西哥也存在收入损失，如对于玉米种植的小农场主来说，他们还不能立刻转向种植更有利可图的作物。同时，对其他群体来说，自由贸易区的建立会给他们带来收入的增加。例如，在农业方面，北美自由贸易区促进了墨西哥向美国的水果和蔬菜出口的大量增加。

北美自由贸易区的另外一个特征也意想不到地引起了大量关注。由于自由贸易区的每个成员国都保留了对区外进口产品的贸易壁垒，成员国还必须在其边境布置警力，以应对那些试图绕道低税成员国以规避高税收国的进口商品征税或者禁止进口。它们的海关官员必须执行原产地原则。这个规则可确定哪些产品是在自由贸易区内生产的，可在自由贸易区内自由流通；同时也能确定哪些产品不是在区内生产的。这个规则可以制约外国公司通过只在区内进行少量的加工而声称产品在本地生产的行为。

9.4.3 亚太经济合作组织

亚太经济合作组织是促进亚太地区经济发展、经济合作、贸易和投资自由化的组织，其产值占世界国民生产总值（GNP）的50%以上，进出口总额占世界贸易总额的41%，人口占世界人口总数的45%以上。

亚太经济合作组织成员中有亚洲国家和地区，也有美洲国家，还包括次级的区域经济一体化组织，如北美自由贸易区、东南亚联盟和澳新自由贸易区。

9.4.3.1 亚太经济合作组织的发展历程

亚太经济合作组织于1989年11月在澳大利亚堪培拉正式宣布成立。亚太地区共12个国家和地区参加了第一届部长级会议。它的根本目的是促进亚太地区的经济增长和繁荣，亚太经济合作组织的主要决策机构是每年一次的各成员领导人非正式会议和部长级会议，下设秘书处、贸易投资委员会等。

1990年第二届新加坡部长级会议正式承认亚太经济合作组织是亚太地区各成员经济高层代表的非正式论坛。

1992年第四届曼谷部长级会议明确把“开放的地区主义”作为组织原则，成立秘书处，标志着亚太经济合作组织向组织化迈出了关键的一步。

1994年发表的《茂物宣言》确定了亚太地区经济合作的道路和方向。其通过削减关税和非关税壁垒，促进亚太地区的经济增长。

1995年发表的《大阪宣言》将贸易投资自由化和便利化与加强经济技术合作作为亚太经济合作的两大支柱。

1998 年会议发表的《走向 21 世纪的亚太经合组织科技产业合作议程》为各成员之间的经济技术合作规划了蓝图。

1999 年奥克兰会议探讨了货币合作及建立次区域自由贸易区的可能性。

随着各国经济逐渐从金融危机的影响中恢复过来，在 2001 年的第八次领导人非正式会议上，亚太经济合作组织重新开始商议全面应对全球化挑战的问题。

2002 年洛斯卡沃斯会议就经济增长、发展新经济等制定了政策措施。

2003 年的会议重点就如何减小发达成员和发展中成员之间的贫富差距，推动中小企业发展等方面达成了协议。

2004 年的会议强调继续深化亚太经济合作组织贸易和投资的自由化。

2005 年的釜山会议强调加快事业贸易组织多哈发展议程谈判，批准“釜山路线图”，营造透明、安全的商业环境，弥合区域鸿沟，缩小差距。

9.4.3.2　亚太经济合作组织的运行

与其他区域经济集团相比，亚太经济合作组织有两个明显的特点。首先，它是一个开放的区域型组织，不仅在内部成员间相互开放，对区域外的其他国家与地区也同样开放。其次，它是一个自愿合作组织。

鉴于亚太经济合作组织成员间经济发展水平、制度、文化、宗教等方面的差异性较大，在一体化进程中遵循着灵活渐进的原则。但各成员要停止采取一切可能导致贸易保护主义升级的措施。

在成立的几十年内，亚太经济合作组织在经济贸易领域合作方面取得了不少进展，到目前为止，它的平均关税率小于世界平均水平，并在持续下降。成员间进行了广泛的协商和信息交流，提高了政策透明度，推动了电子商务、数字经济等新经济领域的贸易和投资自由化。经济技术合作总体框架得以确立，组织机制也不断完善。

但总体而言，亚太经济合作组织的运行还存在着较多问题。作为一个横跨太平洋两岸的大区域组织，其成员在经济制度、发展水平、政治制度和意识形态方面都存在着很大的差异，而且内部又包括多个次区域组织，合作主题利益关系错综复杂，决定了经济合作过程中激烈的利益冲突和艰难的合作进程。

10

Internatioanl Trade and Economic Growth

With the exception of a handful of nations in North America, Western Europe, Japan, Australia, and New Zealand, most nations of the world are classified as less developed or, to put positively, as developing countries. In relation to developed (or more developed) countries, the average developing country is characterized by a low (and sometimes extremely low) average real per capital income, a relatively high proportion of the labor force in agriculture or other primary activities, such as mineral extraction, a low life expectancy, a high rate of illiteracy, and a high rate of population growth. There is, however, no sharp dichotomy between developed and developing nations but a fairly continuous spectrum from the very rich to the very poor.

In the past, the economic relationship between developed and developing nations were characterized by developing nations exporting primarily food and raw materials in exchange for manufactured goods from developed nations. This is still the case for the poorest developing nations, but not for the more advanced developing nations. In 1980, manufactured products were only 25 percent of developing country exports, but by 2003 that figure exceeded 80 percent.

Although the level and rate of economic development depend primarily on internal conditions in developing nations, most economists today believe that international trade can contribute significantly to the development process. This was not always the case. Until the 1980s, a sizable and influential minority of economists strongly believed that international trade and the functioning of the present international economic system hindered rather than facilitated development through secularly declining terms of trade and widely fluctuating export earnings of the developing nations. These economists contended that standard international trade theory based on comparative advantage was completely irrelevant for developing nations and the development process. Therefore, they advocated industrialization through import substitution (i.e., the domestic production of manufactured goods previously imported) and generally placing less reliance on international trade for development. They also advocated reforms of the present international economic system to make it more responsive to the special needs of developing countries.

10.1 Growth and Development Over Time

Over the time, as the scale of labour (L) increases and the accumulation of capital (investment), including human capital (K) and technological progress (T), the international community evolves. An increase in a country's labour and capital endowments and/or technological advances can cause the country's production possibilities curve to shift outward. The shape and magnitude of the movement depend on the growth ratio of L, K and T.

We examine the growth of a country that produces two kinds of commodities (commodity X is labor-intensive and commodity Y is capital-intensive) under conditions of constant technicalconditions and constant economies of scale. When the growth ratio of K and L is the same, the production possibility curve will move outward in both directions according to the growth ratio of the two elements at the same time. As a result, the slopes of the new and old curves (before and after factor growth) are equal. The similarities of the two lines are cut by the ray from the origin. Here is the case for balanced growth (Balanced growth).

The volume of both X and Y goods will increase if it is only the increase of labor force, because labor is invested in the production process of two commodities. Nevertheless, the increase in commodities X (labour-intensive goods) will be faster than the increase in commodities Y (capital-intensive goods). The opposite is true when only this element grows. If labor and capital increase at different rates, the production possibility curve of outward migration can be similarly determined. the same results for technological progress. The following chart shows that the increase in different types of elements is a national development (Figure 10.1).

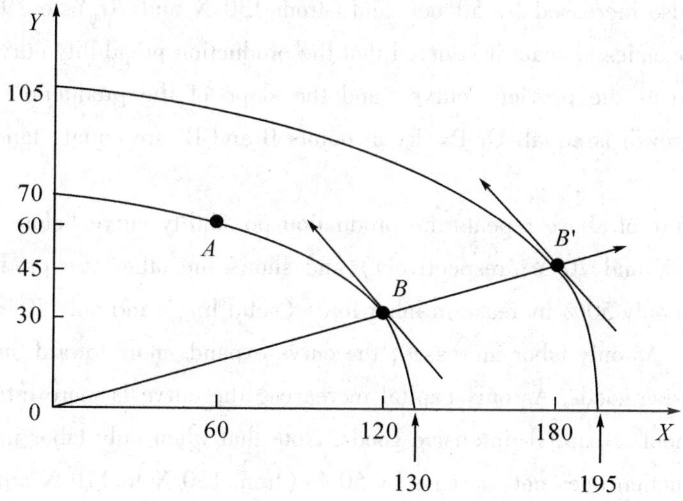

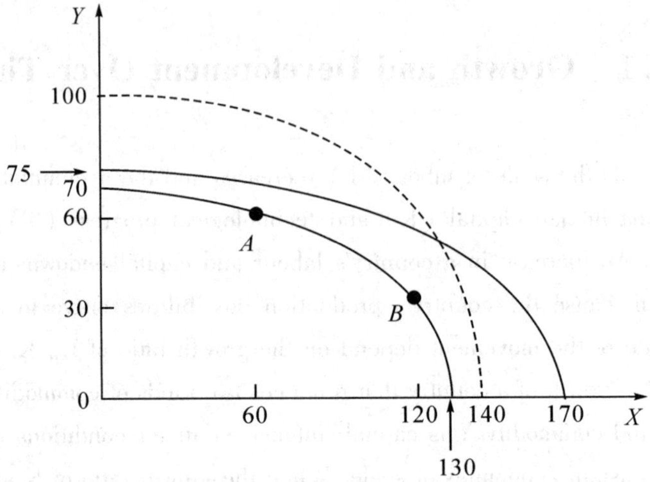

Figure 10. 1 **Growth of labour and capital over time**

The left figure shows a balanced growth of 50% for both labor (L) and capital (K) under conditions of constant returns of scale and technology. both production possibility curves have the same shape and slope (Px/Py) for any ray emitted from the origin. The right picture shows a L increase of only 50 per cent or a K increase of only 50 per cent. Only when L grew by 50 per cent, output of commodities X (labour-intensive products) grew at a rate higher than that of commodity Y (but below 50 per cent). Similarly, when only K increases by 50%, the growth rate of commodity Y output is higher than that of commodity X, but less than 50% (see production possibility curve indicated by dashed line).

In the figure above, the graph on the left assumes a 50 percent increase in the balanced growth of both labour and capital elements of country 1 (see figure 3. 1). Maximum output for each commodity also increased by 50 per cent, from 130 X and 70 Y to 195 X and 105 Y. With constant economies of scale it is noted that the production possibility curve after expansion is the same shape as the previous curve, and the slope of the production possibility curve before and after growth is equal. Or Px/Py at points B and B′ are equal, tangent by rays from the origin.

The right figure of above repeats the production possibility curve before country 1 growth (intercept is 130 X and 70 Y, respectively) and shows the other two production possibility curves, which are only 50% increase in labor force (solid line) and only 50% increase in capital (dashedline). As only labor increases, the curve expands more toward the X axis of measuring labor-intensive goods. As only capital increases, the curve is more intended to measure the Y axis movement of capital-intensive goods. Note that when only labor increases by 50%, X maximum production does not increase by 50% (from 130 X to 170 X only). For X to increase by 50 per cent, both labour and capital must be increased by 50 per cent. Similarly, when capital alone increases by 50%, Y maximum production increases by less than 50% (from 70 Y to 100 Y).

When labor and capital increase at the same rate, if the scale reward is unchanged, and the production technology of both commodities is unchanged, then the rate of return of production efficiency and then labor and capital remains unchanged before and after the growth. If the sequential rate (i.e. the ratio dependent on the total population) is also constant, the real per capita income and standard of living of a country remain the same. If only labor grows (or labor grows faster than capital), the capital/labour ratio and the productivity of labor, the rate of return on labor, the real income per capital will all decline. In turn, excessive capital growth (or capital growth faster than labor) will increase the capital/labour ratio, productivity of labor, returns and average income. Different types of technological progress will have the same impact.

10.2 Trade Theory and Economic Development

According to the traditional trade theory, if countries specialize in the production of their own goods with comparative advantages, the global spread will increase and trade will benefit all countries. According to the current distribution of factor endowments and technologies between developed and developing countries, developing countries should continue to specialize in the production and export of raw materials, fuels, minerals and simple labour-intensive food-grade commodities in exchange for more complex manufactured goods in developed countries, according to the theory of comparative advantage.

While this may maximize benefits in the short term, developing countries believe that this specialized mode of production and trade reduces them to a position of mere subordination to developed countries and leaves them short of maximizing the dynamic benefits and benefits of industry in the long term. This dynamic benefit derived from industrial production (distinguished from static benefits arising from comparative advantage) refers to a more trained workforce, more innovation, higher and stable prices for export products, and higher income levels for the people. Developing countries are accompanied only by poverty, underdevelopment and subordination. Let us look at the reality and confirm this conviction that all developed countries are mainly industrialized, while most developing countries are mainly engaged in agriculture or mining, or in the manufacture of simple products.

Traditional trade theory is thus attacked because it is static and independent of the development process. According to this view, traditional trade theory focuses only on regulating existing conditions, while development requires that existing conditions must be changed. In short, it is believed that traditional trade theory can only maximize welfare at a certain point in a period or in a short period of time, but it cannot be guaranteed in the long term or always.

These are indeed serious accusations, and if they are true, it is true that traditional trade decoupled from economic development. However, as explained in the previous section, traditional trade theory can be expanded by introducing long-term changes in factor supply and technology. This means that the formulation of a country's development model is not a thing once and for all, but must change over time and conditions. For example, as a developing country accumulates capital and advances in technology, its comparative advantage shifts from primary and simple manufactures to more complex manufactures and services. To some extent, Brazil, South Korea, Mexico and a number of other developing countries have undergone this transformation. Traditional trade doctrines therefore remain relevant for developing countries and the development process.

It must be noted, however, that today's international trade can no longer be an "engine of growth" or the most important force driving economic development, although it was once the engine of growth in the neo-colonial areas of the nineteenth century (United States, Canada, Australia, New Zealand, Argentina, Uruguay and South Africa). The reason is that demand for food, raw materials and simple manufactured goods has slowed considerably today compared to the 19th century, and that many developing countries today do not have much natural resources per capita (except oil-exporting countries) compared the countries of the neo-colonial regions a century ago. However, international trade remains a necessary condition for development. No one has forced China to open its doors, but without such openness, it will not have access to capital and technology, nor to a market that has allowed it to grow rapidly over the past decade.

10.3 Immiserizing Growth

If a country's growth leads to more and more exports, while the terms of trade deteriorate a lot, the country's welfare is likely to decline. This is what the trade economist Jagdish (Jagdish Bhagwati) calls poverty growth (immisering growth), and he first discussed this possibility. We will illustrate the growth of poverty through the figure below (Figure 10.2).

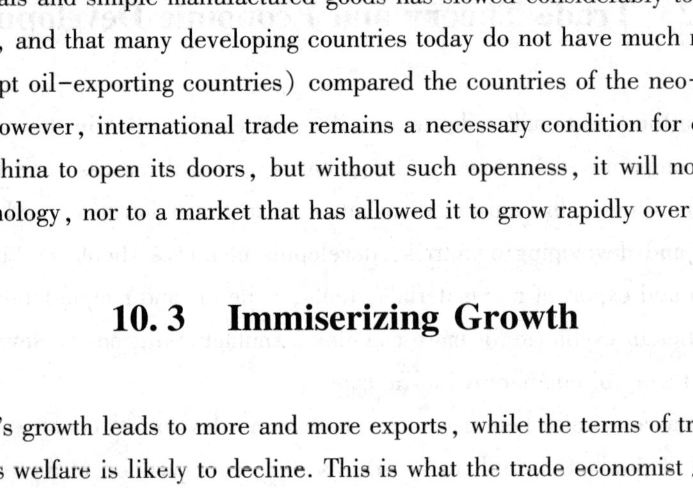

Figure 10.2 **Immiserizing Growth**

The graph (growth in poverty) shows that if country 1 increases the supply of labor by 50%, as in the right graph (growth of labor and capital over time), its production possibility curve moves more outward on the horizontal axis of the measurement X (labour-intensive goods) than on the vertical axis of the measurement Y (capital-intensive goods). The figure below shows that the increase in the number of country 1 export X resulted in terms of trade ranging from $Px/Py = Pb = 1$ to $Px/Py = Pb = Pb^* = 1/2$ and consumption points from the E point on the III of the undifferentiated curve decreases to the E^* point on the II of the undifferentiated curve. For the country, the more it grows, the poorer it becomes (that is, the country becomes poorer after it grows).

Despite the possibilities, poverty-induced growth is rare in the real world. As we have seen in the previous section, as long as enough trade volume increases, even if a country's terms of trade for commodities deteriorate, its welfare will increase.

10.4 Import Substitution Versus Export Orientation

In the 1950s and 1970s, most developing countries considered it necessary to achieve industrialization, rather than continuing the path of specialization in the production and export of products (food, raw materials, mineral products), as traditional trade theory suggests. The realization of industrialization depends on: ①faster technological progress; ②the creation of high-paying jobs free from the severe unemployment and underemployment difficulties faced by most developing countries; ③greater multiplier effects before and after the associated production processes; ④ improved terms of trade to stabilize export prices and incomes; ⑤addressing the problem that demand for manufactured goods in developing countries is growing faster than the growth of national export earnings and from the resulting imbalances. The desire of developing countries to industrialize was justified by the fact that all rich countries were militarily industrialized, while most of the poor countries were predominantly agricultural.

Having set industrialization targets, developing countries must choose between the two paths of industrialization through import substitution and export orientation. Both policies have advantages and disadvantages. Import substitution industrialization (import-substitution industrialization, ISI) has three main advantages: ①the presence of a market for industrial products, as demonstrated by imported goods, reduces the risk of industries to replace imports; ②for developing countries, protecting domestic markets against foreign competition will force developed countries to lower trade barriers and allow them to export manufactured goods more easily; ③ foreign companies are being guided to establish so-called "tariff factories" to counter tariff barriers in developing countries.

The disadvantages of this strategy are: ①domestic industries are accustomed to an environment free of foreign competition and thus lack the incentive to improve efficiency; ②import substitution leads to industrial inefficiency due to the small size of domestic markets in many developing countries, which cannot take advantage of economies of scale; ③ after primary manufactures are replaced by domestic production, as more capital-intensive and technologically advanced imports must be produced by domestic substitution, which becomes increasingly difficult and costly (due to greater protection and less efficient).

Export-oriented industrialization (export-oriented industrialization) strategies also have advantages and disadvantages. Its advantages are: ①that it overcomes the shortcomings of the small domestic market and allows developing countries to take advantage of economies of scale, which is particularly important for many poor and weak developing countries; ②that the production of industrial goods for export requires and stimulates the efficiency of the economy as a whole, which is particularly important when the output of one industry is the input of another; ③that as domestic markets grow, the expansion of manufactured exports is unlimited (and import substitution is limited).

However, there are also two serious shortcomings in this strategy: ①developing countries may find it very difficult to establish export industries because of competition from high-efficiency industries that have been built in developed countries; ②developed countries often take effective protective measures to protect their labour-intensive industries, which are those industries in which developing countries have or can quickly gain a comparative advantage.

In the 1950s and 1970s, many developing countries, especially some large countries, were keen to choose alternative import strategies to industrialize, protecting or stimulating their nascent industries through effective tariffs. The deeper degree of the product processing is, the higher the effective tariff rate. This policy was initially used to encourage relatively simple assembly of foreign components, and it is hoped that more such products and intermediate products will subsequently be produced at home (backward linkages). Strong protective measures in domestic industry have also stimulated the establishment of tariff factories in developing countries.

Industrialization through import substitution has often had only limited success or failure. Such practices often lead to: ①extremely inefficient domestic industrial production and extremely high prices for domestic consumer goods; ②excessive capital consumption but only minimal labour absorption; ③neglect of the agricultural and other primary product sectors, resulting in a decline in income from the traditional export sector, with some countries (such as Brazil) being forced to import food previously exported.

The combined conclusion is that countries with import substitution strategies (e. g. India, Pakistan, Argentina) are much worse off and have a much slower economic growth rate than those with export orientation as early as the 1950s (e. g. Hong Kong, China, South Korea, Singapore). It is also important to note, however, that import substitution may bring certain benefits to developing countries in the early stages of development (especially to large countries), and that export-oriented strategies are the absolutely necessary means of development in the future. In this way, developing countries could benefit from the rotation of both strategies depending on their level of development, particularly in larger developing countries. That is what South Korea actually does.

10.5 The Terms of Trade and Economic Development

We define a country's terms of trade as the ratio of the price of export commodities to the price of imported commodities. We can define the terms of trade (terms of trade) (n) of a commodity (commodity) or a pure exchange (net barter) in a world where many commodities exist, which is equal to the ratio of the national export price index (Px) to the import price index (Pm) multiplied by 100 (the percentage used to indicate the terms of trade). namely:

$N = (Px/Pm) \times 100$

In addition, there are other types of terms of trade, such as terms of income. (income terms of trade) (I), defined as:

$I = (Px/Pm)\ Qx$

Qx refers to the export volume index. Thus, terms of trade income refer to a country's export-based import capacity.

Since the development of developing countries depended to a large extent on the import of capital goods, the change in that indicator was important to them. Trade is beneficial to a country if its N and I increase simultaneously. Trade is bad for a country if its N and I fall at the same time. Should N fall and I increase, the country would have improved in the sense of being able to import more.

According to the economists Prebisch and Singh, the terms of trade of commodities in developing countries in 1870-1983 were deteriorating. The reason they give is that productivity gains in developed countries translate, in whole or in large part, into higher wages for workers (labour is relatively scarce and trade unions are strong), while in developing countries productivity gains are translated, in whole or in large part, into lower prices. As a result, the problem is clear that developed countries have benefited most from both worlds: their productivity gains have led to high incomes for workers, and the low prices that developing countries have brought with them as a result of productivity gains have enabled developed countries to reap the full benefits of paying for agricultural products imported from developing countries.

While Prebisch and Singh's conclusions and reasons have been strongly criticized by other economists, a 2002 study by Cashin (Cashin) and McDermott (McDermott) showed that real prices of primary commodities (raw materials, food and minerals) declined by about 1 per cent annually from 1962 to 1999. They also found evidence that price volatility has increased since the beginning of the 20th century and has become more frequent since the 1970s. these conclusions have been confirmed by D. I. Harvey et al (2010). It was therefore important to see the types of commodities exported by developing countries. For example, developing countries that mainly export raw materials will find their terms of trade slightly better, while developing countries that mainly export energy products will find their terms of trade much better. Moreover, most studies have shown that, regardless of changes in the terms of trade of commodities, the overall terms of trade income of developing countries have improved substantially. The reason is the huge increase in exports.

10　国际贸易与经济增长

除了北美、西欧、日本、澳大利亚和新西兰的少数国家外，世界上大多数国家都被归类为欠发达国家，或者准确地说是发展中国家。就发达国家（或较发达国家）而言，平均来看发展中国家的特点是人均实际收入较低（有时极低），农业或其他主要活动中的劳动力比例相对较高，如采矿、低预期寿命、高文盲率和高人口增长率。然而，发达国家和发展中国家之间没有明显的分别，而是从非常富有的国家到非常贫穷的国家之间有特别明显的连续的范围界定。

过去，发达国家和发展中国家之间的经济关系的特点是，发展中国家主要出口粮食和原材料，以换取发达国家的制成品。对欠发达的发展中国家来说，情况仍然如此，但对较发达的发展中国家则并非如此。1980 年，制成品仅占发展中国家出口的 25%，但到 2003 年，这一数字超过了 80%。

虽然经济发展水平和速度主要取决于发展中国家的内部条件，但今天的大多数经济学家认为，国际贸易可以对发展进程做出重大贡献。但是情况并不总是如此。直到 20 世纪 80 年代，相当数量和少数有影响力的经济学家坚信，国际贸易和目前国际经济体系的运作起到的是阻碍作用而不是促进发展，因为贸易条件长期下降，发展中国家的出口收入波动很大。这些经济学家认为，基于比较优势的标准来看，国际贸易理论与发展中国家和发展进程完全无关。因此，他们主张通过进口替代（以前进口的制成品的国内生产）实现工业化，并减少依赖以促进国际贸易发展。他们还主张改革目前的国际经济体系，使其更能满足发展中国家的特殊需要。

10.1　经济增长的推动力及推动因素

随着时间的推移，因为劳动力（L）规模的增加以及包括人力资本（K）和技术进步（T）在内的资本（投资）的积累，各个国际会逐步发展。一国劳动和资本禀赋的增加和/或技术的进步会引起该国生产可能性曲线向外移动。移动的形状和幅度则取决于 L、K 和 T 的增长比率。

我们考察在技术条件恒定、规模效益不变的条件下一个生产两种商品（商品 X 为劳动密集型，商品 Y 为资本密集型）的国家的增长。如果 K 和 L 两者增长比率相同，生产可能性曲线将按照两要素的增长比率同时向两个方向外移。所以其结果便是新旧两条曲线（要素增长前后）各点的斜率相等，两条线的相同点被源于原点的射线相割，这就是平衡增长（Balanced growth）的情况。

如果仅是劳动力 L 增加，由于劳动投入两种商品的生产过程，X 和 Y 两种商品量均会增加。但是，商品 X（劳动密集型）的增加将快于商品 Y（资本密集型）的增加。在仅有则本要素增长时情况则恰好相反。如果劳动和资本以不同比率增长，外移的生产可能性曲线也可类似地确定。对于技术进步的结果也是一样的。图 10.1（劳动力和资本随时间的增长）表明了不同类型要素增加是国家的发展。

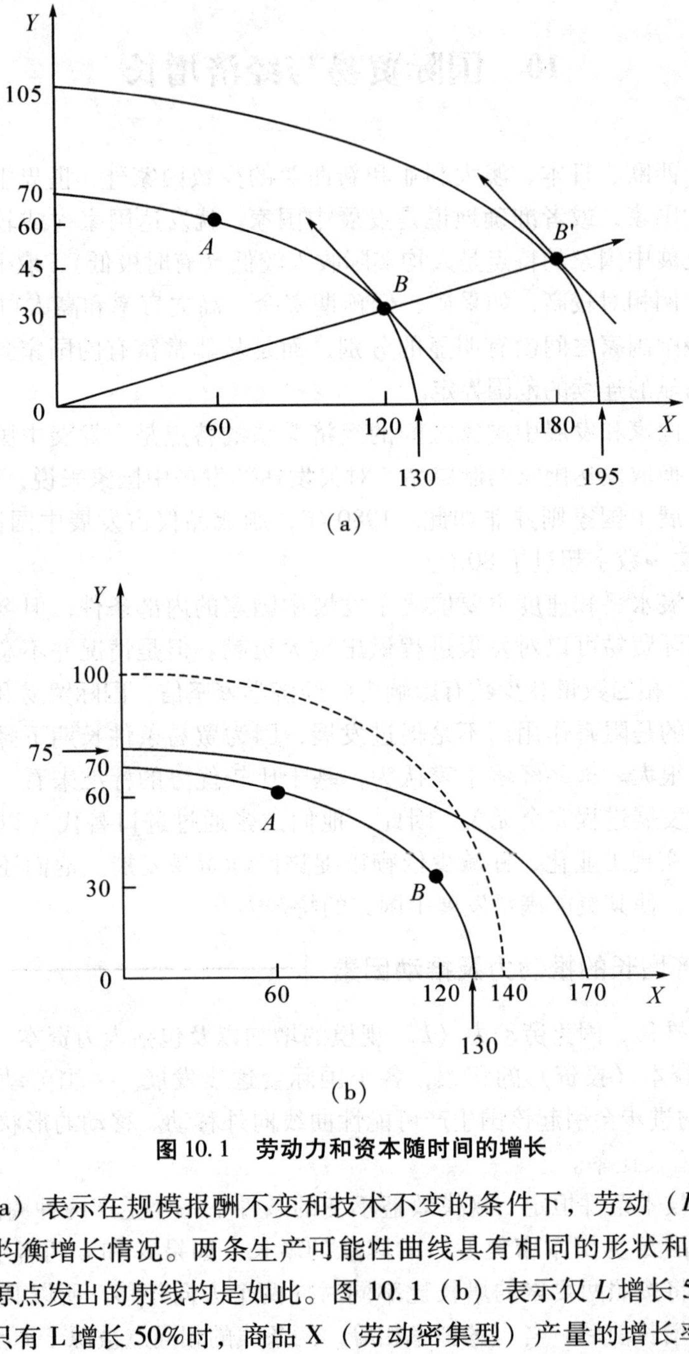

图 10.1　劳动力和资本随时间的增长

图 10.1（a）表示在规模报酬不变和技术不变的条件下，劳动（*L*）和资本（*K*）均增长 50%的均衡增长情况。两条生产可能性曲线具有相同的形状和斜率（*Px/Py*），对任何一条从原点发出的射线均是如此。图 10.1（b）表示仅 *L* 增长 50%或仅 K 增长 50%的情形。只有 L 增长 50%时，商品 X（劳动密集型）产量的增长率高于商品 Y 的增长率（但低于 50%）。同样地，当只有 K 增长 50%时，商品 Y 产量的增长率高于商品 X，但低于 50%（见用虚线表示的生产可能性曲线）。

图 10.1（a）说明假定国家 1（参见前面第 3 章的图 3.1）的劳动与资本两要素都增加 50%的平衡增长情况。在规模效益不变的条件下，每种商品的最大化产量也增加 50%，从 130X 和 70Y 增加到 195X 和 105Y。值得注意的是，扩张后的生产可能性曲线与之前的曲线形状相同，增长前后的生产可能性曲线的斜率相等，或者说 *Px/Py* 在 *B* 点和 *B*’ 点相等，并且被来自原点的射线相切。

图 10.1（b）重复了国家 1 增长前的生产可能性曲线（截距分别为 130X 和 70Y），并显示了另外两条生产可能性曲线，分别是仅劳动力增加 50%（实线）和仅资本增加 50%（虚线）。当只有劳动增加时，曲线更多地向测度劳动密集型商品的 X 轴方向扩展。当只有资本增加时，曲线更多地向测度资本密集型商品的 Y 轴方向移动。注意，当只有劳动增加 50%时，X 的最大化产量并没有增加 50%（只从 130X 增加到 170X）。要使 X 增加 50%，必须要让劳动与资本两要素都在增加 50%。同样，当仅资本增加 50%时，Y 的最大化产量也增加不到 50%（从 70Y 增加到 100Y）。

当劳动与资本以相同比率增长时，如果规模报酬不变，两种商品的生产技术也不变，那么生产效率进而劳动与资本的回报率在增长前后都不变。如果依次从比率（依赖于总人口的比率）也不变来看，则一国的人均真实收入和生活水平也保持不变。如果只有劳动增长（或劳动比资本增长快），则资本/劳动比率及劳动的生产效率、劳动的回报率、人均真实收入都将下降；反过来，资本增长（或资本比劳动增长快），资本/劳动的比率、劳动的生产效率、回报率及平均收入都将上升。不同技术发展的类型下也会有同样的影响。

10.2 国际贸易理论与经济增长

按照传统的贸易理论，如果各国专门生产自己具有比较优势的商品，世界的总出口量将会增加，通过贸易可使各国均受益。按照目前的建设要素禀赋和技术在发达国家与发展中国家的分布，根据比较优势理论，发展中国家就应当继续进行原料、燃料、矿产品、食品及简单的劳动密集型商品的专业化生产和出口，以换取发达国家更为复杂的制造品。

虽然这可能在短期内使福利最大化，但发展中国家认为这种专业化的生产和贸易方式把它们降低到仅从属于发达国家的位置，并使它们在长期中与产业的动态利益和福利最大化无缘。这种源于实业生产的动态利益（区别于比较优势产生的静态受益），是指更加训练有素的劳动力、更多的创新、更高且稳定的出口产品价格，以及人民更高的收入水平。伴随着发展中国家的只是贫穷、不发达、从属于他人。让我们来观察一下实际情况，更会印证这种说法：所有发达国家都主要是工业化国家，而大多数发展中国家则主要从事农业或采矿业，或简单产品的制造。

传统贸易理论因此受到攻击，因为它是静态的，而且与发展进程无关。按照这种观点，传统贸易理论只注重调节现存的条件，而发展则要求必须改变现存的条件。简而言之，人们相信传统贸易理论只可能在某一时期的某一点上或者短时期内使福利最大化，但不能保证长期内或总是如此。

这些确实是严重的问题，如果它们真实存在，确实会使传统贸易理论与经济发展脱钩。然而，如上一节所说明的，传统贸易理论可以引入供给、技术的长期变化等要素从而加以拓展。这就意味着一国发展模式的制定不是一劳永逸的事情，而是必须随时间和条件的变化而改变。例如，随着一个发展中国家的资本积累和技术进步，其比较优势会从初级产品和简单的制造品转向更复杂的制造品和服务。在某种程度上，巴西、韩国、墨西哥和其他一些发展中国家已经发生了这种转变。因此，传统的贸易理论对于发展中国家和发展进程仍然是很有意义的。

不过必须指出的是，今天的国际贸易不可能再是“增长的引擎”，或是成为推动经济发展的最重要的力量，虽然它曾经是 19 世纪新殖民地区（美国、加拿大、澳大利亚、新西兰、阿根廷、乌拉圭和南非）的增长引擎。原因是与 19 世纪相比，今天人们对食品、原材料和简单制造品的需求增长已经放慢了很多，而且今天的很多发展中国家与一个世纪之前的新殖民地区国家相比没有很多的人均自然资源（石油输出国家除外）。然而，国际贸易仍是发展的一个必要条件。没有人强迫中国开放国门，但是如果没有这样的开放，中国不可能得到资金和技术，也得不到这样一个使其在过去 10 年飞速发展的市场。

10.3 贫困化增长

如果一国的增长导致越来越多的出口，同时贸易条件却恶化很多，该国的福利就有可能下降。这种情况被贸易经济学家杰格迪什（Jagdish Bhagwati）称为“贫困化增长”（immisering growth），他最早就讨论了这种可能性。我们将通过图 10.2 说明贫困化增长。

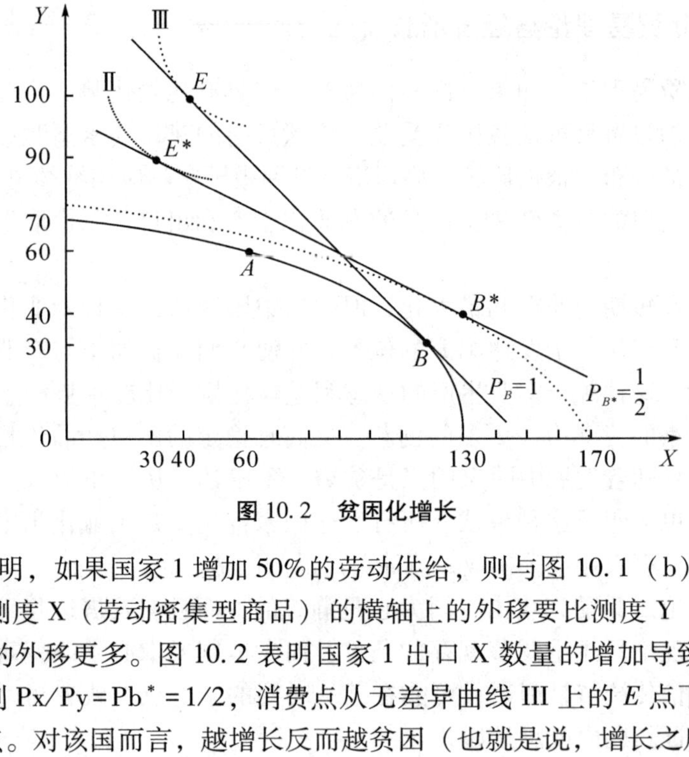

图 10.2 贫困化增长

图 10.2 表明，如果国家 1 增加 50%的劳动供给，则与图 10.1（b）一样，其生产可能性曲线在测度 X（劳动密集型商品）的横轴上的外移要比测度 Y（资本密集型商品）的纵轴上的外移更多。图 10.2 表明国家 1 出口 X 数量的增加导致了贸易条件从 Px/Py = Pb = 1 到 Px/Py = Pb* = 1/2，消费点从无差异曲线 III 上的 E 点下降到无差异曲线 II 上的 E^* 点。对该国而言，越增长反而越贫困（也就是说，增长之后国家 1 反而变得更穷了）。

尽管存在可能性，贫困化的增长在现实世界却很少发生。就像我们在前一节所看到的，只要有足够多的贸易量的增长，即使一个国家的商品贸易条件有所恶化，其福利还是会有所增长。

10.4 进口替代与出口导向

20 世纪 50 年代至 70 年代，大多数发展中国家经过深思熟虑后认为，必须实现工业化，而不能如传统贸易理论所说继续走专业化生产及产品（粮食、原材料、矿产品）以供出口的道路。工业化的实现依赖于：①更快的技术进步；②创造高薪工作岗位，从大多数发展中国家面临的严重失业和未充分就业的困境中解脱出来；③使关联生产过程前后的乘数作用得到更大的发挥；④改善贸易条件，稳定出口价格和收入；⑤解决发展中国家对制造品需求的增长快于国家出口收入增长的问题，从由此造成的收支不平衡的困境中解脱出来。所有发达国家基本是军事工业化国家，而大多数欠发达国家则主要是农业国，从这一事实出发，发展中国家实现工业化的愿望是合乎情理的。

确定了工业化目标后，发展中国家必须在通过进口替代和出口导向来实现工业化这两条道路之间做出抉择。两种政策都各有优缺点。进口替代工业化（import-substitution industrialization，ISI）有三种主要优势：①工业产品市场已经存在，这已被进口商品所证明，从而降低了建立工业取代进口的风险；②对发展中国家来说，保护国内市场以抵制国外竞争，必迫使发达国家降低贸易壁垒，允许它们出口制造品更容易；③国外公司被引导建立了所谓的“关税工厂”以对付发展中国家的关税壁垒。

这种策略的缺点是：①国内工业习惯于无国外竞争的环境，从而缺乏提高效率的动力；②由于许多发展中国家国内市场狭小不能利用规模经济的优势，致使进口替代导致工业的低效率；③在初级制造品被国内生产取代以后，因为更多的资本密集和技术先进的进口必须由国内替代生产，进口替代变得越来越困难且成本高昂（由于保护程度更高、效率更低的缘故）。

出口导向工业化（export-oriented industrialization）策略也有优缺点。其优势在于：①它克服了国内市场狭小的缺陷，允许发展中国家利用规模经济的优势，这对于许多既贫穷又弱小的发展中国家尤为重要；②为出口而进行的工业品生产，需要并刺激了整个经济的高效率，这在一种工业的产出是另一种国内工业的投入时尤为重要；③随国内市场的成长，出口制成品的扩张是无限的（而进口替代下则是受限制的）。

然而，这种策略也有两个严重的缺陷：①由于来自发达国家已建成的高效率工业的竞争，发展中国家建立出口工业可能非常困难；②发达国家经常采取有效的保护措施以保护自己的劳动密集型产业，而这些产业正是发展中国家已经或可以很快取得比较优势的产业。

20世纪50年代至70年代，许多发展中国家特别是一些大国，非常热衷于选择进口替代策略来实现工业化，它们通过有效关税来保护自己的新生工业或刺激它的诞生。产品加工程度越深入，有效关税率就越高。刚开始使用这一政策是为了鼓励相对简单的外国零部件组装，希望随后有更多的这种产品和中间产品在国内生产（后向联系）。国内工业的强保护性措施也刺激了发展中国家关税工厂的建立。

通过进口替代实现工业化通常只取得了有限的成功或遭遇失败。这种做法通常会导致：①国内工业生产的极低效率和国内消费品的极高价格；②过量的资本消耗只能吸收极少的劳动；③忽视农业和其他初级产品部门，引起传统出口部门收入下降，一些国家（如巴西）甚至被迫进口以前出口的食品。

综合结论是，实施进口替代策略的国家（如印度、巴基斯坦、阿根廷）与那些早在20世纪50年代就实行出口导向的国家与地区（如中国香港、韩国、新加坡）相比状况更糟，经济增长率也低得多。但也必须指出，进口替代可能会在发展阶段的早期给发展中国家带来一定好处（特别是大国），而在以后的发展过程中出口导向策略才成为绝对必需的手段。这样看来，发展中国家可视自己的发展程度轮流使用两种策略而获益，特别是较大的发展中国家可以做到这一点。韩国实际就是这样做的。

10.5 贸易条件和经济增长

我们定义一国的贸易条件为出口商品价格相对进口商品价格的比率。在存在许多商品的世界中，我们可以定义商品（commodity）或纯物物交换（net barter）的贸易条件（terms of trade）（N），它等于国家出口价格指数（Px）与进口价格指数（Pm）的比乘以 100（用来表示贸易条件的百分比）。即

$N=(Px/Pm)\times 100$

除此以外，也有其他类型的贸易条件，如贸易的收入条件。我们将一国的贸易收入条件（income terms of trade）（I）定义为

$I=(Px/Pm)\ Qx$

其中，Qx 指的是出口量指数。因而贸易收入条件是指一国以出口为基础的进口能力。

由于发展中国家的发展在很大程度上依赖资本品的进口，因而这项指标的变化对他们来说非常重要。如果一国的 N 和 I 同时增加，贸易对该国是有利的。如果一国的 N 和 I 同时下降，贸易对该国是有害的。假使 N 下降而 I 增加，则该国从能够进口更多的意义上讲是有所改善的。

根据经济学家普雷维什和辛格的研究，发展中国家 1870—1983 年的商品贸易条件是恶化的。他们给出的原因是发达国家生产率的提高全部或大部分转化为工人更高的工资收入（劳动力是相对短缺的，而且工会力量强大），而发展中国家却将生产率的提高全部或大部分转化为更低的价格。这样一来，问题就清楚了，发达国家从两个世界都获得了最多的好处：自身生产率的提高为工人带来高收入，同时，发展中国家随生产率提高而带来的低价格使发达国家在支付从发展中国家进口的农产品方面占尽好处。

尽管普雷维什和辛格的结论及理由受到了其他经济学家的强烈批评，但是 2002 年卡辛（Cashin）和麦克德莫特（McDermott）的一项研究显示，1962—1999 年初级商品（原材料、食品和矿产品）的实际价格每年大约下降 1%。他们还发现有证据表明，从 20 世纪初开始价格波动的幅度在上升，从 20 世纪 70 年代起价格的波动变得更频繁了。这些结论已由 D. I. Harvey et al（2010）证实。因此，重要的是发展中国家出口的商品类型。比如，主要出口原材料的发展中国家会发现其贸易条件只是稍好了一点，而主要出口能源产品的发展中国家则发现其贸易条件好了很多。而且，大多数研究表明，无论商品贸易条件如何变化，发展中国家总体的贸易收入条件是实实在在地改善了。其原因在于出口量有了巨大增长。

11 Trade Policies for Developing Countries

Much of the world's attention focuses on the industrialized economies, especially the United States, Japan, and the countries of Western Europe. The attention is not surprising, given that these areas produce over half of world output and an even greater share of the supply of media services. Yet about 6 billion people (six-sevenths of the world's population) live in countries that are considered developing countries. One surprise is how widely the fortunes of these developing countries vary. Some have succeeded in developing and have experienced high growth rates. Others have experienced serious economic declines. The average product per person has grown faster in the developing countries than it has grown in the industrialized countries since 1990. Yet, even with such a growth advantage, it would still take more than a century for the developing countries to catch up with the average per capita income int the industrialized countries.

The most striking pattern, however, is the wide disparity in growth rates among the developing countries/regions. Some are achieving super-growth, while some have suffered declining income levels since 1990. Income have tended to grow fastest in East Asia. The "Four Dragons" have grown so quickly over the past two decades that they now have relatively high incomes. South Korea's per capita GDP is about $30 000 and those of the other three Dragons are even higher. Several other countries in East Asia also achieved high growth rates. At the rate achieved in 1990—2012, China's per capita income doubles in less than eight years.

However, in one-seventh of the developing countries for which we have data, income per person declined between 1990 and 2012. Most are countries in Africa and countries in Central and Eastern Europe and Central Asia that are making a transition from central planning to a market-based economy. The gaps in growth rates are much wider among developing countries than among high-income countries. Why are the fortunes of developing countries so different, with some growing rapidly with others stay poor? Do diffences in their trade policies play a role? Are there lessons about trade policy to be learned by studying what the supergrowing newly industrializing countries (NICs) did that countries with stagnating or declining incomes did not? This chapter reveals some clear answers and some still-unresolved questions about the trade-policy options for developing countries.

11.1 What Trade Policies Should Developing Countries Adopt?

Trade is important for developing countries. Exports of goods and services on average are about 37 percent of GDP in developing countries. (For developed countries exports are about 28 percent of GDP on average.) Developing countries are the source of about 46 percent of all world export. About 42 percent of exports by developing countries go to industrialized countries, and these are about 38 percent of industrial countries imports.

What role can trade and trade policy play in development? How can trade and trade policy be used to boost incomes and economic growth in poor countries? Many developing countries have comparative advantages based on land (usually with a tropical climate) and in various natural resources "in the ground." Exploiting these comparative advantages would lead to exports of foods, fuels, and other primary products. Developing countries also generally have a comparative advantages based on less-skilled labor. This abundant labor could be used in combination with the land and natural resources in producing primary commodities, or it could be used in the production of less-skilled-labor-intensive manufactures. Developing countries could also seek to develop more advanced manufacturing industries using infant industry policies.

What should the government of, say, Ghana do about inports and exports if it is determined to reverse the economic stagnation that has held down the living standards of its people? To supplement the greater task of reforming its whole economy, Ghana has these basic trade policy choices:

(1) A trade policy that accepts and exploits the country's comparative advantages in land and natural resources. For Ghana this means encouraging greater exports of cocoa, coffee, gold, and other primary products, but offering no encouragement to industrial development by restricting imports or Encouraging exports of manufactured products.

(2) A trade policy that attempts to enhance the gains from exporting primary products by raising the world prices of these products. If the country's exports of a product are large enough, the country could use an export tax in a way that is similar to the nationally optimal import tariff. If the country cannot accomplish much by itself, it could organize or join an international cartel. For Ghana, this means taxing exports of coacoa or organizing a cartel of cocoa producers or coffee producers.

(3) A policy that taxes and restricts imports to protect and subsidize new industries serving the domestic market. For Ghana, this might mean forcing Ghanaians to buy more expensive domestic steel, televisions, and airline services. If the strategy nurtures infant industries successfully, firms in these industries eventually can compete at world prices.

(4) A trade policy that encourages the development of new industries whose products can be readily exported. Most of these new industries would make manufactured products that exploit the country's comparative advantages in less-skilled labor. For Ghana, the new export production would probably be textiles, clothing, or the assembly of electrical products.

A developing country today does indeed face this choice alone, for the most part, without much international help other than negotiated trade liberalizations like the Uruguay Round.

In choosing a trade policy, should a developing country just follow the trade-policy guidelines laid out in Chapter 6 through 8? Or are developing countries so different that they need a separate trade-policy analysis? The basic answer is that the trade policy conclusions of Chapter 6 through 8 do apply to all countries. Whether industrialized or developing. The pros and cons of restricting or subsidizing trade are the same, and the specificity rule still compels us to consider alternatives to trade policy when trade is not the source of the development problem. All that is different in this chapter is the degree of emphasis put on certain points.

Developing countries are different in that they face certain challenges that are less formidable, though still present, in a developed economy. These challenges fall into two categories:

(1) Capital markets work less efficiently in developing countries. A defining characteristic of a lower-income country is that there are more barriers to the lending of money to the most productive uses. As a result, good projects must overcome a higher cost of capital (interest rate) than the rate at which capital is available to less promising sectors. One underlying reason is that property rights are less clearly defined, holding back the willingness to invest in new assets.

(2) Similarly, labor markets work less efficiently in developing countries. The wage gaps between expanding and declining sectors are greater than those in higher-income countries. The wider wage gaps are an indirect clue that some labor is being kept from moving to its most productive use.

These differences imply some special tasks for the government of a developing country. There is a case for considering which sectors to protect or subsidize or give cheap loans to, if the government cannot quickly eliminate the barriers to efficient capital and labor markets. The government must also decide whether it is realistic to try to change the nation's comparative advantage, for instance, by inceasing its investment in education and health care to expand the country's endowment of human skills. The shift from central planning to a market economy has required yet other policy decisions. We now explore the alternatives for trade policy for a developing country in the order that we presented them for Ghana: focus on exporting primary products, use export taxes or international cartels to influence the world prices of these primary products, use import protection to develop new manufacturing industries, or encourage the development of export-oriented new manufacturing industries.

11.2 Are the Long-Run Price Trends Against Primary Producers?

It seems natural that developing countries export primary products (agriculture, forestry, fuels, and minerals), and these are often called traditional exports. The majority of developing countries get half or more of their export revenues from primary products. Many developing countries have exports concentrated in one or a few products like petroleum, coffee, cotton, gold, sugar, timber, diamonds, and bauxite/aluminum.

A recurring idea is that developing countries's growth is held back by relying on exports of primary products. In the 1950s, Raul Prebisch and others argued that developing countries are hurt by a downward trend (and instability) in primary-product prices. International markets, ran the argument, distribute income unfairly. Since developing countries are net expoters of primary products, they are trapped into declining incomes relative to incomes in the industrialized world.

Economic analysis shows that there are at least two major forces depressing, and at least two forces raising, the trend in the pricesof primaries relative to manufactures.

The relative price of primary products is depressed by Engel's law and synthetic substitues.

(1) Engel's law. In the long run, per capita incomes rise. As they rise, demand shifts toward luxuries—goods for which the income elasticity (percent rise in quantity demanded/percent rise in income causing the change in demand) is greater than 1. At the same time, the world's demand shifts away from staples—goods for which the income elasticity of demand is less than 1. The 19th-century German economist Ernst Engel discovered what has become known as Engel's law: The income elasticity of demand for food is less than 1 (food is a staple). Engel's law is the most durable law in economics that does not follow from definitions or axioms. It means trouble for food producers in a prospering world. If the world's supply expanded at the exact same rate for all products, the relative prce of foods would go on dropping because Engel's law says that demand would keep shifting (relatively) away from food toward luxuries.

(2) Synthetic substitues. Another force depressing the relative prices of primary products is the development of new human-made subsititues for these natural materials. The more technology advances, the more we are likely to discover ways to replace minerals and other raw materials. The most dramatic case is the development of synthetic rubber around the time of World War Ⅰ, which ruined the incomes of rubber producers in Braizil, Malaysia, and other countries. Another case is the development of synthetic febers, which has lowered demand for cotton and wool.

On the other hand, two other basic forces tend to raise the relative price of primary products:

(1) Nature's limits. Primary products use land, water, mineral deposits, and other limited natural resources. As population and incomes expand, the natural inputs become increasingly scarce, other things being equal. Nature's scarcity eventually raises the relative price of primary products, which use natural resources more intensively than do manufactures.

(2) Relatively slow productivity growth in the primary sector. For several centuries productivity has advanced more slowly in agriculture, mining, and other primary sectors than in manufacturing. A reason is the tendency for cost-cutting breakthroughs in knowledge to be more important in manufacturing than in primaries. Slow productivity advance translates into a slower relative advance of supply curves in primary-product markets than in manufacturing markets, and therefore a rising relative price of primaries (or a falling relative price of manufactures), other things being equal.

So we have two tendencies that depress the relative price of primary products, and two that raise it. How does the tug-of-war work out in the long run? It depends on when you look at the data and how far back into history you look. We can understand why the fear of falling relative primary prices was greatest in the 1950s (when Prebisch's argument achieved popolarity) and the 1980s. Those were periods of falling primary prices just before World War Ⅰ, the historical heyday of high prices for farm products and other raw materials. Nor was there much discussion of depressed prices during World War Ⅱ, the Korean War of 1950-1953, the boom in primary-product prices in the early 1970s, or the run-up in commodity prices during the 2000s. During such times, many writers revived the Malthusian arguments about the limits to planet Earth.

To stand back from the volatiles swings in commodity prices, let's look over as long a period as possible. We can scan the period 1900-2013, though following some price series back to 1870 would tell a similar story. We also have to allow for the very large increase in energy prices since 1999, which causes a divergence between the relative price of all primary products and the relative price of nonfuel primary products at the end of the time period.

The general trend for relative nonfuel primary-product prices is downward. Statistically, if we fit the best trend line to the data over this entire time period, we find that these prices are declining at about 0.8 percent per year. (For all primary products, including energy fuels, the general trend is also downward, but the spike since the late 1990s pulls the trend line up somewhat. Statistically, the best trend line shows a price decline of about 0.4 percent per year.) Somehow, Engel's law and the technological biases toward replacing primary products have outrun nature's limits and the relative slowness of productivity growth in primary sectors. (Or, in shorthand, Prebisch outran Malthus.)

Some commodities have declined in price more seriously than others. The price of rubber snapped downward between 1910 and 1920 and has never really bounced back since. The relative prices of wool, cocoa, aluminum, rice, cotton, and sugar declined by more than half during the 20th century. In contrast, the relative prices of lamb, timber, and beef more doubled.

While the net downward trend in primary prices stands as a tentative conclusion, there are two biasesin the available measures:

(1) The fall in transport costs. The available data tend to be gathered at markets in the industrial countries. Yet technological improvements in transportation have been great enough to reduce the share of transport costs in those final prices in London, NewYork, or Tokyo. That has left more and more of the final price back in the hands of the primary-product exporters. Quantifying this known change would tilt the trend in the prices received by producers toward a flatter, less downward trend.

(2) Faster unmeasured quality change in manufactures. We are using long runs of price data on products that have been getting better over time. Quality improvements (including those in the form of new products) are thought to have been more impressive in manufactures (and services) than in primary products. So what might look like a rise in the relative price of manufactures might be just a rise in their relative quality, with no trend in the relative price for given quality. This data problem is potentially serious, given that many 20th-century data have, for example, followed the prices of machinery exports per ton of exports, as if a ton of today's computers were the same things as a ton of old electric motors.

When all is said and done, the relative price of primary products may have declined as much as 0.8 percent a year since 1900, or there could have been almost no trend. There is a weak case for worrying about being an exporter of agricultural or extractive products on price-trend grounds.

11.3 International Cartels to Raise Primary-Product Prices

Perhaps the developing-country producers of primary products can take actions to turn the price trends in their favor. Perhaps the primary-product exporters can become more powerful if they cooperate with each other, using international cartels or other types of concerted action.

11.3.1 The OPEC victories

History records many attempts at international cartels (international agreements to restrict competition among sellers). The greatest seizure of monopoly power in world history was the price-raising triumph of the OPEC in 1973-1974 and again in 1979-1980.

A chain of events in late 1973 revolutionized the world oil economy. In a few months' time, the 12 members of OPEC effectively quadrupled the dollar price of crude oil, from \$2.59 to \$10.36 a barrel. Oil-exporting countries became rich almost overnight. The industrial oil-consuming countries sank into their deepest recession since the 1930s. The relative price of oil (what the price of a barrel of oil could buy interms of manufactured exports from industrial nations) tripled.

The sequel was a plateau of OPEC prosperity, a further jump, and then growing signs of weakness. From 1974 to 1978, the relative price of oil dipped by about a sixth, but stayed much higher than it had been at any time before 1973. Next came the second wave of OPEC price hikes, the second "oil shock" in 1979 - 1980. Led by the Iranian Revolution and growing panic among oil buyers, the relative oil price more than doubled. In the mid-1980s, however, OPEC weakened. The relative price of oil dropped suddenly in late 1985, from four to five times the old (pre-1973) real price in 1980-1984 to less than two times the old price for 1986-1989.

The tale of oil and OPEC in the 1970s and 1980s is one of two dramatic cartel victavories and a subsequent retreat. The victories and the retreat both need explanation.

First, the victories. The oil shocks of 1973-1974 and 1979-1980 were not the result of a failure of supply or exhaustion of earth's available resources. The world's "proved reserves" of known and usable oil were growing faster than world oil consumption. Nor were the costs of oil extraction rising much.

The 1973-1974 and 1979-1980oil price jumps were human-made. The key was that world demand was growing far faster than non-OPEC supplies. Oil discoveries had been very unevenly distributed among countries. The share of OPEC countries in world crude oil production rose to over 50 percent by 1972. Furthermore, OPEC's share of proved reserves—roughly, its share of future production—was over two-thirds.

By the early 1970s, the United States was for the first time becoming vulnerable to pressure from oil-exporting countries. Largely immune to oil threatsin earlier Middle East crises, the United States found itself importing a third of its oil consumption, part of it from Arab countries, by 1973. With their growing importance in world production, and with growing U.S. reliance on oil imports, OPEC countries were able to create a scramble among buyers to pay higher prices for oil in 1973 and again in 1979.

11.3.2 Classic monopoly as an extreme model for cartels

How big could the cartel opportunity be? That is, if a group of nations or firms were to from a cartel, as OPEC did, what is the greatest amount of gain they could reap at the expense of their buyers and world efficiency? If all of the cartel members could agree on simply maximizing their collective gain, they would behave aws though they were a perfectly unified profit-maximizing monopolist. Because a commodity like oilis fungtible, they would probably not be able to discriminate by setting different prices to different foreign buyers (excet for standard distinctions by quality that we can safely ignore here). The cartel members acting as a monopoly would try to find the price level that would maximize the gap between their total export sales revenues and their total costs of producing exports. When cutting output back to the level of demand yielded by their optimal price, they would take care to shut down their most costly production units (e. g., oil wells) and keep in operation only those with the lowest operating costs.

To understand what price and output yield that highest level of profits, and what limits those profits, we must first understand that the optimal price lies above the price that perfect competition would yield, yet below the price that would discourage all sales. The cartel members want to set a price higher than the competitive price, but their pricing power is limited by the negative slope of the demand curve for the cartel's product. This point is clear if we just consider the extreme case of a prohibitive price markup. If the cartel were foolish enough to set a very high price (prohibitive price), it would lose all of its export business. Thus, the cartel's best price must be well below the prohibitive price. The cartel price that is optimal for its members is not optimal for the world, of course. At the same time, the cartel causes net world losses by curtailing oil exports that would be worth more to buyers around the world than those exports cost the cartel members themselves to produce.

11.3.3 The limits to and erosion of cartel power

11.3.3.1 Rules of setting price

How high is the cartel's profit-maximizing price if the cartel is functioning at full effectiveness? The theory of cartel provides some rules.

(1) The higher the marginal cost of production, the higher the price.

(2) The higher the elasticity of demand, the lower the price. If demand is elastic, buyers easily find other ways of spending their money if the product price rises much.

(3) The larger the share of world production controlled by the cartel, the higher the price. Controlling more of the world production effectively increases the demand for the cartel's production (rather than having this demand lost to outside producers).

(4) The larger the elasticity of supply of noncartel producers, the lower the price. The elasticity of noncartel supply acts in the same way that the elasticity of demand does. The cartel refrains from raising the price too much because dong so results in too large a loss of its own sales.

11.3.3.2 Anticartel trends

These rules also suggest forces that work increasingly against cartels over time. When the cartel is first set up, it may well enjoy low elasticities and a high market share. Yet its verysuccess in raising price is lilely to set four anticartel trends in motion: sagging demand, new competing supply, declining market share, and cheating.

(1) Sagging demand. The higher price will make buying countries look for new ways to avoid importing the cartel's product. If the search for subsititutes has any success at all, imports of the buying countries will drop over time for any given cartel price. These countries's long-run demand curve for imports of the product is more elastic than their short-run demand curve. This happened to OPEC. As theory predicts, and as some OPEC oil minister had feared, the oil-importing countries slowly came up with ways to conserve on oil use, such as more fuel-efficient cars.

(2) New competing supply. The initial cartel success will addelerate the search for additional supplies in noncartel countries. If the cartel product is an agricultural crop, such as sugar or coffee, the cartel's price hike will cause farmers in other countries to shift increasing

amounts of land, labor, and funds from other crops into sugar or coffee. If the cartel product is a depletable mineral resource, such as oil or cropper, noncartel countries will respond to the higher price by redoubling their explorations in search of new reserves. If the noncartel countries have any luck at all, their competing supply will become increasingly elastic with time. Again, that happened to OPEC—other countries discovered new oil at a faster rate.

(3) Declining market share. The cartel's world market share will fall over time. To raise the product's price without piling up ever-rising unsold inventories, the cartel must cut its output and sales. Since nonmembers will be straining to raise their output and sales, the cartel's share of market will drop even if all of its members cooperate solidly. OPEC's share of world oil production fell from over half in the early 1970s to less than a shird in 1985.

(4) Cheating. Theory and experience add a fourth reason for a decline in cartel power—the incentive for members to cheat on the cartel agreement.

As a cartel member, you have enough oil reserves to pump and sellmoe than your ageed output (OPEC calls this your production quota) for as long in the futures as you need to plan. Raising your output above your production quota might cost you only, say, $6 a barrel at the margin. Buyers are willing to pay close to $100 for each barrel you sell if the other cartel members are faithfully holding down their output. Why not attract some extra buyers to you by shaving your price just a little bit below $100, say, to $98? You can do so in the hope that your individual actions will not cause the cartel price to drop much, if at all. Theory says that this incentive to cheat tends to undermine the whole cartel. Perhaps some large members can keep the cartel effective for a while by drastically cutting their own outputs to offset the extra sales from the cheaters. Their aggregate size determines how long they can hold out.

OPEC members cheated on the cartel, even openly, just as theory would predict. Up to the mid-1980s, the largest producer, Saudi Arabia, had to hold the cartel together by cutting its production while others cheated. Thenthe Saudis themselves shifted to a more competitive stance, and the relative price of oil fell dramatically in late 1985. The usual theory of cartels thus correctly explains why cartel profit margins and profits will erode with time. Yet the theory does not say that cartels are unprofitable or harmless. On the contrary, it underscores the profitability of cartel formation to cartel members. Even a cartel that eventually erodes can bring fortunes to its members.

11.3.4 Other primary products

Do theory and OPEC experience hold out hope developing countries wanting to make large national gains by joining cartels in other primary products besides oil? Not much. There are good reasons for believing that international cartels would collapse faster, with less interim profit, for the non-oil primary products. For agricultural crops in particular, there is the problem of competing supply. Other countries usually can easily expand theacreage they devote to a given crop.

History agrees with this verdict. Of the 72 commodity cartels set up between the two world wars, only 2 survived past 1945. Of the few dozen set up in the 1970s, only 5 lived as late as 1985: cocoa, coffee, rubber, sugar, and tin. These 5 cartels have been so weak that they have had little effect on commodity markets since 1985.

Given the limits of international cartel power, a developing nation could still tax its own primary-product exports for the sake of economic development. In principle, the strategy could work well. A tax on exports of Nigerian oil, Ghanaian cocoa, or Philippine coconuts could generate revenues for building schools, hospital, and roads.

Unfortunately, the political economy of some developing countries seems to diven theexport - tax revenues away from the most productive uses. For example, Nigeria's oil revenues were lost in a swollen government bureaucracy and ravenous corruption. Ghana's cocoa marketing board used its heavy taxation of cocoa farmers to support luxury imports by officials. The Marcos government distributed the Philippine coconut-tax revenues among a handful of Marcos's friend and relatives.

11 发展中国家的贸易政策

全球的注意力大多集中在工业化国家身上，尤其是美国、日本和西欧各国。这不足为奇，因为这些国家生产了全球一半以上的产品。在媒体服务方面，它们还占有更大的份额。然而，全球超过60亿人口（约占世界人口的6/7）都生活在发展中国家。令人惊讶的是，这些发展中国家的经济发展大相径庭。一些国家已经成功地实现了经济的高速增长，而另外一些国家则经历着严重的经济衰退。自1990年以来，发展中国家的人均产出增长率高于工业化国家。即便如此，发展中国家的人均收入若想赶上发达国家水平，仍需要一个多世纪的时间。

然而，最令人震惊的事实是，这些发展中国家和地区之间的经济增长率有很大的差别。部分国家和地区正在实现高速增长，而另一些国家和地区自1990年以来经历了收入水平的衰退。东亚地区有着最快的收入增长趋势。“四小龙”经历过去20年的迅速增长后，现在已经拥有了相对较高的收入水平。韩国的人均GDP已经超过了30 000亿美元，其他“三小龙”甚至更高。东亚的其他一些国家也实现了高增长。按照1990—2012年的增长速度，中国的人均收入只用不到8年的时间就实现了翻番。

但是，就在1990—2012年，数据显示发展中国家和地区中有1/7的国家和地区人均收入下降了。这些国家和地区都在非洲以及中东欧及中亚地区，历经从中央计划经济向市场经济的转型。发展中国家之间的增长差异远大于高收入国家。为什么发展中国家的命运差异如此之大，一些高速增长，而另一些却停留在贫困之中呢？是它们的贸易政策之间的差异起了作用吗？通过研究那些迅速增长的新兴工业化国家（NICs）采取了那些收入陷入停滞甚至开始下降的国家没有采取的政策，我们可以从中得到哪些政策上的经验和教训？本章就发展中国家的贸易政策选择给出一些明晰的答案，并提出一些尚未解决的问题。

11.1 发展中国家应当采用何种贸易政策

贸易对发展中国家是很重要的。商品出口平均占到发展中国家GDP的37%（而对于发达国家，这一比例为28%左右）。全球约有46%的出口源于发展中国家。发展中国家的出口约有42%流向了工业化国家，但是这些出口仅占到工业化国家进口的38%。

贸易和贸易政策在发展中起了什么作用？它们如何能够提高低收入国家的收入，实现经济增长？很多发展中国家在土地上（通常是热带气候）以及地下的自然资源方面具有比较优势。它们利用这些比较优势会形成粮食、燃料以及其他初级产品的出口。发展中国家通常在低技能劳动力上也具有比较优势。丰富的劳动力可以与土地和自然资源结合起来生产初级产品，或者生产低技能劳动密集型商品。发展中国家还可以采取幼稚产业政策发展较为先进的制造业。

一国政府，如加纳政府，如果下定决心扭转经济停滞、人民生活水平下降的局面，应当在商品进出口方面采取哪些措施？除全面改革其整个国民经济体系外，加纳还可以选择实行以下基本的贸易政策：

（1）接受和采取可以充分发挥该国在土地和自然资源上的比较优势的贸易政策。对于加纳而言，这意味着鼓励更多的可可、咖啡、黄金及其他初级产品出口，对于通过限制进口或者鼓励出口工业品来谋求工业发展的做法不予鼓励。

（2）通过提高世界价格来提高出口初级产品收益。如果一国的某一产品的出口量足够大，那么这个国家可以征收出口关税。这在某种程度上类似于国家最优进口关税。如果这个国家无法独自实现这一目标，也可以组织或者加入国际卡特尔。对于加纳，这意味着它对可可出口征收关税或者组织可可及咖啡生产者的卡特尔。

（3）对产品进口征收关税并加以限制，以保护和补贴服务于本国市场的新产业。对于加纳而言，这可能意味着强迫加纳人购买本国更加昂贵的钢铁、电视机和航空服务。如果这个策略成功地培育了本国幼稚产业，那么这些产业的公司最终可以在国际价格水平上参与竞争。

（4）鼓励产品已经可以出口的新产业发展。大部分这一类新兴产业生产的产品都可以发挥该国在低技术劳动力方面的比较优势。对加纳而言，这些新的出口产品很有可能是纺织品、服装或者组装的电子产品。

如今，除了通过类似乌拉圭回合这样的谈判实现贸易自由化的途径外，在大多数情况下，发展中国家事实上是在没有多少国际援助的情况下，独自面对这些选择。

在选择贸易政策的时候，发展中国家是否只需要遵循第 6 章至第 8 章中列出的贸易政策准则？或者发展中国家与发达国家之间有天壤之别，因此它们需要另外一种贸易政策进行分析？对这些问题的基本答案是：第 6 章至第 8 章中给出的贸易政策结论适用于所有的国家，无论是发达国家还是发展中国家。限制或者补贴贸易的正面及负面效应对各个国家都是相同的。当贸易不构成影响发展问题的限制时，对症规则仍旧要求我们考虑贸易政策的替代方案。本章的不同之处只是在于对某些问题给予了更多的关注。

发展中国家所面对的一些挑战与发达国家相比是不同的，虽然这些挑战在发达国家依旧存在而且不再那么艰巨。这些挑战可以分为两类：

（1）发展中国家的资本市场运作效率低下。低收入国家的一个典型特征是在给最有效率的项目提供贷款时存在更多障碍。其结果是好的项目相对于某些前景不明的项目，必须承受更高的资本成本（利率）。一个潜在的原因是产权界定不明晰，这抑制了对新资产投资的意愿。

（2）类似地，发展中国家劳动力市场运行效率低下。扩张行业和衰退行业之间的工资差距大于高收入国家的行业差距。较大的工资差距间接反映了部分劳动力不能流动到更有效率的行业中去。

这些特点意味着发展中国家政府面临着一些特殊的任务。如果政府不能快速地消除实现高效率资本市场和劳动力市场中的障碍，那么便需要考虑对哪些产业给予保护、进行补贴或者提供低息贷款。政府还必须判断是否存在改变本国比较优势的现实性，如通过增加对教育及医疗条件等来增加本国人力资源的要素禀赋。这种从中央计划经济到市场经济的转变还需要其他政策决策。接下来，我们探讨发展中国家贸易政策的选择，以供加纳参考。加纳可以专注于初级产品出口、征收出口税、组织国际卡特尔来影响初级产品的世界价格；运用进口保护的手段来发展新兴制造业，或者鼓励出口导向新兴工业的发展。

11.2 长期价格趋势是否有利于初级产品生产者

发展中国家出口初级产品（农业产品、林业产品以及燃料和矿产）似乎是很自然的，这些产品通常称为“传统出口产品”。大多数发展中国家从初级产品出口中获得一半甚至更多的出口收入。很多发展中国家的出口产品都集中在一种或者几种产品上，如石油、咖啡、棉花、黄金、食糖、木材、钻石以及矾土或者铝矿等。

一个被人们反复提及的观点认为，对初级产品出口的依赖阻碍了发展中国家的经济增长。20 世纪 50 年代，保罗·普雷维什等提出，发展中国家因初级产品的价格下降（以及不稳定）趋势而利益受损。这种观点认为，国际市场收入分配不公平。因为发展中国家是初级产品的净出口国，与工业化国家相比它们更加容易陷入收入下降的困境。

经济学分析显示，初级产品的价格下降趋势相对于制成品而言至少有两种原因导致价格下降，也至少有两种原因导致价格上升。

导致初级产品相对价格下降的原因是恩格尔定律和人工合成的替代品。

（1）恩格尔定律。从长期来看，人均收入是不断上升的。随着收入的上升，人们的需求转向奢侈品——需求收入弹性（需求数量增加的百分比/导致需求变化的收入增加的百分比）大于 1 的商品。同时，世界对必需品（需求收入弹性小于 1 的商品）的需求转移。19 世纪的德国经济学家厄恩斯特·恩格尔提出了恩格尔定律：食品需求收入弹性小于 1（食品为必需品）。在非定理或公理推导出来的经济学定律中，恩格尔定律是最为持久的一个。这意味着在经济繁荣的世界中食品生产者将面临困境。如果所有产品的世界供给以完全相同的速度增长，食品的相对价格将会下降，因为恩格尔定律说明需求将会不断地从食物（相对的）转移到奢侈品。

（2）人工合成的替代品。导致初级产品相对价格下降的另一个因素是替代这些天然材料的新型人造替代品的开发。科技越发达，人们越容易发现代替矿产和其他原材料的途径。最引人注意的一个例子就是第一次世界大战前后人造橡胶的开发，使巴西、马来西亚以及其他国家天然橡胶生产者的收入遭受重大损失。另一个例子是人造纤维的开发，减少了对棉花和羊毛的需求。

此外，还有两个基本因素促使初级产品相对价格上升：

（1）自然资源的有限性。初级产品的生产需要土地、水、矿藏和其他有限储量的自然资源。在其他条件不变的情况下，随着人口和收入的增长，天然投入品变得越来越稀缺。由于初级产品的生产比制造产品的生产更密集地使用自然资源，自然资源的稀缺性最终将提高初级产品的相对价格。

（2）初级产品生产率相对的低速增长。几个世纪以来，农业、矿业和其他初级产业生产效率的进步要比制造业缓慢。原因之一是相对于初级产品的生产，通过知识降低成本已经成为制造业越来越重要的趋势。在其他条件不变的情况下，生产效率提高的速度较为缓慢，则意味着初级产品市场的供给曲线比制造产品市场的供给曲线向右移动得要慢，这也就提高了初级产品的相对价格（或降低了制造产品的相对价格）。

这样一来，我们就得到两种压低初级产品相对价格的趋势，以及两种提高该价格的趋势。从长期来看，这种力量之间的角逐会如何起作用？要回答上述问题，取决于你观察哪一个时期的数据，以及你对历史事实要追溯到何时。我们可以了解到，为什么对初级产品相对价格下降的担忧在20世纪50年代（当时普雷维什的观点被普遍接受）以及在80年代最甚。这正是初级产品价格下降的时期。此外，在第一次世界大战前很少有人研究初级产品价格的下降，当时农产品和其他原材料正处于历史上的最高水平。在第二次世界大战、1950—1953年的朝鲜战争、20世纪70年代初期的初级产品价格高涨以及21世纪前10年的中后期初级产品价格暴涨的时候，也没有多少人讨论价格下降的问题；相反，在这些时期很多评论家重新鼓吹起马尔萨斯关于地球资源有限性的理论。

让我们暂且把关注点从商品价格的不稳定波动移开，从尽可能长的时期进行观察，可以方便地考察到1900—2013年这一较长时期初级产品的价格走向。我们即便是向前追溯到1870年，也能得出类似的结论。同时，我们也需要考虑到自1999年以来能源价格的急剧上升，它引发了在该时期末全部初级产品与非燃料初级产品相对价格之间出现了较大偏离。

非燃料初级产品的相对价格总体趋势是下降的。统计数据表明，如果我们做出符合这一时期全局数据的最佳趋势线，可以发现这些价格年均下降0.8%。对于全部初级产品而言，包括能源燃料，其价格的总体趋势也是下降的。但是20世纪90年代末期的峰回路转在一定程度上拉高了整条趋势线。统计学上，最佳趋势线表明年均下降0.4%。可以说，恩格尔定律和利用新技术替代初级产品这两种因素的作用，超过了自然资源有限性和初级产品产业生产效率相对较慢这两个因素（或者简单地说，普雷维什战胜了马尔萨斯）。

部分产品的价格比其他产品下降得更为严重。橡胶的价格在1910—1920年急剧下降，而且自此再也没有真正意义上反弹过。羊毛、可可、铝、水稻、棉花和食糖的相对价格在20世纪下降了一半以上。相比较而言，羊肉、木材和牛肉的相对价格则翻了一番还要多。

尽管初级产品的相对价格有净下降的趋势，然而用来衡量初级产品价格的方法存在两个偏差：

（1）运输成本的下降。现有数据一半来自工业化国家的市场。运输业的技术进步进一步降低了伦敦、纽约或东京的产品最终价格中运输成本的比重。这使初级产品出口者获得的收益越来越大。如果将这种变化因素计算出来，初级产品生产者所获的收益有上升趋势，这也使得初级产品价格的下降趋势更为平缓，下降幅度也更小。

（2）工业制成品为被度量的更快的品质变化。我们分析产品时使用的是长期价格数据，这些产品随着时间的推移，质量也在不断地改善。工业制成品（以及服务）的质量的进步（包括以新产品形式）比初级产品更明显。因此，一些制成品相对价格的上涨，可能正是因为它相对质量的提高，而不是在给定质量下产品的相对价格变化的趋势。这种数据有十分严重的潜在问题，例如，20世纪的很多价格数据遵循的是每吨出口产品中的机械品出口价格计算的，就好比如今出口的每吨计算机与过去每吨老式电动马达是同样的东西。

总而言之，初级产品的相对价格可能自1900年以来平均每年下降0.8%，但也可能并不存在什么趋势。因此，从价格走势来看，为农产品或矿产品的出口者担忧是缺乏充分依据的。

11.3 提高初级产品价格的国际卡特尔

也许发展中国家的初级产品生产者可以采取一些行动使得价格的变动趋势有利于自己，也许初级产品的出口商可以通过国际卡特尔相互合作或者其他形式的协同行动变得更加强大。

11.3.1 石油输出国组织的胜利

历史上曾经出现了很多这样的卡特尔的尝试（限制销售者之间竞争的国际协定）。世界历史上最大的获取垄断力量的事件，就是 1973—1974 年的石油输出国组织（OPEC）。OPEC 于 1979—1980 年再次成功地提高了国际石油价格。

1973 年年末的一连串事件使世界石油经济发生了重大变革。在几个月的时间里，OPEC 的 12 个成员国成功地使石油的美元价格提升了 4 倍，从每桶 2.59 美元上涨到 10.36 美元。石油输出国几乎一夜之间暴富。消费石油的工业化国家则陷入了自 20 世纪 30 年代以来最为严重的衰退。石油的相对价格（一桶石油的价格可以从工业化国家购买到的工业制成品）是原来的 3 倍。

其结果是 OPEC 各成员国经济上升到一个新的繁荣水平，之后又进一步腾飞，但最终呈现出衰退的迹象。1974—1978 年，石油的实际价格大约下降了 1/6，但仍远高于 1973 年以前的任何一年的水平。1979—1980 年，迎来了 OPEC 石油价格第二波大提价，即第二次“石油冲击”。受伊朗革命和石油购买者日益加重的恐慌的影响，石油价格上涨了一倍以上。然而在 20 世纪 80 年代中期，OPEC 的势力开始变弱，石油的实际价格于 1985 年突然下跌，从 1980—1984 年的约 4 ~ 5 倍的原价格（1973 年之前）下降到 1986—1989 年的不到原价的两倍。

20 世纪七八十年代的石油和 OPEC 的传奇是戏剧性的卡特尔的成功和衰退。这种成功和衰退都需要予以解释。

先谈成功。1973—1974 年和 1979—1980 年的石油冲击，并不是供给不足或地球上可利用资源枯竭的结果。全世界已探明且可利用的石油的增长快于世界石油消费。石油开采成本也并没有提高多少。

1973—1974 年和 1979—1980 年的石油价格的暴涨是人为造成的。关键在于世界需求的增长远远快于非 OPEC 国家供给的增长。石油在各国间的分布极不均衡，OPEC 国家在全球石油生产中所占的比重到 1972 年达到 50% 以上。此外，OPEC 占有已探明石油储量的份额——近似等于未来的生产份额——为 2/3 以上。

到 20 世纪 70 年代初期，美国首次变得易受石油输出国压力的牵制。基本上没有受到早期中东危机威胁的美国，在 1973 年其石油消费有 1/3 要从国外进口，其中部分需要从阿拉伯国家进口。随着 OPEC 在世界石油生产中的地位日趋重要，同时美国对石油进口依赖的日益增强，OPEC 国家得以利用买方竞争而在 1973 年和 1979 年再一次抬高石油价格。

11.3.2 作为卡特尔的极端模型的古典垄断

为理解为什么价格和产出可以带来最大利润以及什么因素制约了这些利润，我们必须先理解最优价格将高于完全自由竞争情况下的产量所对应的价格，且如果低于最优价格则完全没有销售。卡特尔成员想要制定一个比完全竞争时更高的价格，然而，它们的定价能力受限于对石油产品负斜率的需求曲线。如果仅考虑抑制购买的禁止性价格这种极端的情况，这一价格点是很清楚的。即如果卡特尔足够愚蠢，将价格定得非常高（限制性价格），它将失去所有的石油出口业务。因此，卡特尔组织的最优销售价格一定处于禁止性价格以下。当然，对于卡特尔成员来说为最优的卡特尔价格，对于全世界却并非最优。同时，卡特尔通过削减石油出口数量导致了世界福利的净损失，这些被削减出口的石油数量对于购买者具有的价值要高于卡特尔成员的生产成本。

11.3.3 对卡特尔力量的限制和侵蚀

11.3.3.1 定价的规则

如果卡特尔能够完全有效率地运作，那么获得利润最大化的价格能有多高？对此，卡特尔的理论提供了以下一些规则：

（1）产品的边际成本越高，价格越低。

（2）需求弹性越大，价格越低。如果需求是有弹性的，面对卡特尔产品价格上升的时候，购买者无疑就会选择消费其他产品。

（3）卡特尔控制世界产量的份额越大，价格就越高。控制更大的世界产量份额，能有效地增加对卡特尔产品的需求（而这部分需求不会落入非卡特尔的外部生产者处）。

（4）非卡特尔生产者的供给弹性越大，价格越低。非卡特尔生产者的供给弹性与产品需求弹性的作用是一样的。卡特尔会避免大幅提价，因为这么做将导致自己的销售量大幅减少。

11.3.3.2 不利于卡特尔的趋势

这些规则也意味着随着时间的推移，逐渐会产生不利于卡特尔的力量。当卡特尔刚刚建立时，它可能会舒适地享受低价格弹性和高市场份额。然而，一旦它成功地抬高了价格，反而很可能使得四种不利于卡特尔的趋势发生：低迷的需求、新的竞争性供给、下降的市场份额和作弊。

（1）低迷的需求。更高的价格将使购买国寻求新的途径，避免进口卡特尔的产品。如果它们可以成功地找到替代品，那么随着时间的推移，对于任何给定的卡特尔价格，购买国的进口需求都将下降。这些国家对进口产品的长期需求曲线比短期需求曲线更具弹性。这正是 OPEC 经历过的。正如理论所预期的，也正如一些 OPEC 国家的石油部长们所担忧的，各石油进口国慢慢地找到了降低石油消费的多种途径，如更多地使用节能型轿车。

（2）新的竞争性供给。卡特尔最初的成功会激励非卡特尔国家增加产品供给。如果卡特尔产品为农产品，如糖或咖啡，卡特尔的价格上涨将促使其他国家的农民将越来越多的土地、劳动力以及资金从其他农作物转向糖和咖啡。如果卡特尔产品为可耗竭的矿物资源，如石油或铜，非卡特尔国家对更高价格所做出的反应是加倍努力地勘探新的储量。如果非卡特尔国家幸运的话，其竞争性供给将随着时间的推移更加具有弹性。这又是 OPEC 所经历的——其他国家以更快的速度发现了新的石油储备。

（3）下降的市场份额。卡特尔所占有的世界市场份额随着时间推移会下降。为了在提高价格的同时不造成库存积压，卡特尔必须削减其产出与销售。由于非卡特尔国家将竭力增加其产出和销售，即使卡特尔成员同心协力，卡特尔的市场份额也将会下降。

OPEC 占世界石油市场的份额从 20 世纪 70 年代的一半多，下跌到 1985 年的不到 1/3。

（4）作弊。理论与经验还增加了卡特尔力量衰退的第四个原因——卡特尔成员有违反卡特尔协定，进行作弊的动机。

假定你是其中的一个成员国，作为一个典型的卡特尔成员，你拥有足够的石油储量，有能力按照自己的计划开采和销售超过协议数量（OPEC 称之为“产品配额”）的石油。超过配额增加产出只会提高你的边际成本，如每桶 6 美元。假设其他卡特尔成员如实地维持其产出，购买者则愿意为你卖的每一桶石油支付将近 100 美元。为什么不通过将价格略微下降至 98 美元及以下（如 98 美元）来吸引额外的购买者呢？你这么做，是因为你认为你的个体行为不会使卡特尔价格下降多少。从理论上讲，作弊行为会削弱进而瓦解整个卡特尔组织。各个大型成员国可以通过大幅削减自己产量的方式来抵消其他作弊者增加的产量，进而维持卡特尔的效率。因此，这些大型成员国的总体规模决定了卡特尔可以维持多久。

正如理论所预期的，OPEC 成员的确在卡特尔组织内作弊，甚至公开作弊。直至 20 世纪 80 年代中期，最大的生产者——沙特阿拉伯不得不在别国作弊时削减自己的产量以维持卡特尔。到了 1985 年后期，沙特阿拉伯转而采取了具有竞争力的石油价格，石油的相对价格一落千丈。因此，卡特尔理论正确地解释了为什么卡特尔的利润和利润率会随着时间的推移而下降。然而该理论并没有说卡特尔是无法盈利或是无害的；相反，它强调了卡特尔组织给其他成员所带来的收益。即使是一个终将瓦解的卡特尔，也会给其成员带来巨大的收益。

11.3.4 其他初级产品

对于发展中国家而言，经济理论记忆 OPEC 的经验是否意味着他们有希望通过加入除石油以外的其他初级产品卡特尔组织而获取更大的国家利益？实际情况并非如此。这里有充分的理由使人相信，对于非石油的初级产品，卡特尔瓦解得会更快，中期收益也更少，其中以农产品尤甚。因为存在着供给竞争问题，其他国家可以很容易地扩大相应的农产品的种植面积。

历史证实了这个结论。在两次世界大战之间建立的 72 个商品卡特尔中，只有 2 个存活过了 1945 年。在 20 世纪 70 年代新建立的十几个卡特尔中，只有 5 个生存至 1985 年：可可、咖啡、橡胶、糖和锡。自 1985 年以来，这 5 种商品的卡特尔影响力微小，以至于它们对商品市场几乎没有什么影响。

由于国际卡特尔的垄断力量受到这些限制，发展中国家为了经济发展仍旧可以对本国的初级产品的出口征税。大体上，这种战略可以很好地发挥作用。对尼日利亚的石油、加纳的可可、菲律宾椰子的出口征税可以用于修建学校、医院和道路。遗憾的是，某些发展中国家，由于一些政治经济的原因，将出口征税收入从生产率最高的用途上挪为他用。例如：尼日利亚的石油收入消失在日益臃肿的政府官僚机构和贪婪的腐败之中；加纳可可营销局用对可可种植者的重税收入来进口政府官员们所需要的奢侈品；马科斯政府将菲律宾的椰子果税收分配给马科斯的少数几个朋友和亲戚。

12 Multinationals and International Factor Movements

12.1 Types of Foreign Investments

There are mainly two types of foreign investments: portfolio investments and direct investments. Portfolio investments are purely financial assets, such as stocks and bonds denominated in a national currency. Regarding bonds, the investor simply leads capital to get fixed payouts or a return at regular intervals and then receives the face value of the bond onf a fixed date. Most foreign investments prior to World War I were of this type and were flowed primarily from the United Kingdom to the new colonies, such as the United States and Canada, for railroad construction, land reclamation and development of raw materials. According to the regulation of the U.S. government, the percentage of stocks purchased in a portfolio investment shall be less than 10% of the voting stock of a corporation (a purchase of 10% or more of the voting stock of a corporation is regarded as a direct investment). As for stocks, the investor purchases the equity, or the ownership of the company net assets. Portfolio or financial investments take place primarily through financial institutions such as banks and investment funds. International portfolio investments collapsed after World War I and had not revived until the 1960s.

Direct investments are real investments in factories, capital goods, land and inventories where both capital and management are directly arranged by the investors who keep the control over the use of the invested capital. Direct investment usually takes the forms of setting up a branch or taking over another firm (e. g., purchasing a majority of the stock in a company). Any purchase of 10% or more stock of a firm, however, is regarded as direct investment by the U.S. government. In the international environment, direct investments are usually undertaken by multinational corporations engaged in industries like manufacturing, resource extraction, or services. As important as portfolio investments, direct investments are now the main forms or channels for international private capital flows.

12.2 Motives for Direct Foreign Investments

The motives for direct investments abroad are generally the same as for portfolio investments —that is, to earn higher returns (possibly resulting from higher growth rates abroad, more favorable tax treatment, or greater availability of infrastructures) and to diversify risks. Indeed, it has been found that firms with a strong international orientation (either through exports or through foreign production and / or sales facilities) are more profitable and have a much smaller variability in profits than purely domestic firms.

Although these reasons are sufficient to explain international portfolio investments, they leave unanswered the basic question of why the residents of a nation do not borrow from other nations and themselves make real investments in their own nation rather than accept direct investments from abroad. There are several possible explanations for this. The most important is that many large corporations often have some unique production knowledge or managerial skills that could easily and profitably be utilized abroad and over which the corporation wants to retain direct control. In such a situation, the firm will make direct investments abroad. This involves horizontal integration, or the production abroad of a differentiated product that is also produced at home.

Another important reason for direct foreign investments is to obtain control of a needed raw material and thus ensure an uninterrupted supply at the lowest possible cost. This is referred to as vertical integration and was the form of most direct foreign investments in developing countries and in some mineral-rich developed countries. Thus, American and the foreign corporations own mines in Canada, Jamaica, Venezuela, Australia, and other nations, and foreigners own some coal mines in the United States. Vertical integration involving multinational corporations can also go forward into the ownership of sales or distribution networks abroad, as is the case with most of the world's major automobile producers.

Still other reasons for direct foreign investments are to avoid tariffs and other restrictions that nations impose on imports or to take advantage of various government subsidies to encourage direct investments made by U.S. firms in the EU countries and some direct foreign investments in manufacturing in developing nations. Examples of the latter are the direct foreign investments nations. Other possible reasons for direct foreign investments are to enter a foreign market so as to share in the profits, to purchase a promising foreign firm to avoid its future competition and the possible loss of export markets, or because only a large foreign multinational corporation can obtain the necessary financing to enter the market.

Two-way direct foreign investments can then be explained by some industries being more advanced in one nation (such as theAI industry in the United States), while other industries are more efficient in other nations (such as the automobile industry in Japan). Direct foreign investments have been greatly facilitated (in a sense made possible) by the very rapid advances in transportation (i.e., jet travel) and communication (i.e., international telephone lines and international data transmission,) that have occurred since the end of World War II. These advances permit the headquarters of multinational corporations to exert immediate and direct control over the operations of their subsidiaries around the world, and thus facilitate and encourage direct investments abroad.

12.3 Reasons Why Multinationals Exist

Why do multinational enterprises exist? The answer seems simple-because they are profitable. But the issue is more complicated than it sounds.

We should first dispose of one possible explanation that multinationals are simply a way of shifting financial capital between countries based on national differences in returns and risks. Although return and risk must play a role in the decisions by firms about whether to make direct investments, this financial theory of direct investment is not adequate. It does not explain why these international investments would be large enough to establish managerial control to another, international portfolio investment can accomplish this task better than direct investment by firms whose major preoccupation lies in production and marketing.

There is some agreement that five different pieces together provide a good explanation of why multinational firms exist (and why they are as large as they are). The five pieces are: ①Inherent disadvantages of being foreign. ②Firm-specific advantages (to overcome the inherent disadvantages). ③Location factors (that favor foreign production over exporting). ④Internalization advantages (that favor direct investment over contracting with independent firms). ⑤Obligation rivalry (among multinational enterprises).

The combination of these pieces into a framework for understanding the multinational enterprise is often called the eclectic approach, with credit for the synthesis going to John Duning.

12.3.1 Inherent Disadvantages

Our first step is to recognize that there are good reasons why multinational enterprises should not exist. An MNE has inherent disadvantages in trying to compete against foreign rivals by operation on their own turf. The multinational is at a disadvantage in this foreign production environment because it does not initially have the native understanding of local laws, customs, procedures, practices, and relationships. In addition, the firm has the extra costs of maintaining management control. It is expensive to operate at a distance, expensive in travel and communications, and especially expensive in misunderstanding. Furthermore, the MNE may lack useful connections with political leaders in the foreign country, or it could face actual or potential hostility from the foreign country's government.

12.3.2 Firm-Specific Advantages

What makes it possible for a multinational to overcome the inherent disadvantages of being foreign? To be successful, the multinational must have one or more firm-specific advantages—that is, one or more assets of the multinational enterprise that are not assets held by its local competitors in the host country (or, perhaps, by any other firm in the world). A firm's secret technology or its patents are a firm-specific advantage, or as in the case of petroleum refining (Royal Dutch Shell) or metal processing (Alcoa), the firm may gain advantage by coordinating operations and capital investments at various stages in a vertical production process. Because of heavy inventory costs and its knowledge of the requirements at each stage, the firm may be able to economize through synchronizing operations. Or the firm may have marketing advantages based on skilled use of advertising and other promotional methods that establish product differentiation—for instance, through highly regarded brand names (examples: Nestle, Procter & Gamble). Or an advantage may inhere in superior management techniques (example: GeneralElectric). Or, as for many of these large MNEs, it has access to very large amounts of financial capital, amounts far larger than the ordinary national firm can command. Some special advantage is necessary for the firm to overcome the disadvantages of operating at a distance in a foreign environment. It is costly for the firm to develop these assets (for instance, the cost of research and development to develop new technology, the marketing expenses to establish and maintain a strong brand name). The challenge to the firm is to maximize its returns on these assets.

We now have an enterprise that has firm-specific advantages such that it could operate profitably as a multinational. But should it? Even for the firm that has firm-specific advantages, it must also consider alternatives to foreign direct investment for earning profits from activities in a foreign market. It must be more profitable for a multinational enterprise to own and manage a foreign operation, rather than adopting some other way of earning profits. Let's focus on the situation in which a firm wants to earn profits by selling to local buyers in the foreign country. Here are two questions for the firm's managers:

(1) Should the firm sell to foreign buyers by exporting from its home country, or should the firm set up local production in the foreign country to produce the products that are sold to the foreign buyers?

(2) Should the firm license local firms in the foreign country to use its advantages in their own operations that serve the foreign buyers, or should the firm set up foreign operations that it owns and controls?

The answers to these questions bring location factors and internationalization advantages into the explanation.

12.3.3 Local Factors

Local factors are all of the advantages and disadvantages of producing in one country (the home country) or in another country (the foreign country). We have already developed, in the previous chapters of the book, many of the location factors that we need to answer the questions "Export or FDI?" Here are four key location factors from our previous explorations:

(1) Comparative advantage: the effects of resource availability (labor, land, and so forth) on the costs of producing in different countries.

(2) Scale economies: size advantages that favor concentrating production in a few locations and serving other national markets by exporting.

(3) Governmental barriers to importing into the foreign country: tariffs and nontariff barriers that make it difficult to export from the home country.

(4) Trade bloc: setup that favors FDI if the foreign country is a member of a free-trade area (or similar arrangement) but the home country is not a member because production in the foreign country can also be used to serve buyers in the other member countries.

There are other location factors that are important in some industries. High costs oftransporting a product favor FDI to locate production units close to foreign buyers, rather than serving faraway buyers by exporting. Government taxes, subsidies, and regulations affect the profitability of producing in different countries. The need to adapt products to the specific tastes of foreign buyers can favor FDI because it is more effective to have close links among the local marketing group, the product redesign group, and the operations group that must produce the redesigned products at acceptable costs.

Location factors are key to answering the questions "Export or FDI?" Note that the answer could go either way for a specific firm and product. In some cases, it is more profitable to export from the home country, for instance, because the home country has a comparative advantage in the availability and low cost of the most important resource needed in producing the product. In other cases, foreign production in an affiliate established by direct investment is more profitable, for instance, because the foreign country has high tariffs on imports of the product.

12.3.4 International Advantages

Even if the firm rules out exporting as a way of serving the foreign market, it still has alternatives for earning profits from that foreign market. Instead of using foreign direct investment to set up an affiliate, the firm could sell or rent its firm-specific advantages to foreign firms for them to use in their own production. For instance, if the advantages are based on superior technology, a strong brand name, or better management practices, the firm could license one or more foreign firms to use these assets. A license is an agreement for one firm to use another firm's asset, with restrictions on how the asset can be used, and with payments for the right to use the asset.

In making the decision between FDI and licensing of foreign firms, the firm with the asset must weigh the advantages and disadvantages of each alternative. An important advantage of licensing foreign and firms is that the firm avoid (most of) the inherent disadvantages of establishing and managing its own foreign operations. On the other hand, there are advantages to keeping the use of the firm-specific advantages within (internal to) the enterprise. International advantages are the advantages of using an asset. International advantages exist because there are drawbacks to using the market for many firm-specific advantages, particularly intangible assets like technology, brand names, marketing techniques, and management practices.

Internalization advantages arise from avoiding the transaction costs and risks of licensing an independent firm. Negotiating the license is often costly and difficult. The licensor wants a high payment, and the license wants a low payment. The licensee is likely to be skeptical of claims by the licensors also wants to put various restrictions on how the licensee can use the asset, but the licensee wants to have as few restrictions as possible. The, even if the license agreement can be negotiated, the licensor still faces some importance risks. The licensee may not be as careful with the asset as the licensor would be. For instance, the licensee may let secret technology to otheractivities not covered by the other competitors, or the licensee may fail to maintain product quality, leading to news reports ("brand-name cola causes widespread illness in Austria") that harm the global reputation and value of the brand.

Foreign direct investment keeps the use of the assets under the control of the enterprise itself. It avoids many of the drawbacks of using the market for these kinds of assets. The advantages of internalization are based on the ability of the MNE's management of set the terms for the use of the assets in its foreign affiliate. The returns to the use of the assets are part of the profits earned by the affiliate, and the enterprise can enforce policies to safeguard the ongoing value of its intangible assets. The multinational enterprise uses FDI to better appropriate the returns to its intangible assets.

The importance of internalized use o firm-specific intangible assets explains why foreign direct investment occurs to a greater extent in high-technology industries (electronic products or pharmaceuticals, for example) and marketing-intensive industries (food products or automobiles, for example) than it does in standard-technology industries (clothing, for example) or less marketing-intensive industries (paper products, for example).

12.3.5 Oligopolistic Rivalry

Many multinational enterprises are not the tiny firms that populate perfectly competitive markets. Instead, they are large firms that often compete among themselves for market shares and profits. They have used their intangible assets (like new technologies and strong brand names) obtain large market shares. The same intangible assets drive their FDI.

Multinationals can use their decisions about foreign direct investment as part of their strategies for competing. For instance, multinationals compete for location. A multinational sometimes seems to set up an affiliate that looks only marginally profitable, yet it does so with the stated purpose of beating its main competitors to the same national market. General Motors may set up a foreign affiliate in a developing country mainly because it fears that if it doesn't, Toyota will. With some regularity, other multinational rivals then quickly respond by setting up their own affiliates in this country, to prevent the first mover from gaining any lasting advantage. Such follow-the-leader behavior results in a bunching of the timing of entries by rival multinationals into a host country. Most of the affiliates may have a tough time earning profits.

Multinationals can also use FDI to try to mute competition and enhance their market power. First, a multinational may acquire foreign firms that are beginning to challenge their international market position. Second, a multinational may set up an affiliate in the home country of one of its rivals, to establish a competitive threat to this rival. The message is "Don' t compete too vigorously against me in other countries, or I will make life tough for you in your own home market."

12.4 Problems Created by Multinational Corporations in the Home Country

By efficiently organizing production and distribution on a worldwide basis, while MNCs can increase world output and welfare, they can create serious problems in both home and host countries. The most controversial of the alleged harmful effects of MNCs on home country is the loss of domestic jobs resulting from foreign direct investments. There are likely to be unskilled and semiskilled production jobs in which home countries have comparative disadvantages, it is for this reason that organized labor in the United States and other major home country oppose direct foreign investments by MNCs. However, some clerical, managerial, and technical jobs are also likely to be created in the headquarters of the MNCs in home country as a result of foreign direct investments. Even if the home country would have lost these jobs anyway to foreign competitors and would have had no jobs created at home without direct foreign investments. The extent to which this may be true depends on the type of direct foreign investment and the circumstances under which it takes place.

A related problem is the export of advanced technology to be combined with other cheaper foreign factors to maximize corporate profits. It is claimed that this may undermine the technological superiority and future of the home country. However, against this possible harmful effect is the tendency of MNCs to concentrate their R&D in the home country, thus allowing it to maintain its technological lead. In any case, whether MNCs undermine the technological leadership of its home country is still a controversial issue and there is no clear answer.

Another possible harmful effect of MNCs on the home country can result from transfer pricing and similar practices, and from shifting their operations to lower-tax nations, which reduce tax revenues and erode the tax base of the home country. This results from common international taxing practice. Specially, the host country taxes the subsidiary's profits first. To avoid double taxation of foreign subsidiaries, the home country then usually taxes only repatriated profits (if its tax rate is higher than in the host country), and only by the difference in the tax rates.

An example will clarify this point. Suppose that the corporate profit tax is 40% in the home country and 30% in the host country, and the before-tax risk-adjusted profit rate is 20% abroad but 16% at home. The MNC will then invest abroad. When 20% is earned abroad, the host country get 6 % in taxes (at 30% tax rate) and the MNC retains 14%. When the MNC repatriates this 14% profit, the home country will tax it at the rate of 10% (the difference between the domestic and the foreign corporate tax profit rate). Thus, the home country gets only 1.4% and only when the profits are repatriated. The reinvestment of profits abroad in the MNC's affiliate thus amounts to an interest-free loan from the home country. If the corporate profit tax rates of the home and host countries were equal, the home country would collect no tax at all even when the MNC repatriates its profits. Had the MNC invested in the home country to begin with and earned a profit of 16%, the home country would have collected a tax of 6.4% (at the 40% tax rate). Thus, MNCs reduce tax revenues and erode the tax base of the home country.

Finally, because of their access to international capital markets, MNCs can circumvent domestic monetary policies and make government control over the economy in the home nation more difficult. There alleged harmful effects of MNCs are of crucial importance to the United States, since it is home for about 1/3of the largest MNCs. In general, home country does impose some restrictions on the activities of MNCs, either for balance-of-payment reasons or, more recently, for employment reasons.

12.5 Problems Created by Multinational Corporations in the Host Country

Host countries have even more serious complaints against MNCs than home countries. First and foremost is the allegation that MNCs dominate their economies. This is certainly true for Canada, where almost 60% of the total capital in manufacturing is owned or controlled by foreigners (40% by Americans). It is also true for some of the smaller developing countries. Foreign domination is felt in many different ways in host countries, including ① the unwillingness of a local affiliate of an MNC to export to a nation deemed unfriendly to the home country or the requirement to comply with a home-country lar prohibiting such exports; ② the borrowing of funds abroad to circumvent tight domestic credit conditions and the lending of funds abroad when interest rates are low at home; and ③ the effect on national tastes of large-scale advertising for such products as Coca-Cola, McDonald's and so on.

Another alleged harmful effect of MNCs on the host country is the siphoning of R&D funds to the home country. While this may be more efficient for the MNC and the world as a whole, it also keeps the host country technologically dependent. This is especially true and serious for developing countries. MNCs may also absorb local saving and entrepreneurial talent, thus preventing them from being used to establish domestic enterprises that might be more important for national growth and development. The extent to which this occurs, however, is not clear. MNCs may also extract most of the benefits resulting from their investments in host countries, either through tax and tariff benefits or through tax avoidance. In developing countries, foreign direct investments by MNCs in mineral and raw material production has often given rise to complaints of foreign exploitation in the form of low techniques inappropriate for labor - abundant developing nations, ignorance of labor training, overexploitation of natural resources, and creating highly dualistic "enclave" economies.

Most of these complaints are to some extent true, particularly in the case of developing host countries, and they have led many host nations to regulate foreign investments in order to mitigate the harmful effects and increase the possible benefits. Thus, Canada imposed higher taxes on foreign affiliates with less than 25% Canadian interest. India specifies the sectors in which direct foreign investments are allowed and sets rules to regulate their operation. Some developing countries allow only joint ventures (i.e., local equity participation) and se rules for the transfer oftechnology and training of domestic labor, impose limits on the use of imported inputs and the remission of profits, set environmental regulations, and so on. In extreme cases, the host country can nationalize foreign factories. However, it is likely to seriously impact the future direct foreign investments to the country.

Even in the United States, the home country of the third largest MNCs, greatly concerned about foreigners' control towards economics which is brought by the high investments from the foreign countries during the late 1980s. The worries vanished in the light of the sharp reduction in foreign direct investments in the early 1990s. Efforts are currently made by the EU, OECD, the UN, and UNCTAD to devise an international contract. Therefore, it is impossible to succeed in solving the problems created by MNCs in home and host countries by strict restriction.

In recent years, Chinese MNCs purchase energy companies in developing countries and high-tech companies in developed countries are attracting the attention of host countries.

12.6 Financial Crisis

Another important and serious problem facing the international monetary system at present is that it seems to be powerless to prevent international financial crisis, especially in emerging markets. Six financial crises occurred since the mid-1990s, including: the Mexican financial crisis from 1994 to 1995; the Southeast Asian financial crisis from 1997 to 1999; the Russian financial crisis of the summer of 1998; the Brazilian financial crisis of 1999; Financial crisis in Turkey and Argentina. The International Monetary Fund estimates that in recent financial crises, the loss of total output of each country as a percentage of GDP was 82% in Indonesia, 57% in Thailand, 39% in Malaysia, 30% in Mexico, and 27% in South Korea (there are no estimated data for Brazil, Russia, Turkey and Argentina).

Although the basic causes of several financial crises are different, the process is very similar. After detecting signs of weakness in a country's economy, a large number of hot money has moved out of the market, causing the crisis to erupt. In the early 1990s, many countries opened their capital markets, and foreign investors invested heavily in these emerging markets to obtain high capital reports and score their investment portfolios. However, when they found problems in their economies, these countries immediately withdrew their capital on a large scale, which caused a sudden economic crisis. The danger is that the crisis will spread to other countries, including developed countries.

A number of measures have been proposed, and some steps have already been taken to avoid or minimize such crises in the future and thus greatly strengthen the architecture of the present international monetary system and improve its functioning. including: ①strengthen the links between international currencies; ②strengthen the banking and financial systems of emerging markets; ③encourage more private sector participation.

Without accurate, credible and timely information, the market will not be able to operateeffectively. Therefore, market transparency is becoming increasingly important. Financial warning indicators (such as budget and frequent project deficits, long-term and short-term external debt, and the share of international saves in GDP) can alert which emerging markets are likely to have problems. Through early warning, foreign investors can understand the potential problems in the market, avoid blindly excessive capital inflows, and prevent crises.

It is also critical to strengthen the banking and financial systems in emerging markets. All emerging markets involved in the financial crisis over the past decades have fragile banking and financial systems. The International Monetary Fund has formulated standards in accounting, auditing, corporate governance, payment and settlement systems, security, and banking. Some of these have been performed as part of the IMF's oversight functions.

The private sectors are more involved in taking responsibility for resolving emerging market crises by rebuilding and rolling out loans or providing new funding rather than escaping quickly, which is a prerequisite for official IMF assistance. The reason for this is that private investors have invested too much short-term funds in emerging markets for non-constructive purposes. Therefore, they should be held accountable for the crisis they create.

Meanwhile, we shall realize that even if all the reform measures we have considered can be put intopractice, we still cannot eradicate the possible financial crisis in the future. We can only hope that these reforms will reduce the number of financial crises and reduce their severity. The instability and crisis of international finance are an inevitable product of financial market liberalization. It is also the price we must pay while enjoying the benefits of financial market liberalization for industrialization and the development of emerging markets.

The financial crisis is not limited to emerging market economies. From 2008 to 2009, most United States and the other advanced economies fell into a severe financial crisis. The recent global financial crisis began in 2007 in the US real estate industry. The reason is that banks provide large (sub) loans or mortgages to individuals or families who cannot pay back. When many individuals and families default on loans, American banks were in deep crisis. The crisis then spread to the entire financial industry in 2008, and then from the financial industry to the physical industry in the United States, and even the rest of the world, leading to the "Great Recession" in 2009 (this was the worst economic recession since World War II).

There are four basic reasons that lead to therecent global financial crisis: ①Insufficient financial supervision, especially in the field of investment banking; ②Existing financial supervision measures have not been implemented; ③ Greed. Bankers and other financial professionals pursue profits regardless of cost; ④Fraud. Madoff's Ponzi scheme defrauded $65 billion.

The problems arising from these present exchange rate arrangements are closely related to other serious problems that the present world confronts. They are: ①Low growth and high unemployment in developed economies after the Great Recession; ② Trade protection in developed countries in the context of rapid globalization; ③A large number of structural imbalances in the United States and inadequate economic structural transformation in the transition economies of Central and Eastern Europe; ④Extreme poverty in many developing countries; ⑤Lack of resources, environmental degradation and climate change threaten global sustainable development.

12 跨国公司与国际要素流动

12.1 对外投资的形式

对外投资主要有两种形式：组合投资和直接投资。组合投资是指投资于用一国货币计量的纯金融资产，如股票和债券。对于债券，投资者只是借出其资本以便获得固定的报酬，或者定期获得收益并在一个预定的日期收回债券的面值。第一次世界大战以前，大多数外国投资都是这种类型，资金主要从英国流向新殖民地地区，如美国和加拿大，投资于铁路的修建、土地的开垦和原材料资源的开发。美国政府也规定，组合投资中购买一个公司股票的数量应低于该公司有投票权股票的10%（达到或超过10%就变成直接投资了）。对于股票，投资者购买的是权益，或者说得到了对公司净资产的一份所有权。组合或金融投资开始是通过一些金融机构（如银行和投资基金）完成的。国际组合投资在第一次世界大战结束后垮掉了，直到20世纪60年代以后才又开始复兴。

直接投资是对工厂、资本货物、土地和存货的直接投资，资本和管理都由投资者一手安排，投资者保留对已投资资本使用的控制权。直接投资通常以一家公司成立分公司或接管另一家公司的形式出现（如购买另一家公司绝大多数股权）。然而，美国政府的规定是购买任何一家公司的股票超10%就视为直接投资。在国际环境中，直接投资通常被一些跨国公司用来介入制造、资源提取、服务等行业。直接投资和组合投资一样，是当前国际私人资本流动的主要形式或渠道。

12.2 对外直接投资的动因

对外直接投资的动机基本上与组合投资的动机一样，是为了获得更高的收益（可能是因为国外有更高的经济增长率、更吸引人的税收优待政策，或是更优越的基础设施）和分散风险。事实上，那些有很强国际业务的公司（或通过出口，或利用国外的生产销售设施），比完全在国内发展的公司有更多的赢利，而且收益的波动更小。

这些原因足以解释为什么有国际组合投资。然而，对于对外直接投资还有一个基本问题未回答，即为什么还不能解释一国的居民不从其他国家借钱而后对本国进行实际投资，却要接受从国外来的直接投资？对此有几种可能的解释。最重要的原因在于许多大公司往往具有一些独特的生产知识和管理技能可以很容易在国外经营获利，而且这些公司也希望保留直接控制权。在这种情况下，这些公司就会对国外直接投资。这涉及一个横向一体化的问题或者说在国内外都生产差别产品的问题。

直接投资的另外一个重要原因是为了获得所需原材料的控制权，以保证按尽可能低的成本得到不间断的供给。这被称为“纵向一体化”，它是在发展中国家和一些产矿丰富的发达国家大多数外国直接投资形成的原因。因此，美国和其他外国公司拥有了加拿大、牙买加、委内瑞拉、澳大利亚及其他国家的矿井，一些外国公司拥有了美国的煤矿。跨国公司的纵向一体化也能向前延伸到拥有国外的运输和销售网。世界上多数主要的汽车制造商都是这样做的。

对外直接投资还有其他一些原因，如避开关税和国家对进出口商品的其他限制，或是为了得到政府对各种鼓励外国直接投资的补贴。前者的例子是美国公司对欧盟国家所进行的大规模直接投资，以及在发展中国家制造中的一些直接投资。后者的例子是在发展中国家和一些发达国家的经济衰退地区的外国直接投资。对外直接投资的另一个可能的原因是进入国外一个寡头市场以求分享利润、购买一个有前景的外国公司以避免未来的竞争及在出口市场上未来可能的损失，或者仅是因为只有大型跨国公司才能获得进入市场所必需的融资。

双向直接投资也可以这样解释：一国的某些行业比较先进（如美国的人工智能工业），而另一国的其他行业效率更高（如日本的汽车工业），这也会促进双向投资。同时应该注意到第二次世界大战结束以后到交通（如喷气式飞机旅行）和通信（如国际电话网和国际信息传输及处理）获得了飞速发展，这也是为双向直接投资创造了便利的条件。由于跨国公司的总部能对全世界的下属机构的运营实现即时的直接控制，从而方便和鼓励了对外直接投资活动。

12.3 跨国公司存在的原因

为什么会有跨国公司？答案听起来很简单——因为跨国公司可以更好地盈利。但实际上问题远比听上去复杂。

我们先排除一个可能的解释，即跨国公司不过就是利用国家之间受益和风险的差异，在国家间进行金融资产转移的一种方式。尽管收益和风险的差异在企业是否进行直接投资的决策上起到了一定的作用，但这样直接投资的金融理论并不足以站得住脚。因为它解释不了国际投资为什么要达到可以控制国外公司管理权的规模。如果只是要进行金融资产的国家之间的转移，那么国际间接投资可以比主要从事产品生产和营销企业所进行的直接投资能更好地实现这个目标。

有五个如下理由可以解释跨国公司为什么存在且规模如此巨大：①跨国公司固有的劣势；②跨国公司持有的优势（克服上述固有劣势）；③地区优势（这使在外国生产优于对其出口）；④内部化优势（使得直接投资优于其他公司签订合同和联盟）；⑤寡头垄断竞争（在跨国公司之间）。

将这些因素结合起来理解跨国公司的框架通常被称为“折中理论”，由约翰·邓宁首次系统提出。

12.3.1 固有的劣势

首先，我们应当认识到，有很多理由能够说明跨国公司不应该存在。因为跨国公司在东道国与本土企业进行竞争时有其固有劣势：跨国公司不熟悉东道国的法律、风俗习惯、程序、惯例以及各种关系。因此，在这种外国环境中，跨国公司与本土公司的竞争处于不利的地位。其次，跨国公司在管理控制上也会发生额外成本。远距离的运营代价昂贵，交通和沟通的成本也非常昂贵，特别是沟通的成本甚高。最后，跨国公司与东道国正式领袖之间缺乏有效的联系，从而可能面临来自东道国政府切实的或潜在的敌意。

12.3.2 跨国公司持有的优势

跨国公司如何克服作为外国企业在东道国经营而带来的固有劣势？要想成功克服其固有劣势，跨国公司必须有一个甚至更多的公司特有优势，即具有一项甚至更多项东道国本土企业所不具备的资产（或者可能是世界上其他企业所不具备的资产）。企业的秘密技术或者专利可以是特有优势。或者企业在垂直生产过程的不同阶段，协同运作以及资产投资可能有的优势，如石油精炼、金属加工等。由于巨大的存货成本和每阶段所需要的专门知识，公司可以通过同步运营来节省费用。或者跨国公司基于其熟练的广告运用和其他可以建立产品差异化的促销手段，如通过被高度认可的品牌（如雀巢和宝洁），可能会获得营销优势；或者是卓越的金融资本数量，远远大于普通企业可以控制的数额。某些特定优势对跨国公司克服在外国环境中远距离运作的劣势是必须具有的。当然，拥有这些资产需要消耗高额成本，如开发新技术需要研发费用，确立和维持一个强大品牌需要市场投入等。跨国公司所面临的挑战就是将这些产品带来的收益最大化。

假设一个拥有特定优势的企业跨国经营是有利可图的，那么它应该成为跨国公司吗？即使是对于具备了特定优势的公司，仍必须考虑除了对外直接投资，是否还有其他投资方式使它从国外市场活动中获得利润。对跨国公司来说，拥有和管理国外业务运用的利润必须超过采用其他经营方式挣得的利润。让我们重点思考这样一个情景：假设一家公司试图通过向外国的消费者出售商品来盈利，公司的经理们将面临两个问题：

（1）公司是在从本国生产，然后出口卖给外国消费者，还是到外国建厂生产向外国消费者提供产品？

（2）是通过许可证形式，准许国外当地企业使用本公司运营上的优势来为外国消费者提供服务，还是到外国建立一个拥有所有权和控制权的企业？

回答这两个问题，需要引入区位因素和内部化优势来解释。

12.3.3 区位优势

区位优势是一个国家（母国）和另一个国家（东道国）生产的所有优势和劣势。在之前的章节里，我们已经研究过很多区位因素来回答“出口还是外国直接投资”这个问题。以下是四个已经提及的比较关键的区位因素：

（1）比较优势，即在不同国家生产成本中的可利用资源（劳动力、土地等）的效应。

（2）规模经济，即在一些区域集中生产并通过出口为其他国家市场服务的规模优势。

（3）阻碍商品进出口的东道国政府壁垒，即不利于出口的关税和非关税壁垒。

（4）贸易集团，即如果外国是某个自由贸易区（或类似集团的成员国），而母国是非成员国，这将有利于外国直接投资，因为在该外国生产的产品还可以便捷地提供给其他成员国的消费者。

在某些行业，还有其他重要的区位因素，如高额运输成本有利于通过外国直接投资使生产地点更接近外国消费者，而不是通过出口卖给距离遥远的消费者；政府的税收和补贴政策会影响在不同国家生产的利润率；外国直接投资有利于让产品更加适应外国消费者特定需求的要求。因为这样可以有效地与本土销售部门、产品重新设计部门进行密切的联系，营运部门可以在可接受的成本下生产重新设计的产品。

区位因素是回答“出口还是外国直接投资”问题的关键。但需要注意的是，对于某一特定的公司或者产品，答案也可能是从母国生产并出口更加有利。例如，因为生产某一产品所需的非常重要的资源在母国获取的成本比较低。但是也有例外，通过直接投资在外国建立子公司生产更加有利，因为外国对这种产品设置了很高的进口关税。

12.3.4 内部化优势

即使一个企业不通过出口这种方式服务于外国市场，它依然有其他可替代的选择从外国市场中获得利润。除了通过外国直接投资建立子公司，跨国公司还可以通过出售或者出租其特有优势给东道国的公司让它们生产产品。例如，如果一家公司的优势来自其卓越的技术、强大的品牌或更好的经营管理实践，那么它可以通过许可方式使一家或者多家东道国公司使用这些资产。许可证允许一家公司可以在某些条件下使用另一公司的资产，并对这种使用权支付报酬。

外国公司要在外国直接投资和许可证两种形式之间做出选择时，必须权衡两者的优势与劣势。授予外国公司许可证的一个重要优势是跨国公司可以避免（大部分的）在东道国投资设厂和管理带来的内在劣势；而外国直接投资则能确保本公司的特有优势，即只限制在公司内部（内部化）使用的优势。内部化优势是指公司内部使用某些特定资产而获得的优势，不需要得到其他公司购买、租赁或者得到许可证去使用这些资产。之所以存在内部化优势，是因为公司的许多特有优势，特别是无形资产，如技术、商标、市场营销技术以及管理实践等地的定价市场存在缺陷。

内部化优势来源于可以规避授予一家独立公司许可证时产生的交易费用和风险。许可证的谈判成本通常颇高，且困难重重。许可证想要获得高额报酬，而被许可方则想尽量少付出代价。被许可方很可能对许可方声称的无形资产的价值和索要的高价表示怀疑。许可方还希望对被许可方如何使用资产设置重重设限，而被许可方则希望这种限制尽可能少。然后，即使协议达成，许可方还会面临很多重大风险。被许可方不会像许可方那样谨慎对待这些产品。例如，它们可能会把机密技术泄漏给其他的竞争者；或者自作主张将这些技术运用到协议中不允许的活动中去；或许被许可方不能维持产品质量而引发了损害品牌的全球声誉和价值的新闻报道（如“奥地利的可口可乐导致广为传播的疾病”等）。

外国直接投资可以保持资产在公司控制范围内使用，可以克服市场缺陷带来的弊病。内部化优势来源于跨国公司管理其子公司使用这些资产的能力。跨国公司不仅能通过其子公司使用这些无形资产获得回报，而且能够实行严格的政策维护这些无形资产的价值。跨国公司通知外国直接投资保证了无形资产的收益最大化。

在内部使用公司特有的无形资产解释了为什么外国直接投资更多地出现在高科技行业（如电子产品和制药产品）和市场密集行业（例如食品和汽车），而不是标准技术行业（如服装业）或者市场密集程度不高的行业（如纸制品行业）。

12.3.5 寡头垄断竞争

很多跨国公司都不是那种处于完全竞争市场的小公司，而是彼此竞争市场份额和利润的巨头。它们使用无形资产（如新技术和大品牌）攫取大量的市场份额。这些无形资产驱动它们进行对外直接投资。

跨国公司把对外直接投资的决策作为它们竞争策略的一部分。例如，跨国公司在特定区域的竞争。跨国公司建立子公司，看起来似乎只有蝇头小利，但它这么做的特定目标是在同一国市场上打击其主要竞争对手。通用汽车也许会在一个发展中国家成立外国子公司，主要是因为担心如果它不那么做，丰田就会做。在某些特定规则下，其他的竞争对手也通过在这个国家建立它们的子公司而做出响应，以阻止竞争对手的行动获得持久的优势。这种跟随领先者行为引起的竞争表现为跨国公司在进入东道国时一拥而上。因此，大多数跨国公司的分支机构都需要度过一个艰难时期才能获利。

跨国公司也能通过对外直接投资来减少竞争和提高它们的市场力量。首先，跨国公司可以收购那些开始挑战其国际市场地位的外国公司。其次，跨国公司可能在某个竞争对手的国家设立子公司，从而形成对竞争对手的威胁，大致的意思是“在其他国家不要和我竞争得太过分，否则我在你的家门口给你好看”！

12.4　跨国公司对母国的影响

跨国公司通过在世界范围内有效地组织生产和销售来增加世界产出与福利，同时它们也为其母国和东道国带来了严重的影响。跨国公司对其母国最有争议的损害就是由于它的对外直接投资使本国的就业机会减少了。减少的很可能是本国处于竞争劣势的非熟练或半熟练工作岗位。由此，美国和其他一些主要的母国的工会组织非常反对跨国公司的直接对外投资活动。当然直接对外投资很可能也要求跨国公司总部中相应地增加一些文秘、管理和技术方面的工作。然而，即便失去的工作机会比增加的多，如果没有外国直接投资，很可能母国的这些工作岗位也会被国外竞争者抢走，而在国内也不会产生新的就业机会。当然，在失业程度上，这取决于对外直接投资的类型和投资发生的环境。

一个相关的问题是出口先进技术与国外便宜的其他要素相结合，使得公司的利润最大化的战略。这一做法被认为会损害母国的技术领先地位与未来利益。然而，为防止可能的危害，跨国公司总是把研究与开发工作集中于本国，以保持技术领先的趋势。无论如何，跨国公司是否有损其母国的技术领先地位，仍然是一个充满争议的问题，还没有明确的答案。

跨国公司的另一种可能的有害作用是转移定价及其他类似活动带来的。跨国公司把经营活动转移到低税率国家，从而减少了母国的税基和税收收入。这一结果的根源是国际税务实践。具体来讲，子公司东道国将先对子公司征税，为避免双重征税，母国通常只对汇回国内的利润征收两国税率的税差（这里假设母国的税率比东道国的税率高）。

举例来说，假设母国的公司所得税为40%，而在子公司的东道国，这一税率为30%，税前风险调节利润率在国外是20%，国内只有16%。那么一家跨国公司将进行海外投资。如果它在国外得到的利润率为20%，子公司东道国得到6%的税收（30%的税率），跨国公司保留了14%的税。如果跨国公司用利润对国外子公司进行再投资，就等于从母国利润汇回国内时，母国就不能对此再征税了。如果跨国公司投资于其母国，哪怕只有16%的利润率，母国都能收到6.4%的税（以40%的税率计算）。因此，跨国公司的海外投资减少了母国的税收收入，侵蚀了它的税基。

最后，由于跨国公司能进入国际资本市场，所以它能绕过国内的货币政策，从而增加了本国政府调控经济的难度。以上论及的跨国公司的有害作用对美国影响最大，因为它是超过1/3最大的大型跨国公司的母国。总体来说，或者是出于国际收支平衡的原因，或者最近出于对就业问题的考虑，跨国公司的母国确实加强了对跨国公司活动的限制。

12.5 跨国公司对东道国的影响

跨国公司的东道国有时会比其母国抱怨得更加强烈。最重要的是，这些国家断言，跨国公司在操纵着国家的经济生活。如加拿大，本国60%的制造业资本为外国人所有或控制。同样，对一些小的发展中国家来说也是如此。外国人对东道国经济对干预和控制有多种不同的途径，包括：①不愿让当地的子公司向那些被认为对母国不友好的国家或母国法律禁止出口的国家出口产品；②当东道国金融政策紧缩时从国外借款，当母国利率低时向海外贷款；③大规模做广告，如可口可乐和麦当劳公司等，以影响当地国家的消费偏好。

跨国公司对东道国有害的另一种说法是这些跨国公司将研发基金吸收到自己的母国。这一行为从跨国公司以及世界整体来看可能更有效率，然而它确实造成了东道国在技术上不得不持续地依赖于跨国公司母国的局面。这对于发展中国家来说的确是很现实而且很严重的问题。跨国公司也可能会吸纳当地的储蓄及企业的高级人才，从而阻碍民族企业的建立，而这对发展中国家的经济发展是更重要的。不过这种情况的严重程度目前尚不清楚。跨国公司通过它们的投资，从税收或关税优惠抑或通过避税从东道国攫取了几乎所有的收益。在发展中国家，跨国公司在采矿业及原材料产业的直接投资屡遭批评。人们越来越多地抱怨它们以低价收购产品，对劳动力资源丰富的发展中国家不恰当使用高资本密集度的生产技术，不重视当地劳工的培训，过度开采自然资源及造成高度二元性的“飞地”经济。

大部分的这类抱怨在某种程度上是确切存在的，特别是在发展中国家。这些抱怨促使许多东道国规范、调整外国的投资活动，使之减少危害，增加可能的收益。为此，加拿大对在本国的外国子公司征收高于加拿大公司但不超过其25%的税收。印度设有专门的部门来引导和规范外国的投资和经营活动。许多发展中国家只允许合资企业（有本地资本参与）的存在，并就技术转让和培训国内劳工制定了规则，限制使用进口部件，并制定了环境方面的法规等。在极端情形下，东道国可以把外国的生产机构收归国有。但是，这很可能会严重影响将来外国对该国的直接投资。

甚至在美国，三个最大跨国公司的母国，20世纪80年代后期也曾对高额的外国直接投资流入带来的外国人对经济的控制表示了极大的关注。到了90年代前期，由于外国的直接投资锐减，这种担心才消失。欧盟、经济合作发展组织、联合国以及联合国贸易发展会议目前都在为制定跨国公司的国际性协议而努力。然而，由于母国与东道国的利益总是冲突的，在实践中很难达成一个非常适合各方的国际性协议。因此，采用严格限制的方法来解决由跨国公司在母国与东道国间产生的问题以及因此引发的相互指责是不可能成功的。

最近几年，中国的跨国公司对发展中国家的能源公司和发达国家的高科技公司的收购正在引起东道国的关注。

12.6 金融危机

目前，国际货币体系所面临的另一个重要严重问题是，它对于防止国际性，特别是新兴市场的金融危机似乎无能为力。自20世纪90年代中期以来出现了6次金融危机，包括：1994—1995年的墨西哥金融危机，1997—1999年的东南亚金融危机，1998年的俄罗斯金融危机，1999年的巴西金融危机，2001—2002年的土耳其金融危机和阿根廷金融危机。国际货币基金组织估计，近年来的数次金融危机中，各国总产出的损失占GDP的比重分别为：印度尼西亚82%，泰国57%，马来西亚39%，墨西哥30%，韩国27%（无巴西、俄罗斯、土耳其及阿根廷的数据估计）。

尽管造成数次金融危机的根本原因各不相同，但其过程却很相似。察觉到某国的经济有疲软的迹象后，大量的短期流动资金纷纷搬出市场，从而使得危机接连爆发。20世纪90年代初期，很多国家开放了资本市场，外国投资者将资金大量投入这些新兴市场以获得高资本汇报。然而，当发现这些国家经济出现问题后，它们会立即将资本大规模撤出，从而使得经济危机突然爆发。其危险在于，危机会传播到包括发达国家在内的其他国家。

为了避免可能发生的危机，或将危机的规模减小至最低限度，人们也提出了一些方法，并逐步实施了某些措施以强化现有的国际货币体系的结构，完善其功能，其中包括：①加强国际货币之间联系的透明性；②强化新兴市场的银行和金融体系；③鼓励更多私有部门的参与。

缺少了准确、可信、及时的信息，市场将无法有效运行。因此，市场的透明性显得越来越重要。财务预警指标（如预算及精彩项目赤字、长期和短期外债以及国际储备在国内生产总值中所占的份额）可以警示哪些新兴市场可能出现的问题。通过预警，国外投资者可以了解市场潜在的问题，避免资金盲目地过度流入，从而防止危机的产生。

强化新兴市场的银行及金融体制也是非常关键的。过去10年卷入金融危机的所有新兴市场，其银行和金融体制都很脆弱。国际货币基金组织制定了会计、审计、公司治理、支付及结算体制、保安、银行等各个方面良好的规范标准。其中，某些已经被作为国际货币基金组织监督职能的一部分加以履行。

私有部门更多的是参与承担解决新兴市场危机的责任，即通过贷款重建和展期或提供新的资金，而不是迅速逃离，并将此作为获得国际货币基金组织官方援助的先决条件，这也是至关重要的。这样做的理由是私人投资者出于并无建设性的目的，将过多短期资金投入新兴市场。因此，他们必须对自己造成的危机负责。

同时，我们必须认识到，即使我们所考虑到的所有改革措施都能付诸实践，仍无法根除将来可能发生的金融危机。我们只能希望这些改革措施可以减少金融危机发生的次数，降低其严重性。国际金融的不稳定以及危机是金融市场自由化不可避免的产物，也是我们在享受金融市场自由化带给工业化和新兴市场发展好处的同时必须付出的代价。

金融危机并不仅限于新兴市场经济体。2008—2009 年，美国和大多数其他发达经济体陷入严重的金融和经济危机。2007 年，发端于美国的房地产行业，其起因是银行将大量（次级）贷款或抵押贷款提供给无法偿付的个人或家庭。当很多个人和家庭拖欠贷款时，美国的银行陷入深度危机。随后危机在 2008 年蔓延到整个金融行业，进而从金融行业蔓延到美国的实体行业，甚至世界其他地区，导致 2009 年的“大衰退”（这是第二次世界大战结束后最为严重的经济衰退）。

近期全球金融危机有四个基本的原因：①金融监管不充分，尤其是在投资银行领域；②已有的金融监管措施没有实施；③贪婪，银行家和其他金融专业人士为求利润不计成本；④欺诈，麦道夫的庞氏骗局涉及 650 亿美元。

现行汇率制度产生的问题是与当今世界所面临的其他一些严重问题密切相关的。这些问题包括：①大衰退后发达经济体的低增长和高失业率；②在快速全球化背景下发达国家的贸易保护主义；③美国大量的结构失衡和中东欧转轨经济体经济结构改造不充分；④很多发展中国家的极度贫困问题；⑤资源匮乏、环境恶化和气候变化对全球的可持续发展形成威胁。

Bibliography
参考文献

PAUL R KRUGMAN, MAURICE OBSTFELD, 2011. International Economics Theory and Policy: 8th edition [M]. Beijing: China Renmin University Press.

ROBERT JCARBAUGH, 2017. International Economics: 15th edition [M]. Beijing: China Renmin University Press.

PUGEL, THOMAS, 2018. International Trade: 16th edition [M]. Beijing: China Renmin University Press.

SALVATORE, DOMINICK, 2019. Introduction to International Economics: 3rd edition [M]. Beijing: Tsinghua University Press.

海闻, P. 林德特, 王新奎, 2012. 国际贸易 [M]. 上海: 格致出版社.

保罗·R. 克鲁格曼, 茅瑞斯·奥伯斯法尔德, 2013. 国际经济学理论与政策: 第8版 [M]. 黄卫平, 等译. 北京: 中国人民大学出版社.

多米尼克·萨尔瓦多, 2013. 国际经济学基础: 第3版 [M]. 高峰, 译. 北京: 清华大学出版社.

托马斯·A. 普格尔, 2014. 国际贸易: 第15版 [M]. 赵曙东, 沈艳枝, 译. 北京: 中国人民大学出版社.

薛荣久, 2015. 国际贸易 [M]. 第5版. 北京: 对外经济贸易大学出版社.

罗伯特·J. 凯伯, 2017. 国际经济学: 第15版 [M]. 侯锦慎, 刘兴坤, 译. 北京: 中国人民大学出版社.